# THE COMMUNICATION COACH
## Business Communication Tips from the Pros

*by*

**Jeffrey Tobe**
**Sandie Akerman**
**Mary Maloney Cronin**
**Debbie Gracey**
**Deb Haggerty**
**Cyndi Maxey**
**Laurel Bellows**
**Vicki Niebrugge**
**Kevin E. O'Connor, CSP**
**Janet Sue Rush**
**James R. Kwaiser**
**Cathy Burnham**
**Judy Tobe**

ISBN: 0-9662689-0-3
Manufactured in the United States of America

# Foreword

The wind was swirling as it often does in semi-enclosed venues, whipping the rain and sleet into our faces from all directions. Even if the weather had cooperated, the din of the environment made a simple spoken statement difficult to understand as the words were blown away before they could reach the intended recipient.

Each person was prepared for this possibility. "Keep it simple, clear and to the point," were our instructions. We were focused as we strained to hear the instructions. Upon receiving our directions, we were to set to complete the job at hand. We had a task to accomplish, we knew our assignments and what was expected of us. We even had a contingency plan—if the spoken word failed, a little hand signal, a nod of the head was all that was needed to make the adjustment.

This was communication at its best. This was a typical Sunday in the NFL!

Often, I find myself wishing that it was that simple to communicate today. In today's world of information overload, it has become more and more difficult to communicate effectively. Assumptions seem to rule our perceptions. We speak and people hear us but nobody really listens. People hear what they want to hear. Or they hear from their point of view. Or they assume what you said is what they heard. Rarely does anyone say, "Let me get this straight. Is this what I heard you say? Is this how you would like it to be?" People assume!

We are all guilty of assuming. We do it with our spouses, with our kids, with our friends and in business every day. Why? Because we have been trained to believe that it is necessary in the communication process. We do not want to spend the time it takes to keep things simple, clear and to the point. It takes a commitment to focus on the situation and the task at hand without letting our minds wander to the next challenge.

Research has shown that our minds process over fifty thousand thoughts each day. Even when we say we are *listening*, only part of our brain is committed to the process; the rest is actively considering other things. We are very active people. How many times have you said, "There are just not enough hours in a day to get the job done."? It all comes down to focus. Focus on us, our lives, our jobs and our careers. The focus should be on how we excel and how we get ahead.

My wife and I recently did some redecorating in our home and it was a frustrating experience. Nothing was done correctly the first time.

In ordering curtains with a salesperson in our house, we decided on three panels for each curtain. The salesperson wrote down two but explained that, "she would communicate with the workroom that there should be three." When the curtains arrived they were too long for the windows and they only had two panels. Of course, we sent them back only to have them returned two weeks later with two-and-one-half panels. When we inquired as to how this could happen when material for three panels was ordered originally, we were told that, "They wasted too much fabric in making the two panels and the extra length. Not enough was left over to make the third, so we only added a half a panel." We explained that it was not what we had ordered. They proceeded to inform us that they would have to order more material and that they could not guarantee that it would be from the same dye lot.

Well, it took them three orders to get the same dye lot which translated to a turnaround time of three months before the curtains were finally finished. All of this because nobody focused on the situation. Nobody wrote down proper instructions, and when there was the initial mistake, no one picked up the phone to communicate the error.

I get the sense that many people pass things off as complete, when they are not. Had they taken the time to focus in the first place, they wouldn't have to suffer the embarrassment of costly mistakes. To make matters worse, many of us have just accepted mediocre. Mediocre service, mediocre quality and mediocre accuracy in communications. We don't want to rock the boat and we want to avoid conflict in any situation. I know this because I was one of those people willing to accept mediocrity in communications. I have changed. I can put my foot down and ask myself, "Does it have to be like this? Why can't people focus on the challenge at hand?"

I have more stories about the chairs, the ottoman and the rug, but I won't bore you with the details. Communication issues are typically at the root of all challenges, both personally and professionally. My psychiatrist says I have an identity problem and that's why people don't listen to me. My mother tells me not to let people take advantage. My wife tells me to stand up for myself. My parish priest tells me to pray more and it will all work out.

But, it is my eight-year-old niece Maggie who hit the proverbial nail on the head when she asked, "Wasn't it more fun playing football?" It was more fun playing football. At least in that world we all had a common interest and we were all focused on the same result; to help one another get the job done. What an amazing concept. If only we could translate this to communicating more effectively!

*Rocky Bleier was picked by the Pittsburgh Steelers late in the 1968 draft. Before he could prove himself as a rookie, he was drafted again – this time, for combat duty in Vietnam. A few months later, crippled by enemy fire and grenade wounds in both legs, Bleier faced his biggest challenge. He could barely walk and his professional football career seemed doomed.*

*But Rocky Bleier did the impossible. The story of Bleier's agonizing two year battle to overcome his injuries and return to the Pittsburgh Steelers is described in the book Fighting Back and recreated in a TV movie of the same name. He went on to become one of the Steelers' top leading ground gainers, contributing to four Super Bowl victories.*

*Rocky is now in demand as a speaker, motivating audiences around the world. His presentation, "Be the Best You Can Be" encourages participants to keep on striving for greater accomplishments. He resides in Pittsburgh Pa. and can be reached at (412) 621-2351*

# Table of Contents

❖ **Chapter 1** ❖

# The First Step...

# Creativity in Communications

*by*
*Jeffrey Tobe*

When the capacity to use your creativity and imagination is harnessed and used to enhance your communication skills in business, you will find an amazing tool that can literally make you more money, change the way you manage your internal and external clients, and even alter the way you parent, as well.

—*Jeffrey Tobe*

# The First Step...

Human beings have the amazing capacity to imagine situations that have never existed. Expecting the unexpected can be something as simple as having a contingency plan for your outdoor picnic if it rains or as complicated as dreaming of space tourism in the year 2025. When the capacity to use your creativity and imagination is harnessed and used to enhance your communication skills in business, you will find an amazing tool that can literally make you more money, change the way you manage your internal and external clients ("internal" meaning those to whom you sell your ideas within your organization or those other than the obvious "external" client or customer) and even alter the way you parent as well. "All of this from using your imagination?" you ask.

All of my sales training and creativity sessions are based on the premise of the "21-day rule." It had its roots in Alcoholics Anonymous (AA) which apparently operates on the premise that if you could stop drinking for 21 days, you wouldn't *break* the habit, but you would *change* the habit. People started to accept this rule outside of the realm of AA and embrace it today as a great guideline to accept a new challenge. If it takes 21 days to form a new habit, then *your* challenge is to try the things I am going to suggest in this chapter—the things that are suggested throughout this entire book—with an open mind over a 21-day period. On that premise, continue reading if you dare to be more creative in your communication skills.

Imagine that gravity stops for 30 seconds every single day. Imagine also that this phenomenon is not new. In this scenario, this brief stoppage of the earth's force always has happened and always will happen. Gravity stops every day at the exact same time; you can set your watch by it. Now, if you are a "black and white" thinker, you are imagining yourself floating. For the sake of this chapter, you will have to loosen your imagination and become a "colorful" thinker. Besides the clear fact that you would float, what is one benefit that you can imagine to floating every day for 30 seconds?

What did you imagine? A stress-free respite every day? Having a bird's-eye perspective of the world? Dunking that basketball you have been trying to dunk for the past 30 years or so? An excuse for that messy desk of yours? Maybe you pictured the opportunity for a new product in the padding business: what goes up must eventually come down!

Now, how many times have you actually been in outer space? Literally, not figuratively! I have never found anyone to answer this affirmatively in any of my creativity sessions. Yet, you have the capacity to vividly imagine this situation without much effort and this is where the power lies in being more creative in your communication skills. By the way, humans are the only species able to use our imaginations in this respect. If you asked your dog to "imagine gravity stopping every day for 30 seconds," the dog looks up at you with sad eyes as if to respond, "Are they going to pet me or feed me? Pet me or feed me?" A dog does not have the capacity to imagine anything, let alone dream about floating in space.

The advantages to imagining situations which do not presently exist with your clients are numerous. This chapter will help you get started in trying skills that you may not have considered in the past. These skills will require your imagination and your commitment to trying them for the next 21 days, but the results will speak for themselves. There are only two things that you are going to be asked to consider. First, how do you use your imagination to establish instant rapport with your internal and external clients? Second, once you are on the same wave length, how do you get them to buy into your ideas every time?

# The Power of Reflection

Although various studies have suggested diverse percentages, most researchers agree that when humans communicate with each other, much more emphasis is placed on the tone of the voice and body language than on the words themselves. If you don't believe this, try something that my associate and fellow speaker, Timothy Quinn, claims will drive this point home. Place your hands in front of yourself as if you are cradling a newborn baby and sing (yes, I said "sing!") that famous lullaby that your mother may have sung to you as an infant on many a restless night: *Rock-a-bye-baby*. Pay close attention to the words. Paraphrased, they proclaim to a child that the singer is going to place them in a treetop, the branch will surely break and the child will fall to the ground with the cradle not far behind! If, as a baby, you had been able to comprehend the words, you may have grown up with a different perspective of this very popular song! No, instead the child is comforted by the tone of the singer's voice and their body language. This is no different than when you engage in any typical conversation. So, why not use the power of this knowledge to your advantage whenever you communicate with your clients? By reflecting both the body language and the tone of voice of your clients, you establish instant rapport and create an even playing field on which to communicate.

## The Communication Waltz

In all of my training sessions, I encourage participants to return to their place of business and try something that they sometimes consider to be outside the lines. Leave your comfort zone behind for the next 21 days and practice one of the most powerful rapport builders available to you: *REFLECTION*.

If you have ever had the opportunity to observe two people engaged in conversation, you may have noticed the communication waltz. The pair will automatically begin to reflect each other's gestures, mannerisms and body language without even being aware that they are mirroring one another. Subconsciously, you have experienced this when you walk away from somebody and you feel like you really had a great conversation. Chances are you were in conversational sync like two people waltzing around the ballroom floor.

If humans do this subconsciously, why not speed up the process and take control of the waltz right from the start? *Consciously* reflect the other person's gestures, body language and mannerisms right from the start of a conversation. If they sit cross-legged with their arms folded over their chest, you reflect the same position. If they lean across their desk and bang their fist, you do the same.

*WARNING! WARNING! WARNING!* There is a very fine line here between reflection and rejection! Timing is of the utmost importance. If you were to reflect another person's gestures immediately after they had moved to that position, your encounter would more resemble a kid's game of copy-cat than a business dialogue. Reflect the other person's body language sometime *after* they have assumed another position. If you do this consciously for the first few minutes of your conversation, you will find that an instant rapport is built between you and the subconscious waltz will occur naturally. What happens is that the other person has a feeling that they like what they see in you. And, what do they see reflected in you? *THEMSELVES!*

# Speak Up (or Down)

By the way, reflection actually has a second phase to it. Not only can you reflect the physical attributes of the other person, but by reflecting their vocal characteristics as well, you create the communication you require to establish instant rapport. In other words, if the other person tends to have a loud, booming voice (and we all know one of those people), if they speak quickly or slowly, you must match their tone or inflection and speak to them in the same manner. If their tone is rather timid, you may have to soften your conversation. Start your conversation at the same level as the other person and then adjust to a level at which you both feel comfortable. Again, humans do this naturally. You are simply speeding up the process.

Reflecting the other person's tone of voice and rate of speech is especially effective on the telephone. Some time ago, a very quiet and obviously shy woman called the office to inquire about creativity training workshops for her company. I tend to get excited about conducting workshops. I exuberantly explained how attendees are taught to color outside the lines, how all participants are required to have fun and how everyone participates in the entire experience. On the other end of the line, I heard CLICK! The prospect hung up. About two minutes later, the phone rang again. When my assistant answered, she was stunned to hear the same meek voice on the other end, asking if there was somebody *more serious* to whom she could talk.

Reflection, as it relates to voice, can immediately establish clear communication between two parties. If your work involves handling irate callers, the best way to diffuse the situation is to begin at the same level as they. A few years ago, I worked with one of the "Baby Bell" telephone companies. The employees of this particular department had the unenviable job of diffusing complaints. Every time the phone rang, they prepared themselves for someone complaining about something. (Next to air traffic controllers, I can't think of a more stressful job!) You can guess that the most effective service representatives in the group had discovered *reflection* on their own. For the most part, the telephone company representative's personality made it especially difficult to raise their tone of voice to a customer. The customer service representative found that if they started the conversation at the exact same vocal level, pitch, rate, and intensity as the caller, success was achieved in focusing on the challenge and solving the issue.

Try this with your kids. I have found that ever since my daughters were toddlers, I could diffuse any temper tantrum, not by raising my voice to be heard or to sound angry, but by raising my voice to the same level of urgency or whining as theirs. As you will discover later in this chapter,

I have learned a great deal about effective communication skills from my children!

## Mirror, Mirror on the Wall

Are you still thinking that reflection might not be for you; that it might not be as effective as the examples indicate? Here is a personal example of how powerful reflection really is as a means to establish instant rapport and open communications.

In 1986, when I first began to research the effectiveness of reflection presented by motivational guru, Anthony Robbins, as "mirroring and imaging," I decided to put the idea to the test. I was president of a full-service, promotional agency in Dallas, Texas. One day I received a call from the marketing director of one of the top 10 companies in the region. Because of a rather bizarre direct mail piece that the caller had received from us, she invited me to meet with her and the director of advertising and promotions for the company. I agreed, but on the spur of the moment, I suggested that I bring my partner with me. A mutually agreeable time was scheduled. I decided to put the theory of reflection to the test.

I warned my partner, Laurence, of my intention. I informed him that he was to reflect the advertising director's gestures and voice. I had decided to do the same with the director of marketing with whom I had spoken. The important meeting day arrived. Pam, the director of marketing, and Sue Ann, the director of advertising, sat across from us at a small conference table. Pam began the formal portion of the meeting by standing up and, in a very loud, commanding voice, proclaimed, "Look. I invited you here today because your mail piece caught our attention. We normally do not seek out new vendors, so you have about five minutes to tell us why you are different, and why we should use your services."

What did I do? I STOOD UP, and in a matching loud, commanding voice stated, "You're right Pam. We ARE different and let me tell you why."

As I glanced over at Sue Ann, I noticed her looking at Laurence and rolling her eyes as if to say, "Good grief. Another loud, obnoxious salesperson!" Laurence sat there and eventually rolled his eyes at her as if to agree. When it was the advertising director's turn to speak, she sat with her hands cupped under her chin. She spoke softly and directly to her new friend, Laurence. "Yes, I agree with Pam. In the advertising department…".

By the end of the meeting, Laurence and Sue Ann were exchanging recipes. Pam and I were arranging to meet for a power lunch, and Laurence and I knew that we had landed a new account. As proof that using the skill of reflection is what secured this new account, for the next week when Sue Ann called the office, she would ask to speak to Laurence only. The opposite with Pam. Even though either Laurence or I could help them, the clients felt more comfortable with their reflecting partner. As a postscript to all of this, we also received one of the largest contracts we had ever, or would ever receive—FROM PAM!

# The Two Most Powerful Words in the English Language

Now that you have reflection as a tool to establish instant rapport with a client or prospect, the next step in effective communications is to maintain that rapport. You have additional things on which to concentrate other than reflecting the other person's gestures/body language throughout what you hope will be a very long relationship. Let us look at a technique to get the client to "buy into" your ideas and feel comfortable whenever you communicate with them.

Consider only two words. That's all! Two simple words that can literally change the way you do business. They are, without a doubt, the most powerful words when it comes to being a more creative communicator. What are they?

## "What if"

Using "what iffing" at a very basic level will help to shatter stereotypes: from the stereotype that your internal and external clients have of the experience of doing business with you, to the stereotype someone might have of your title or rank.

In your memory, travel back to your days in elementary school. Your fondest memories are typically of those teachers who broke with tradition. Perhaps they suggested holding the class outside, or going on an unplanned field trip. Why do you remember these experiences so vividly? Because they changed the environment—the stereotype—in which you expected to learn. Your first challenge in being a better business communicator is to constantly change the environment in which your clients expect you to operate.

I recently received a letter from Charles, a manufacturer's representative in the Midwest. A representative's job is to get a distributor excited about selling their line of products over somebody else's.

Charles received an invitation from his largest distributor in Ann Arbor, Michigan, to attend a company's national sales meeting and present his line of goods to the entire sales force of about 65 people. He was informed that he would be number three to present and would have a one-and-a-half hour time slot right before lunch. Well, it didn't take any rocket scientist to figure out that these people would have been sitting for more than three hours (with short breaks between each presentation) before this guy ever had a chance to address the group. Charles remembered hearing me say, "Change the environment. Shatter the stereotype."

He walked into the meeting and announced to everyone that they should pack up their things because he was taking them on a field trip. Excitement built as he led them out to waiting vans which transported them only a few blocks away to the University of Michigan football stadium. Now, college football fans would be the first to recognize that this is one of the largest stadiums in the country. Charles had arranged to hold his entire presentation at the 50-yard line of an empty, 107,000-seat stadium with box lunches for everyone. Which one of the presentations do think the salespeople remembered?

Perhaps renting the local football stadium for your next meeting is a little too far outside the lines, but you should to be aware of how to shatter the stereotype your clients have when communicating with you and your firm. Spending time asking "what if" will help you change the environment in which you communicate.

In the context of creativity, using the "what if" technique is a means to an end. By using "what if" to open the minds of your clients, you can begin to see how powerful it is to have them buy into your ideas, your concepts and, ultimately, purchase your solutions.

The power of using "what if" can increase your bottom line, change the way you interact with your internal and external customers, and alter the way you deal with your children—no matter what their age.

## "See the world through your client's eyes and discover the way your client buys."

In deference to my friends and clients who are in the industry, take a moment to mentally list the characteristics of the stereotypical automobile salesperson. Think of as many adjectives as you can. What did you come up with?

Here is my list:

- ✓ Pushy
- ✓ Fast talker
- ✓ Relentless
- ✓ Poorly dressed
- ✓ Insincere
- ✓ Aggressive
- ✓ Smooth
- ✓ Untrustworthy
- ✓ Scheming
- ✓ Money hungry

Again, apologies to the many automobile salespeople who do not fit the mold. I would venture to guess that this list is not unlike your mental one. So, if you were to be successful in selling cars, you would have to break the stereotype. Do you think that your clients—both internal and external—have a stereotype of the experience they have with you when communicating ideas, concepts or solutions? Start seeing the world through your clients' eyes and attempt to shatter that stereotype.

Try taking the "what if" challenge at your next meeting. Appoint someone the "'*What if* 'questioner-of-the-day." Their role is to begin the meeting with the most bizarre, unreal, non-work-related, *What if* question they can think of. "What if humans did not need to sleep?" "What if hair grew inward instead of outward?" Or, a personal favorite, "What if you had seven fingers on each hand?" When I ask this last question in my creativity workshops, I love the answers I get because they illustrate the openness and fun that "what if" questions will inspire in your group.

With seven fingers on each hand…

"I could play the piano better."

"The Pittsburgh Pirates might have had a chance at the pennant."

"I could wear more jewelry."

"I could count higher."

"We could give high sevens."

My favorite answer was from a gentleman in New York who explained that, "…with seven fingers, I could name each one after a day of the week: Monday through Sunday. When I miss my taxi in downtown Manhattan, I'd give the guy a 'Wednesday'!" This may require some visualization on your part, but I think you get the point.

The key to appointing the "what if" questioner is to have everyone answer the bizarre question. You will be surprised at the results. People begin to laugh and the creative juices begin to flow. You will find the environment one in which creativity can now flourish. Additionally, people will begin to have fun.

The idea of having fun at work seems to be foreign to so many companies. You may have grown up in an age where work and fun did not go together. I grew up in retail. My Dad used to work six days a week and at six o'clock he closed the store to come home to have fun with his family. On Sundays, the store was closed and the whole family participated in fun activities. And, two weeks a year, he took a vacation so we could have FUN! It's little wonder that we have a society that grew up believing that you couldn't possibly have fun and work at the same time.

Wouldn't you agree that people want to work with, work for, conduct business with, communicate with, people who seem to enjoy what they are doing for a living? So, "what iffing" allows people to have some fun while altering the environment in which they meet.

In my soon-to-be-released book, *Coloring Outside the Lines*, I researched several highly creative companies in the United States and Canada. The goal was to discover just what these firms had in common. Why did I consider them to be so creative? I found out something very simple. All of these companies have discovered that there is very little difference between, *"Ah ha!"* (the discovery of a new idea or a new way of doing something) and *"Ha ha!"* (which is having fun). Loosen up and allow yourself and your clients to have fun at work through "what iffing"

Let us take "what iffing" a step further. Years ago, I remember being perplexed over the challenge of retaining good people in my firm. I knew it wasn't standard business practice to leave a job after one month! I quickly diagnosed the challenge and recognized the need to concentrate on my communication skills and look at the big picture. The challenge was in the way I communicated my intentions, desires and expectations to my employees.

The answer came to light one day when I approached Vic, my sales manager, saying, "Hey, Vic. Did you get a chance to finish that proposal for the ABC account? I need it to complete my quote for this Friday."

Tentatively, Vic replied, "Well, I didn't get a chance to finish it."

Abruptly, I retorted, "Listen, I know you normally get in at 8:00 AM, but I want you here at 6:00 AM tomorrow to finish that thing." And I walked away.

How would this make you feel? Maybe a "Wednesday" came to mind? Do you have a boss who approaches you like this? Maybe you approach your internal clients in the same manner. I can only imagine that the question of how Vic was going to satisfy my demands was constantly on his mind. Then I discovered the power of "what if"

Replaying the same scenario, the conversation would change dramatically when "what if" was incorporated.

"Hey, Vic. Did you get a chance to finish that proposal for the ABC account? I need it to complete my quote for this Friday."

Tentatively, Vic replied, "Well, I didn't get a chance to finish it."

To which I now reply, "I know you normally get here about 8:00 AM, but what if you came in at 6:00 AM to finish it?" Then you need to bite your tongue (B.Y.T.) and LISTEN to the answer.

Vic thinks it over and replies, "Well, I can't Jeff. I can't get my kids to the babysitter's house before 6:30, which means I couldn't get here until seven o'clock."

I volley, "What if you came in every day this week at seven o'clock until you get it done?"

Now he offers, "Yeah, and if I don't get it finished by Thursday, I can plan to stay late and get it done."

By simply adding "what if" and listening (refer to chapter 2, Listening is Your Choice by Sandie Akerman), I opened up a dialogue. A dialogue that never existed in my previous way of communicating. It was then I realized that, with a joint effort, my employees and I could come up with a mutually beneficial solution to any challenge.

My learning curve was still being developed. My wife and I use a common discipline technique with our kids called "Time Out." You may be familiar with the concept. We do not believe in corporal punishment and would prefer our children to be sent to a quiet place, by themselves, to consider what they have done. My parents think that we are totally out of our minds. Their response when one of our children act out? "Just hit the kid!" Different generation, different approaches!

About five-and-a-half years ago, I realized that I must have sounded very threatening to my then three-year-old daughter when I ordered her into a time out after she carelessly knocked over a vase, flowers, water and all. "Get into time and out and figure out why you don't listen when you are told not to climb up on the coffee table." Then I started using "what if" To this day, no matter how angry I am with my daughters' behavior, I will always preface my demands with "what if" What if you go into your room and figure out why you hit your little sister? In her mind, this is far less threatening than I had always sounded in the past *and* it opens up the opportunity for a dialogue. There are times now, as she is going on nine years old, that I will practice this and she will reply, "I'll tell you why, Dad…" and we have a conversation about the challenge! Why? Because I opened myself up to a dialogue when I began by asking a question. And remember, when you ask a question, be prepared for an answer.

Finally, I realized that this powerful new communication tool that I had uncovered would work with my external clients as well. The best way to illustrate this is to share a typical presentation from my former advertising days. One profit center of the company was in the arena of Promotional Products; e.g., giveaways with your company logo or slogan printed on them. I think you will recognize this "selling" style whether you sell a product, service or yourself to external clients.

My presentation would begin with, "Bob, thanks for meeting with me again. After our conversation last week, I went back to brainspark with my colleagues about your trade show challenge and what to give away at your booth to attract more business. We think you should use imprinted coffee mugs. We can imprint your logo on one side and your mission statement on the other. What do you think?"

Bob would typically reply, "Great idea, Jeff. What else do you have?"

To which I would defensively answer, "You don't understand. You see, I have been in the business 12 years and I have seen your challenge dozens of times before. Coffee mugs are definitely the answer to this challenge."

What's happening here? Is it fairly typical of the dialogue you have when you are trying to sell one of your ideas? If you choose to go head-to-head in communicating your ideas, only one thing can happen. YOU END UP WITH A HEADACHE and, usually, without the sale! Unfortunately, many people use this communication style on a daily basis, with their internal and external clients, with their kids and even with their spouses.

Years ago, I realized that perhaps I sounded a little threatening to my customers. Perhaps there is a subconscious power struggle that occurs when selling ideas and perhaps it was in my best interest to let the client win! That's when "what iffing" came to the forefront once again. This allowed the presentation to become a two-way dialogue opening up all kinds of possibilities.

JEFF: Bob, thanks for meeting with me again. After our conversation last week, I went back to brainspark with my colleagues about your trade show challenge and what to give away at your booth to attract more business. "What if" you used ceramic coffee mugs for your next trade show giveaway? (Now, B.Y.T.!)

BOB: Jeff, that's a great idea but we can't use ceramic. They're too fragile and I could never ship them in one piece to all of my shows.

JEFF: "What if" we used plastic mugs?

BOB: Wait a second. Do you have plastic beer steins? Our theme this year is 'Flow Through Ideas' and plastic beer steins just might work.

JEFF: Yea, I do have a plastic beer stein, and the logo changes color when you add cold liquid... .

BOB: "What if" we put our old logo on it and it would change to the new logo when filled?

The conversation in this example went back and forth like this. After I left, what do you suppose Bob said to all of the people with whom he worked? Something to the effect of, "I have a great idea and I want to work with Jeff Tobe because we work well together." By being willing to explore other ideas and options with my client, he had won the power struggle immediately by making it *HIS* idea. In chapter 5, Deb Haggerty deals with different personality traits of your clients, the ability to make the solution *their idea* is even more powerful depending on who it is you are dealing with.

Remember, there is always a stereotype of the communications experience one expects to have with you, based on your past reputation or the reputation of your industry, your company, your product or your service. Your objective in using some of these techniques over the next 21 days is simply to shatter that stereotype. Make the experience a unique one every single time by adapting, reflecting and making it the customer's idea.

*The Communication Coach... Business Communication Tips from the Pros* will give you the tips you need to improve and even excel in your daily communication with your internal and external clients. I look at it like the "connect the dots" puzzles many children love to complete. Treat this chapter, The First Step, as one of those dots and the following chapters as the other dots. When you have finished the book, you should be able to connect the dots—metaphorically, of course—and have the entire communication picture. With this in mind, read the following...

## Connecting the Communication Dots

Sometimes you connect with an internal or external client... like that!

No big thing maybe, but there is something deeper than communicating the same message to the same people.

A spark comes and goes quickly so you have to pay attention.

There's a change in the eyes when you inquire about family.

Pain flickers behind the statistics concerning how well the business is performing.

An older client talks about his bride of 25 years with an obvious affectation.

An eagle-eyed achiever laughs before you want her to.

Someone tells about his wife's job and how proud he is of her.

An old joker needs another laugh on his way to retirement.

A woman says she spends a lot of salary on daycare and a good one is hard to find.

In every conversation with your clients, you hear the dots of love, joy, fear, and guilt.

You hear the cries of celebration and reassurance, and somehow know that when those dots are connected, business will take care of itself.

***Listen...Listen...and Communicate Well!***

*©Coloring Outside the Lines 1997*

# About Jeffrey Tobe

*I*nsider *Magazine* recently dubbed Jeffrey Tobe "the guru of creativity." Prior to his professional speaking career, Jeff had been involved in the advertising industry. During his last three years in that business, he won five International Golden Pyramid Awards for creativity in promotions. Jeff was also recognized as a leader in the sales management arena by Sales & Marketing Executives, International.

Jeff was born in Fergus, Ontario, Canada, and now resides in Pittsburgh, Pennsylvania, with his wife, Judy, and their two daughters. He is a Certified Speaking Professional candidate with the National Speakers Association and a member of the Pennsylvania Speakers Association.

It is Jeff's innovative and entrepreneurial spirit that has made *The Coach* series come to fruition.

For more information and a free marketing video, contact:

200 James Place, Suite 400
Monroeville, PA 15146
Toll free:   1-800-875-7106
Phone:   (412) 373-6592
Fax:   (412) 373-8773
E-mail:   cre8iva@aol.com
Web site:   www.jefftobe.com

# Company Profile . . . Coloring Outside the Lines™

Coloring Outside the Lines offers customized creativity keynotes, seminars, and training for diverse organizations around the world. From your meeting's opening and motivational address, to a long-term program for your sales force, Jeffrey Tobe and his associates bring you fast-paced, up-to-the-minute, participatory programs. The premise behind all of this is that you need to be willing to get outside of your comfort zone and "stop looking in your rear view mirror" at what you have always done in the past. Instead, start looking through your windshield to see what's coming down the road ahead.

## Most Requested Programs

*Coloring Outside the Lines™*
This is Jeff's signature presentation encouraging participants to look at their challenges from a whole new perspective in managing the change that is inevitable with innovation.
■ Keynote or half-day to two-day workshop.

*Listening Between the Lines... Effective Listening Techniques*
Information is power! Yet, this communication tool is the least studied, the least practiced, and the least understood. Learn how to become an empathetic listener and real tools to maintain the competitive edge by keeping your mouth closed and your ears open more often.
■ Keynote or three- to six-hour module.

*DiSC™... Who are you Dealing With Anyway?*
By discovering your unique behavior in business, you can better understand how to relate to your "internal" and "external" customer, your spouse, your children, and your friends. Building long-term relationships is the key to success in business today. This session enables you to understand others while giving you an insight into your individual work style.
■ Keynote or three- to six-hour module.

*C.O.L.O.R. Selling*
Asking the right kinds of probing questions is second only to effective listening techniques in succeeding in business today. This proprietary, five-step questioning approach to sales is a step-by-step process to take you to the next plateau in your selling career. Learn to identify the "basic" versus "specific" needs of your client.
■ Keynote or three- to six-hour module.

❖ **Chapter 2** ❖

# Listening is
# YOUR Choice

*by*

*Sandie Akerman*

A skilled listener
does not just allow listening to happen.
One must actively participate
in the process.

—*Sandie Akerman*

"You haven't heard a word I've said." "Sometimes I feel like I'm talking to myself." "Why don't you ever listen to me?"

Listening… a skill you use everyday—yet one that most people are willing to admit is not done very well. In this chapter, you will start to understand what prevents effective listening and to explore how you can improve your listening capabilities. Tips and techniques, when used appropriately at the proper time, can improve your listening dramatically.

# What is listening?

Many would consider that a simple question. If it is so easy to define listening, why is it so difficult to do? Studies indicate that 70% of what individuals hear is misunderstood or misinterpreted. Understanding what happens when you listen will be beneficial.

While listening may sound like a simple act, it is actually quite complex. In this chapter the assumption is made that the listener is someone without a hearing impairment. Hearing impairment is a physical condition; listening impairment is not. What is the difference between hearing and listening? Keep reading to learn about the process associated with hearing and listening.

Part one of the process is the perception that sound equals hearing. Hearing is the physical ability to accept and transmit sound waves from the eardrum to the brain. Part two of the process is being attuned to sound. This is what listening involves.

Amazingly enough, the ear has muscles. The middle ear muscles are the "listening muscles." Listening is the act of focusing on sound that permits you to receive information that you think is important and reject that which you believe is unimportant. The ability to attach meaning to the transmission of sound creates the impact of the message for each individual.

Numerous studies have been conducted on how much of a person's day is spent in some form of communication. Communication may come in the form of writing, reading, talking or listening. According to communications research conducted by Dr. Ralph Nichols from the University of Minnesota in the 1940s, on average, you will spend 75 percent of your day verbally communicating, either talking or listening. The results of his study remain true today. The breakdown of how much of your day is spent using various communication methods is shown below.

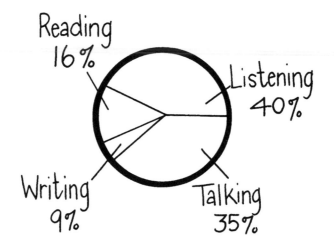

The pie chart clearly confirms that the largest part of communication is listening. How much of your formal education was devoted to the art of listening? Probably none, unless you voluntarily registered for a class offered outside the traditional education curriculum. Listening is the primary means of how information is absorbed and assimilated. The skill of listening is used far more than both reading and writing. Yet, few curriculums focus specifically and singly on the skill of listening. No wonder actively listening to colleagues, subordinates, managers, family members and friends causes such a dilemma.

Listening is a learned skill that usually comes from the school of hard knocks. The first step to becoming an effective listener is to realize that listening is an active, versus a passive, process. A skilled listener does not just allow listening to happen. One must actively participate in the process. To fully understand what active participation is and how to achieve it, let's review some basics.

# The Communication Process

The communication process is comprised of four main components:
1. the sender of the message,
2. the message itself,
3. the channel used to deliver the message, and
4. the receiver of the message.

Communicating sounds simple, right? Then why is effective listening so difficult? Because underneath the obvious exists layers of possible opportunities where roadblocks can occur.

The sender begins the communication process by sharing information with another person or by encouraging that person to perform an action or change a behavior. The sender must translate the message into something the receiver will understand. Translating a message is often called encoding.

Words, either written or spoken, are the mediums that form a message. The medium you use is called the "channel of communication." Let us look at the spoken medium. The sender uses vocal signals that affect the word's meaning. How the sender expresses their words can be as important, if not more important, than the words themselves. How loudly someone speaks, what words are emphasized, the rate of their speech, and the tone of voice all contribute to the meaning of the message.

The meaning of the message relies very little on the words used to deliver the message. Much more important is the nonverbal communication as perceived by the listener. Meanings cannot be transferred from one mind to another via thought transmission... words are the only vehicle by which thoughts can be transmitted. People assign meanings to the words.

For example, Don, Mary's supervisor, is told by his manager to tell Mary she is doing a great job for the company. Don does not believe Mary has done a great job but knows he must deliver the message. He approaches Mary sluggishly, eyes downcast and softly says, "Mary, I just want you to know that we appreciate the job you have been doing for us. Keep up the good work." Don turns and quickly walks away. Did the words Don used convey the message he was asked to deliver? Yes. Did his nonverbal language convey the same message? No. How do you think Mary felt after this encounter?

What makes up a message? There are three components: body language, tone of voice and the words. Can you guess what part each of these play in the reception of the message by the listener? Believe it or not, body language makes up 55 percent of the communicated message, tone of voice accounts for 38 percent and words the remaining 7 percent.

These statistics come from "Communication Without Words" published in *Psychology Today* in 1968 based on research done by Albert Mehrabain. This means that 93 percent of all communication is expressed nonverbally. Nonverbal communication includes eye contact, facial expressions, gestures, inflection, tone, and rate of speech. In order for the message to be accurately received, the sender needs to be sure the nonverbal and verbal communication are congruent.

If inconsistency exists, the receiver will assign meaning to the sender's words based on the 93 percent coming from the nonverbal clues. In the example, Mary assigned meaning to the words Don communicated. The words conveyed one meaning and the nonverbals a totally different message. Mary assigned her meaning based on Don's sluggish approach, downcast eyes and unenthusiastic delivery.

When the message reaches the receiver, the basic communication process, described earlier, occurs in reverse. The receiver must try to understand from the words transmitted what the sender was trying to express. The receiver's role in the process is to decode the message. Decoding involves four parts:

1. Sensing or becoming aware of the message;
2. Interpreting and understanding the meaning and purpose of the message;
3. Evaluating whether or not the message is worth responding to or acting upon; and
4. Responding to the message by performing an action, changing a behavior or sending a message.

# The Listener's Responsibility

The listener has several responsibilities. As soon as the communication process is initiated, the listener decides whether or not to focus on the sender. Next, the listener interprets what the sender has said and then determines, "Do I want to retain that information" in order to respond, make a decision, perform an act, or change a behavior. Each decision impacts the listening process.

Listening with focus requires expending extra energy because you are blocking everything else that is going on around you (externally) and inside you (internally). You cannot possibly listen to and process every sound you hear. Every day you are bombarded by thousands of messages and sounds and it is impossible to concentrate on and put energy into all of them. Consequently, you become selective about where you will invest your time and energy.

Noise and distractions that are occurring around you during a conversation can have a dramatic impact on how well you focus on the communication. Have you ever tried to talk on the phone when people in the same room are laughing or talking? Do you find yourself distracted by the conversation going on around you? Even if you can hear the person on the phone, you probably find yourself trying to listen to both conversations; the conversation with the person on the phone and the conversation with the people in the room. You learn very quickly that you cannot do a good job of listening to anyone this way. You are not able to concentrate on the phone conversation nor on the room conversation. Tune one out (preferably the one in the room) and focus on the caller.

Equally important is the noise or chatter that goes on within your mind. You may be hearing the other person talk and all the while you are thinking, "I wonder if her eyes are that blue naturally or if she wears tinted contacts?" What usually happens next is that it's your turn to talk and you have no idea what to say because you weren't listening.

Did you know that the average person speaks at a rate of 125 to 150 words per minute? Yet, your mind can comprehend and process information at an average rate of 500 words per minute. The question becomes then, "What are you doing during the time lapse of 350 words?" Where does your attention wander? Do you stay focused on the sender of the message? Being aware of the length of your attention span and these questions will help you focus more closely on the whole message. Additionally, understanding the answers may give you clues as to how you can become better at focusing your attention.

The second listener responsibility is to interpret what the sender has said. Remember, meaning is not in the words, it is assigned by the receiver of the communication. You place your own interpretation on what the person is saying. The meanings you assign to the spoken and unspoken message often come from your own background or previous experiences.

Misinterpretation is a frequent occurrence. You are *assuming* that you and the other person have the same message interpretation. You are sure you know what the other person is communicating because the message fits with something you already know. Sometimes you are correct in your assumption, and sometimes you are not. When you are not correct, communication becomes derailed.

To be more effective at interpreting the meaning the sender is conveying, you need to focus on two aspects of the message: emotions and facts. Every message that is sent contains both. Facts make up the content or what is being said. Emotions express feelings or how the person is delivering the message. Focusing on both is important to fully understanding what is being communicated.

When there is a low degree of emotion, it is easier to focus on the facts to determine how you will respond. When you listen for facts you make a decision about what you will do next based on the message. You make the decision concerning how you will listen while the speaker is communicating.

In order to make that decision, ask yourself some questions: "Do I need to comprehend this information in order to do something?" (instructions); "Am I listening to gather complete and accurate information?" (lecture, gathering research, taking notes at a meeting); or "Do I need to evaluate what I am hearing so I can make a decision?" (deciding on a issue, drawing conclusions, making a buying decision). If you are only listening to pure facts it is easier to be an effective listener. However, communication is rarely based on pure fact. Emotions can change the whole dynamic of what is being communicated.

Two listening approaches are more emotion-based. The first is listening to appreciate. This can be used in situations such as a concert, speech, comedy routine, or a discussion where no decision is required. The second is listening to support the sender as he or she talks through their concerns. Empathetic listening is used when counseling a coworker, friend or family member, letting someone vent a frustrating experience or providing the opportunity to blow off steam. Remember most messages have a combination of both facts and emotions and you need to listen for both in order to gain the full meaning.

The third listener responsibility is to determine what portion of the message to retain. You make decisions all the time about what information is important to retain. Because you are flooded with numerous daily messages, you must make decisions about which deserve your undivided attention so you can capture the complete message. Once the entire message has been received, the listener needs to acknowledge the accuracy of the interpretation. Several factors block your ability to focus on, interpret and retain messages.

# What Blocks Your Listening?

Factors which have an impact on your ability to retain information and your listening effectiveness are the filters through which you listen. These listening filters include: the environment where the communication is taking place; your opinions about the subject or the person speaking; and, your physical/mental state at the time of the communication. Whether or not you are aware of it, communication and listening takes place all the time.

The degree to which you grasp the message that is being sent will be impacted by your filters. Everyone has a favorite listening filter called your Preferred Listening Interrupter (PLI). Over the course of the next several days, focus on the conversations you have with others and, when you find yourself not listening, identify what caused your mind to drift/what caused the interruption? After several days, determine whether certain interrupters appear regularly. You have just identified your Preferred Listening Interrupter.

Let's explore each filter type in a little more detail to help you identify the different types of Preferred Listening Interrupters. Is your PLI caused by environmental conditions? Environmental filters are those things that have to do with the conditions under which you are listening.

Examples of environmental filters are: the level of background noise that is present; the temperature of the room; your physical comfort; the speaker's communication style (talking too softly); rate of speech (too fast or slow); vocal variety (monotone, sing-songy, unfamiliar accent); the mannerisms or appearance of the speaker; faulty acoustics which make it difficult to hear; interruptions (telephone calls, outside noises, outside activity or scenery); time pressures or deadlines; and/or distractions. With the myriad of potential interrupters, is it any wonder you may not listen effectively at times? This covers only the environmental filters.

One of my associates has identified that when she catches herself not listening, her PLI is outside noise or distraction. She is one of the best listeners I know. She gives her undivided attention to what the speaker is saying. However, if there is a distraction—perhaps someone walks by the room or someone in the room drops something—her concentration is broken and she stops listening. Did you find your PLI in environmental filters? If not, you may find yours in one of the next two sections.

Physical or mental filters comprise the next major category of Personal Listening Interrupters. You are more physically and mentally alert at certain times of the day. During these peak time periods, you are a more effective listener. Listening at the end of a long day, or when you have had too little sleep, will have a negative impact on your ability to listen. Listening takes total concentration and high energy. When you feel physically and mentally impoverished, you have a difficult time being attentive. When your energy is low, it is easier to daydream or become preoccupied than it is to stay focused on the speaker.

Another factor that can cause listening fatigue is the gap that is created between the speaker's rate of delivery and your ability to comprehend information. Earlier in this chapter the questions were posed, "What are you doing during the time lapse of 350 words? Where does your attention wander? Do you stay focused on the sender of the message?" The time lapse makes it easy to spend this time thinking about other things and be off on a mental tangent. This time lag also may be a factor if you are bored with the situation or the speaker. To stay focused on the listener and use the time lag productively expends a great deal of energy.

My personal PLI is usually associated with this time lapse. In the middle of an important meeting I will hear a small voice in my head saying, "don't forget to...." People who know me say that I have several tracks running simultaneously in my head so I can think about multiple tasks, ideas or situations. This "multiple tracks syndrome", as I call it, is often related to feeling overwhelmed by too many tasks to accomplish every day. Since I have identified my PLI, I have learned to turn off the other tracks so I can focus completely on the speaker's message. I use the time lag for more productive activities like associating what is being said with something that was previously stated or summarizing what the speaker is saying.

The third filter is the category of personal experiences. Everyone has a great deal of history based on past and present experiences which are both positive and negative. These experiences impact your ability to listen effectively. In some situations, your opinions about a certain topic, especially if the opinion is based on a negative emotional experience, prevent you from listening to what the speaker is saying. Usually these past experiences are stored in the subconscious mind. These experiences block you from being in the present moment with the speaker and create an atmosphere of biased listening. A biased listener can distort the message to such a great extent that the likelihood of communication occurring is nonexistent.

In addition, negative or positive words, phrases, and/or topics can elicit an emotional response and keep you from listening effectively. What are the words, phrases or topics that can create these situations for you? By identifying what interrupts your listening, you can take more control the next time you are in a conversation and they come up.

When you disagree with what the other person is saying or when you agree and have additional information to add, another popular Preferred Listening Interrupter is triggered, detouring to another tangent. The personal experience filter can be described as opinions, prejudices, current personal situations, past experiences, and personal agendas. Any of these filters can cause you to begin a separate tangent of thought. A friend of mine found that her dominant PLI is thinking about whether or not she agreed or disagreed with the speaker's message and, based on the outcome, determining how she would respond. Sound familiar to any of you?

Hundreds of PLI variations exist for each of the three major listening filter categories. I would be curious to hear about yours. After you discover what interrupts your listening, please communicate with me about your PLI. (Information regarding how to share your feedback is given at the end of this chapter.)

# Techniques for Improving Listening

Five techniques can be used to improve the effectiveness of your listening dramatically. They are: reflection, clarifying, silence, restatement, and summarizing.

## 1. Reflection

Reflection is best used in situations where you need to play back the speaker's feelings. When you reflect, you demonstrate empathy for the person and the situation. Three components comprise an effective reflective response: tentative statement, defining the feeling being expressed by the speaker, and the summary of the situation.

The *tentative* statement may be something like "It appears that... " or "I am sensing that...." The tentative statement is followed by your statement of what you think the speaker is *feeling*, such as "you are very frustrated" or "you are upset." The definition of feeling is followed by your summary of the situation which may sound like "because of the poor results achieved for the current promotion" or "because your telephone service was disconnected." Putting it all together as a situation summary, it will sound like this, "It appears that you are very frustrated because of the poor results achieved for the current promotion," or "I am sensing that you are upset because your telephone service was disconnected."

*Here are a few for you to try:*
"I am very frustrated with the timeliness of our last order. I'm not sure we are willing to take that risk again."

Tentative Statement: _____

_____

Feeling Statement: _____

_____

Situation Summary: _____

_____

"We have a real problem and I am not sure how we are going to solve it. You have been late the last three nights. This can't continue. I need to know where you are and when you will be home.

TENTATIVE STATEMENT: _____

_____

FEELING STATEMENT: _____

_____

SITUATION SUMMARY: _____

_____

# 2. Clarifying

Clarifying ensures that you and the speaker have the same perception or understanding of what is being communicated. Confirmation is usually formatted as a question. An example is, "When you say 'competitive' what exactly do you mean?" This allows you and the speaker to mirror your perceptions. Everyone has their own meanings for words based on experience, beliefs, knowledge, education, and background. As a result, rarely do two people have the exact same definition for a word or expression. Remember what was said earlier, "Meanings are not in the words. Meanings are attached to the words by people."

The dictionary contains thousands of words. Studies have shown that an average adult uses about 500 of these words most often and that each word has somewhere between 20 and 25 meanings. Therefore, two people that use an average of 500 words with 20 to 25 meanings each means that there are 12,500 possible different meanings.

*Try clarifying these situations.*

SITUATION: The speaker says that your prices are too high.

POSSIBLE RESPONSE: _____

SITUATION: The speaker says that they are frustrated with the level of service they are receiving.

POSSIBLE RESPONSE: _____

SITUATION: The speaker says that they need to think it over and get back to you in a couple of weeks.

POSSIBLE RESPONSE:_____

# 3. Silence

The third effective listening technique is the use of silence. Silence is golden, after all. Frequently, when you are listening to someone speak you have so many thoughts to share that you interrupt or interject when the speaker takes a breath. A good lesson to keep in mind is to remain focused on the message, let there be a silent pause after the speaker stops talking, and then respond. Sometimes the person speaking needs to collect their thoughts before continuing. By jumping in you may be missing the opportunity to learn more. This is especially true in selling, servicing, or negotiating situations. Silence during a conversation is really acceptable. Try it and see what you learn.

# 4. Restatement

Restatement is paraphrasing what you think you have heard the speaker say. This is not parroting. Parroting means you repeat back word-for-word what the person has said. It can be extremely annoying and insulting. Paraphrasing is expressing what the person has said in your own words to be certain you share the same understanding. This is similar to clarifying. The difference is when you use restatement you are stating what was said, not asking a question to clarify. Let us try two restatements.

STATEMENT: "I think selling is a good career because it is one of the primary ways to get to the top of the business world."

RESTATEMENT:  _____

_____

_____

_____

STATEMENT:   "One of the things that I didn't like about college was that my professors didn't give me much freedom to make decisions on my own."

RESTATEMENT:   _____

_____

_____

_____

## 5. Summarizing

The last listening technique is summarizing. Summarizing is best used when you want to recap the main points of the discussion because both parties have a good handle on what has transpired. Together, you can agree about what to do next. An example of a summary statement may be "You have mentioned three priorities so far and they are...." Summarization is a good technique to use when you are in a lengthy discussion which covers several topics and/or decisions.

Using these five effective listening techniques will dramatically improve your communication with others and reduce the amount of misunderstanding.

# Three Key Traits of a Good Listener

*Let me share with you a story about two men.*

❝Two men were walking along a crowded sidewalk in a downtown business area. Suddenly one exclaimed, 'Listen to the lovely sound of that cricket!' But the other could not hear. He asked his companion how he could detect the sound of the cricket amidst the din of people and traffic. The first man, who was a zoologist, had trained himself to listen to the voices of nature, but he did not explain. He simply took a coin out of his pocket and dropped it on the sidewalk, whereupon a dozen people began to look about them. 'We hear,' he said, 'what we listen for.'❞

—Bhagwan Shree Rajneesh
*The Discipline of Transcendence*

What do you listen for? Surveys show individuals listen about 25 percent of the time. You recall only 50 percent of what you hear when you actually listen. And, 70 percent of all misunderstandings happen because people do not listen to each other. If listening skills are not upgraded, there is a high probability that frustration, conflict and miscommunication will be generated. So, what can you do about it? There are three key traits associated with good listeners: patience, focus and open-mindedness.

# 1. Patience

Patience is a virtue, or so we have been told. When you are listening, be patient with the speaker while they are formulating their thoughts and ideas. Time plays a big role in communication. Human beings are in such a hurry that they lack the patience to allow the speaker to fully explore and communicate their idea. Slowing your own internal voice to give the speaker an opportunity to deliver the message in full will improve your listening. Be patient with yourself and the speaker, and your communication will improve.

# 2. Focus

Focusing has two aspects. One aspect is what you do physically, the other is what you do mentally. Focus physically by taking notes and giving verbal and nonverbal clues to indicate that you are listening. When you take notes you let the speaker know that what they are saying is important enough for you to write it down. It tells them that you are concentrating on what they are saying so you can understand. Also, the physical act of writing will keep your mind from wandering during the course of the conversation.

Verbal and nonverbal clues are reinforcements to the speaker that you are listening to them. Some examples of verbal clues are "I see," "please continue," "tell me more," and "uh huh." Nonverbal clues include leaning forward to show interest, nodding your head, giving appropriate facial expressions like smiling or frowning, and direct eye contact. By using, but not overusing, a combination of these clues you will provide the speaker with a congruent message that says you are concentrating on them and what they are saying.

Mentally focus on the speaker to avoid being distracted by anything or anyone while you are listening. To mentally focus on the speaker turn off your own worries. If you have other thoughts while you are trying to listen to someone share their ideas and you believe what you are thinking about is more important, you will not be able to focus on the speaker's message.

Asking questions is another good technique to use when trying to focus. If you know that to fully understand what the other person is saying you will need to ask questions, you will be able to focus. Sometimes you must make yourself listen even when there are distractions.

Focus on both the content of the message and feelings behind the message so you can get the complete communication. The way the speaker says something is often more important than what they say. Listen for the emotions that accompany the words like irritation, frustration, sarcasm, happiness or enthusiasm. The exact same words can be delivered and have entirely different meanings depending on how they are said.

# 3. Open-mindedness

The final key trait of an effective listener is being open-minded. You will not always agree with what the other person says. That is why keeping an open mind is important. By remaining open-minded you may uncover a new opportunity, new information, more support for your position, or a different perspective. Earlier, you discovered that listening blocks can cause you to jump to conclusions and, more times than not, the wrong conclusions. An effective listener hears the speaker out even if they disagree with what is being said. You know the old saying about assuming, "When you assume, you make an ass out of you and me." Eliminate your biases and listen with an open mind.

The old adage of "walk a mile in the other man's shoes" is an appropriate one here. In order for you to remain open-minded you must put yourself in the shoes of the other person to truly understand what it is they are communicating. Their message is important to them. You will be able to understand them better if you listen from their point of view.

Remaining open-minded also includes reacting and responding to *the ideas* the person is communicating and not to *the person*. Emotions are easily engaged in a conversation. When you become emotional, you lose the ability to evaluate objectively what is being said and you stop listening with an open mind. Analyze what the person has said that "hooked" you and begin listening again. Gaining control of your own thoughts and emotions can increase the effectiveness you have in communicating with others. Keep an open mind until you have heard everything they have to say then you can communicate your point.

Limit your talking while the other person is expressing their thoughts. That's easier said than done, right? You cannot listen and talk at the same time and have an effective dialogue with another person. If you are not open-minded, focused and patient, you will probably do one of the following: interrupt the other person or finish their sentences for them. Neither tactic will win you a gold medal as a star listener.

Think about why your best friends are your best friends. When asked whom you would identify as good listeners in your life, most people choose their best friends. Why? It is usually because they are unselfish listeners who demonstrate the three key traits of a good listener. How most people describe their best friends would fit this quote "They are patient, focused on me and what I am saying, and are open-minded enough to let me share anything." Do your friends say that about you?

A way to ensure your friends and colleagues view you as a genuine listener include practicing good listening skills regularly. Practice with everyone you know, such as: friends, family and associates; those people you like and, especially, those you do not like. If you can be a good listener with someone that, in the past, you have had a difficult time listening to for any of the reasons covered, then you can listen to anyone. Practice the ideas that have been discussed in this chapter, such as note taking, verbal and nonverbal reinforcements, the five listening techniques, patience, focus, and being open-minded.

Challenge yourself to listen to material that is new or unfamiliar to you and build those listening muscles. If you concentrate and practice regularly, you will notice marked improvement over time. Effective listening takes effort and concentration and is well worth the investment. Try it and find out what you have been missing by not listening effectively. Remember… listening is your choice!

*One last thought…*

**"God gave us two ears but only one mouth. Some people say that's because he wanted us to spend twice as much time listening as talking. Others claim it's because he knew listening was twice as hard as talking."**

—*Unknown*

# About Sandie Akerman

Sandie Akerman, President of Akerman Consulting & Training, Inc., began her business in May 1995. The business is focused on assisting organizations and individuals improve relationships with self and others through the design and development of customized curriculums.

Sandie has over twenty years of progressive management, training, and sales experience. Innovative and energetic best describe her style in working with people.

Prior to starting her own organization, Sandie was Director of Training & Development, Architectural Finishes, PPG Industries, Inc. She won the Special Achievement Award for developing a customer training program.

Other past employers include Dictaphone Corporation, where Sandie was awarded New Sales Representative, 1983 and Top Sales Manager, 1986; United Telephone Systems, Ponderosa Training Institute, and WISH-TV.

She received Bachelor of Science degrees in Broadcast Journalism and Political Science from Butler University, Indianapolis, Indiana.

Sandie is President of Pittsburgh's chapter of the American Society for Training and Development. She is a member of the National Speakers Association (NSA) and Pennsylvania Speakers Association (PSA).

# Company Profile

kerman Consulting & Training, Inc. specializes in assisting organizations and individuals in creating positive personal results and
increasing organizational effectiveness by improving relationships
with self and others. The staff of Akerman Consulting & Training, Inc.
believe that people are at the heart of the bottom line and what is behind
every issue is how we relate to ourselves and others.

We deploy tools and training to enhance a participant's skills by presenting customized programs in the areas of sales/sales management,
customer service, relationship building and communications.

We do not believe in doing training for training's sake. We are
committed to you leaving our seminars with usable information that is
customized to your situation. We also believe that no matter what the
seminar length, it is critical that you leave with next step actions defined in
order to implement the new knowledge and behaviors immediately.

Other organizational and individual development areas: needs assessment, group facilitation, attitudes and values, change management,
strategic planning, coping/stress techniques, person listening, and team
building. We are an award-winning distributor for Carlson Learning
products.

Akerman Consulting & Training, Inc. works with for-profit and not-
for-profit organizations. Clients include: Mellon Bank, N.A., Pepsi-Cola
Company, National City Bank, Interstate Hotels Corporation, USAirways,
Southwest Bank, Fisher Scientific, Robroy Industries, RPS, Inc., United
Way of Allegheny County, Franklin Interiors, TRACO, and CTAC.

**Sandie Akerman**
**Akerman Consulting & Training, Inc.**

Franklin Park Corporate Center
2000 Corporate Drive, Suite 320
Wexford, PA 15090

Toll-free: 800-253-7626
Phone: 724-933-3113
Fax: 724-933-9164
E-mail: Sandie@akermancenter.com

❖ **Chapter 3** ❖

# Networking Skills
# for the
# New Millennium

*by*
*Mary Maloney Cronin*

Networking is more about
GIVING than it is receiving.

—*Mary Maloney Cronin*

Kevin Bacon, a noted actor who became famous appearing in the movie *Footloose*, is also a very smart business man. Why? Because of the incredible network of people he has built for himself. His circle of influence on the Hollywood circuit and in the entertainment industry has earned him more roles in more movies than any other actor alive. As a matter of fact, *Footloose* was one of the few movies where he was billed as the front-runner. His strategy was not to play the lead in every film, rather it was to take as many secondary roles as he could and play them to the best of his ability. Secondary role playing gave him more opportunity to work in the acting field. This strategy has paid off handsomely. Ironically, a "game" was created that illustrates the success of knowing so many people. The game is called "Six Degrees to Kevin Bacon," and the premise is that within six moves of naming any actor or actress, you can link to Kevin Bacon.

Wouldn't it be nice to drop the name of anyone in the world and in less than six moves they could be connected to you? Remember the Broadway show and movie *Six Degrees of Separation*? The title refers to the fact that there's a chain of no more than six people that links every person on this planet to every other person. Believe it or not, it can be done. All you have to do is NETWORK.

What is networking anyhow? In this chapter you will learn the value of creating a strong network, how to approach, build and maintain your networking base in a proactive manner, the best places to network, who to include on your networking list, the networking no-no's and nuggets, and most importantly, how to continuously network to reap great dividends.

# The Value of Creating a Strong Network

No matter who you are, what level of the organization you have reached, and what business or industry you are in, having a strong network is critical. YOU CAN'T DO IT ALONE. Whether you need a recommendation for a good sales rep or a contact in Portugal by tomorrow, you have to rely on other people to help you get what you need. If you're looking for financial assistance, need intellectual resources, or are seeking to form strategic alliances, networking is a way to make this happen.

Maybe you're relocating to a new area. Networking is the best way to make these challenges happen smoothly.

Defining the value of networking depends on what drives you — pain or pleasure. If it's pain that drives you, then consider the following as valuable reasons to network:

- **Downsizing:** Since 1979, more than 43 million jobs have been lost in America. I know. I lost my job twice before I became self-employed. Those who were lucky enough to find new jobs are earning two-thirds less than they originally earned. Harvey Mackay, in his book *Dig a Well Before You're Thirsty*, says that you should dig your well even if you don't think you need one, and more importantly, you should never wait until you're dying of thirst to start clawing at the ground.

- **Financial Assistance:** Statistics show that the average American family is one step away from financial disaster. It's not that we don't earn enough. We simply don't save enough or plan well enough for the future. What is your relationship like with your banker? Your financial planner? Who can you call on for advice on how to make your money work for you? Do you have a good lawyer in case you're sued? Do you have a good accountant who will manage your money along the way? Do the names of good people immediately come to mind or is it a struggle? Not being able to pay your mortgage on time and constantly having to make excuses when the bill collectors come knocking on your door generates tremendous discomfort. The last thing you want to do is work with incompetent people that might cause you to lose your life savings.

If pleasure drives you, consider the following as valuable ideas to network:

- **Improving Yourself:** Everyone has a unique and viable talent to share with the world. You can always learn something from everyone you meet. By networking, you can significantly increase your knowledge banks and be exposed to things you might never have thought about on your own. Perhaps you know someone who has lived all over the world. You should have conversations with them about diversity and culture contrasts. Maybe you would like to become a wine connoisseur or learn more about how to play the stock market. Books and magazines can offer you a wealth of information; however, networking with the right people can offer valuable, insightful perspectives from someone who has "been there." Keep in mind that people love to share their knowledge with others.

- **Helping Others:** People make careers out of volunteering for various organizations. Their thrill is in helping others. Tremendous opportunity lies in networking with people who share the same mission. Remember, YOU CAN'T DO IT ALONE. Perhaps you have a passion for building self-esteem in children, or conservation, or animal rights. Networking can help you connect with like-minded people. Together you can accomplish a worthy goal. The AIDS Memorial Quilt displayed in Washington, D.C. in 1996 started out as an informal networking group of people who had loved ones die of AIDS. They wanted to do something to make other people aware and educate them of the far-reaching effects of this disease. They began making a quilt in their memory. More than 20,000 quilt panels later, representing almost every state and some parts of the world, the AIDS Memorial Quilt was carried by train to be displayed in front of the White House in October 1996. The ceremony and display received international media attention. All of this occurred through the power of networking.

# Who Should You Include on Your Networking List?

If asked who you should include on your networking list, the answer is simply, EVERYONE. You can benefit from everyone you meet and vice versa. If you're just beginning, don't be discouraged. The average person can sit down and list at least 400 contacts that are immediately at their disposal. For example, you have friends, family, coworkers, teammates, neighbors, classmates, fellow church or synagogue members, and on and on. Go through your receipts in your wallet. Identify the people in the places where you write checks. Where do you go and who do you see regularly? Are you a good customer? Do you know these people by name? Many folks belong to several different organizations, all with directories and mailing lists. Therefore, how many people do you know in the association? Do they know you? The following is a sample list of people who potentially could appear on your networking list. See if you can name at least two people in each area within your own circle of influence as you develop your list.

|  | NAME | NAME |
|---|---|---|
| Accountants |  |  |
| Alumni |  |  |
| Attorneys |  |  |
| Authors |  |  |
| Auto mechanics |  |  |
| Bankers |  |  |
| Beauticians/Barbers |  |  |
| Board of directors |  |  |
| Celebrities |  |  |
| College professors |  |  |
| CEO's |  |  |
| Coaches |  |  |
| Community leaders |  |  |
| Detectives |  |  |
| Doctors |  |  |
| Firefighters |  |  |
| Headhunters |  |  |
| Insurance agents |  |  |

| | NAME | NAME |
|---|---|---|
| Librarians | | |
| Media | | |
| Peers in your business | | |
| Philanthropists | | |
| Pilots | | |
| Police officers | | |
| Political leaders | | |
| Real estate brokers | | |
| Religious leaders | | |
| Restaurant owners | | |
| Secretaries | | |
| Speakers | | |
| Stockbrokers | | |
| Teachers | | |
| Travel agents | | |
| Veterinarians | | |
| | | |

*If you have an unusual story about networking, send it to Cronin Communications at 709 Tally Drive, Pittsburgh, PA 15237, call at 1-800-798-4702, or send via E-mail to MMCronin@aol.com. You'll receive a free copy of The Communication Coach.*

After you've made a list of all the people you know, begin seeking out new people to add to your list on a daily basis. One way to do this is to go to the people section of your local newspaper and cut out the picture and article of "people on the move." These are people that you would like to meet. Send the article to them with a note. Many times I've seen networkers laminate the article, which is inexpensive and adds a nice touch. Call the person to make sure they've received it. Flatter them about their recognition in the paper and ask to set up a phone conference or a meeting. The goal of the meeting is to: 1) find out more about what they do to network, and 2) share the names of at least two people who could help them in their position. They'll respond favorably to the attention they've received. Remember: Networking is more about GIVING than it is receiving. Ask not what they can do for you—ask what you can do *for them!*

Another way to add people to your list is to tap into other people's networks. Everyone on your list has their own circle of influence. Ask to be introduced to some of their contacts and in return, make sure you introduce them to some of yours. Always keep a "wish list" of people you would like to meet. When you're tapping other people's networks, ask them if they know the people on your wish list. Make it a game to figure out how to get to them. Remember, YOU CAN'T DO IT ALONE.

Some other good ways to meet and get to know people are by volunteering your time to serve for a group—any group, participating on an awards committee or offering your services or expert advice for free. Do what you feel comfortable with.

As your circle of influence starts to increase, begin to ask yourself, what's my network look like? Is it global? Do I have people from other states and countries in my network? Why/why not? Who can I help?

Keep in mind, it is not the *quantity* of names that is valuable. It is the QUALITY. Cold names should not appear on your networking list—cold names are those people that you have never had any contact with, and should be listed in a separate file, perhaps as part of your "wish list." Every name in your networking list should be "hot." Hot means you've met them, interfaced and want to continue the relationship. Some people use cold, warm and hot names. I use hot and cold to keep it simple. If you're adding new names and are not sure where they belong, ask yourself—"does this person know me/recognize my name?" If not, they're cold and they go on your wish list of people (individuals) to get to know better in the near future. Hot names are those you've connected with and became people you can count on down the road. You should have made some type of connection with each and every contact listed. People you know are people you can count on down the road.

# Where do you go to Network?

Once again, the list could be endless. The following are some examples of places you can network. As you scan the list, think about conversation topics that go along with these places. (For example, when standing in line for lunch and you see a person reading a book on San Francisco, start a networking conversation by asking if they're going on a trip.)

Associations/organizations
Social clubs
Hobbies
Churches
Restaurants
Bookstores
Dry cleaners
Clothing stores
Health food stores
Trade shows
Conventions
Golf courses/shops
Grocery stores
Elevators

What are some other places where *you* network?

# How do you Network?

Networking is a proactive process and should become part of your day just like brushing your teeth and taking a shower. It truly is a necessity for you to get ahead and become a standout in your profession. To network most effectively, use the following tips.

1. **SET GOALS**
   - Meet one new person each day and follow up. Ask how you can help them. The gentleman behind the counter who fills your coffee cup every morning on your way to work qualifies as a new person. The most important element is to learn their name, and use it every time you see them. Learn something interesting about them. Continue learning about them. Capture their name and interesting information in your database.
   - Seek out and attend at least two networking functions each month. Sitting in the bleachers at your son's baseball game also

counts as a networking function, as long as you are meeting someone new.

- Each month, set a goal for new people you are going to meet. If you're planning on going to two networking functions, then plan to collect at least 10 new business cards at each or 20 new people each month and follow up. Again, ask how you can help them. It is not enough for you to remember them—they must remember you.

## 2. FOLLOW UP

For many people, it can be uncomfortable to talk to strangers, to strike up a conversation with someone new, to ask to exchange business cards. Networking isn't a habit for most; therefore, it may be difficult at first. Many times, just getting through a meeting or networking function is energy consuming, and many people wipe their brow and decide that they've made it through. Then they forget to follow up. Or many people get into a numbers marathon, where they're in a race to build the quantity, not the quality of their networking database. They simply begin adding names without following up. A follow-up system will keep you on track, keep your database solid and keep you excited and motivated to continue building. Your follow up should be systematic. For example:

**STEP 1:** Collect information (name, company, address, phone, fax, e-mail, significant information such as what you talked about, their profession, interests like fishing or golf, etc.) however you can get it without forgetting it. Write it on a napkin or collect their business card.

**STEP 2:** Within 24 hours, drop a quick note to your new contact, asking how you can help them.

**STEP 3:** Enter them into your database. This could be your little black book, time management system, or a computerized contact management software program version—whatever works for you.

**STEP 4:** Schedule a time to call your new contact again in less than two weeks. When you contact them, ask them for their advice on something and ask how you can help them. Keep the conversation short. Let them know you don't want to waste their time, while remembering you want to make a good, lasting impression.

**STEP 5:** Two weeks after the second contact, send them something —an e-mail, a note, a newsletter, etc. For example, I've clipped articles from the *Wall Street Journal* and sent them to people I've just met with a short "for your information (FYI)" note.

STEP 6: Update the contact every three months. Keep in contact with them periodically, systematically. Everyone on your list should be contacted in some fashion a minimum of twice per year, if not more often.

**3. THINK ABOUT HELPING *THEM*, RATHER THAN HOW THEY CAN HELP YOU.**

The best networkers don't talk about themselves until they're asked. After all, you're on a mission to find out interesting information about the new people you meet. To do that, you must ask questions: open-ended questions using "who, what, where, when, why, how." Some other conversation starters include "tell me, describe for me, show me." For many people, the most difficult part of networking is breaking the ice. Here are some examples on how to get a networking conversation started. You'll be guaranteed to get people talking about themselves.

For example, at a cocktail party where spouses are invited: "How did you two meet?"

—At a business luncheon, while seated: "When you're not working, what do you like to do?"

—At an association meeting: "I need your advice. If I were a prospective member, what would you say to convince me to join this group?"

—At a social function: "Where are you from originally? Tell me more about it…"

Another way to break the ice is to notice something about a person. For example, a class ring or unusual jewelry. Ask about it. The goal is to find common ground and to give people a reason to remember you. Even extroverts plan ahead for conversation starters. After a long day, even the most outgoing sometimes find it difficult to walk up to a stranger and start a conversation. One suggestion is to grab a current news magazine and read/skim it so you can sound well-informed when talking to strangers.

# Tools for Networking

Capture the following information as part of your network database to make your database "come alive." It should be a list of interesting, diverse, fascinating people. Your networking database should always go beyond a name and number. In order to maximize your effectiveness in networking, you must know more about them than the basics. For example, this is what I like to note about new people that I meet:

**NAME:** I always list the name before the company, because you're communicating with a person, not a business. Listing the name is more personal. The company may be significant, however it's the person that's most important.

**TITLE:** The title/position is important to know, particularly if a job promotion or a job change occurs. A transition offers an opportunity to network with this contact again to say congratulations.

**COMPANY:** Jot down what the company does, any other information that makes the company unique. For example, the average stay for an employee may be 11 years which is unusually long.

**ADDRESS:** Keep it current. If the address changes, send a congratulatory note. It projects the image that you are "on the ball" and in the playing field.

**PHONE/FAX/E-MAIL:** E-mail is becoming exceptionally important. Most people are happier to answer an e-mail than the phone. In addition, broadcast faxing and broadcast e-mailing are a great way to keep in touch on a systematic basis. (Note: Always check FCC regulations.) It sure beats writing 1000 notes!

**DATE:** List the date you met the person and where. It helps to jog your memory, particularly when your network database gets to be quite large.

**INTERESTS:** Hopefully, when you connected with this person, you found out more about them than their title. Some people break it down into topics such as alma mater, hobbies, family/kids names, awards/recognitions.

**JUICE:** Meaning "juicy information." This is the one thing you can think of that made this person a standout in your mind. You'll refer to it quite frequently. For example, maybe they go on safari every year or want to learn how to fly helicopters.

After you have collected this valuable information, house it in one place that can be accessed easily and updated without too much hassle. The rule of thumb is simply: whatever works for you. I know sales reps that insist on using their little black book, a Rolodex and a Franklin Planner section just for networking. I personally use ACT! contact management software made by Symantec™. It's easy to use and has powerful features for broadcast faxing/e-mailing, logging contact information, scheduling reminders to network again and to-do activities, updating information, listing things you've done for them (like referring business, which gives you an excuse to network again to see how things worked out) recording key conversations, charting a history of every phone call you make, etc. There are a variety of software packages available on the market to organize this data. Again, it doesn't matter how you do it—just do it.

# Networking No-No's

—Avoid talking about salary, politics and gender issues. These are topics where you simply cannot win. Someone is going to disagree with you and probably will take a strong stand on it.

—Don't walk around a room and simply collect business cards. It's better to meet and get to know two people rather than have a handful of cards of people about whom you know nothing. If you don't know anything about them, they certainly don't know anything about you. Plus, they don't qualify for your hot list and that's what you're networking for —to build your hot list!

# How to be a Standout Networker: Networking Nuggets

- Make sure your business card is a mini-advertisement; e.g., who you are, what you do and the benefit you can provide to them. Too often, a business card only has a person's name, address, phone number and company name. Sometimes company names don't immediately imply the business purpose. Have a tagline benefit to trigger the memory of the person who carries the card.

- Develop and use a 30-second "commercial." Be prepared when people ask, "what do you do?" Rather than stumble over the answer to that question, you'll know exactly what to say and deliver your commercial without hesitating. Tell people who you are, what you do, and how you help people. Say it succinctly and with confidence. You will impress people because you portray an image of being focused. People gravitate to people who know what they want out of life.

- Step beyond your comfort zone. Don't be afraid to hear "no." Quite honestly, if you ask for someone's business card after you've had a good conversation with them, they will rarely refuse. Keep in mind that most folks are just as nervous as you are about networking.

Being nervous about networking could be a conversation starter to break the ice as well.

- Be proactive. Don't wait for people to come to you. Go to them. Try to meet and connect with at least 10 new business card contacts each time you're out at a function. You'll be amazed at how fast your network circle begins to grow.

- Have fun. Sing a song in your head. My mentor, Harvey, taught me this slight-edge secret—every time you walk into a room or a new place, make sure you are singing a song in your head. The song must be upbeat, have rhythm and energy, and have a little bit of attitude. Harvey was 71 years old and his song was the Blues Brothers, "I'm a Soul Man." He played that song over and over in his head and when he walked into the room, people noticed. He didn't even have to speak to command respect and attention. Plus he had a great deal of fun.

- Choose another holiday besides Christmas and Hanukkah to send cards, or create one of your own. I get more attention from sending business St. Patty's Day cards than from any other mailing I do. You'll be surprised at how many people will call and say, "I've never received a card for this holiday before. Thank you."

- Read, read, read. Know what's going on in your world. Current events offer you a wealth of conversation starters and options to find common ground with people.

- Never, ever pass up the opportunity to meet a new person. Uncommon things have happened when meetings occur on the spur of the moment. Whether you're waiting for the parking shuttle or you're attending a conference out-of-state, seek out opportunities to meet new people.

- Remember people's names. The most magical sound in the world is the sound of a person's own name. Use it whenever you can. However, if you're unsure of a person's name, refrain from guessing. Also, don't be afraid to ask if you can't remember. People will respect you for admitting that you don't remember their name.

- Be a resource and use other people as a resource. The next time you're going out of town, scan your network of people and call someone you haven't talked to in a while to see what the best restaurants are, etc., then send them a note saying that you liked it. Bring newspapers or send postcards to people on your list.

- Keep a wish list of people you want to meet. You never know what will happen. My husband, Chris, had always wanted to meet Lou

Holtz, the former coach of Notre Dame's football team. One evening Chris was at a dinner party and bumped into someone who knew Lou Holtz's personal secretary. After a lengthy conversation, Chris discovered that like himself, Lou was a huge Pittsburgh Pirate's baseball fan. My husband was able to call Lou's secretary to let her know that he was sending some Pirate memorabilia. He also extended an invitation to a ballgame the next time Lou was in town. Chris never expected anything to materialize. Shortly thereafter, he received a handwritten note from Lou and an invitation to join him on the sidelines for the University of Pittsburgh/Notre Dame football game the following fall so they could meet. Not only did Chris spend time on the sidelines, but he spoke at length with Lou in the locker room and on the field after the game. Since then they have exchanged holiday cards every year. My husband still helps Lou get Pirate tickets and they keep in touch.

- Be creative. A friend of mine sent a box of Cracker Jacks along with an article about Cracker Jack's 100th celebration as a congratulations to the CEO of the company for its own 100th anniversary celebration. The CEO still talks about it.

*A rule to live by:*

> **"It's not what others can do for you.
> It's what you can do for them.
> The ultimate goal in networking
> is making a connection that will be
> remembered and treasured."**

Are you a good networker? Take this quiz to determine your networking level.

# Your Networking Quotient

TO SCORE: Give yourself 10 points for every "yes" you check.

|  | YES | NO |
|---|---|---|
| 1. Do you belong to a business group? (i.e. Chamber of Commerce, etc.) | — | — |
| 2. Do you attend the functions or meetings of your group regularly? | — | — |
| 3. Are you making at least one or two new contacts a month who are in a position to refer business to you? | — | — |
| 4. Do you have "Centers of Influence" who send you more than one referral per year? | — | — |
| 5. When you attend a networking function, do you meet at least five new people? | — | — |
| 6. Do you follow up on contacts you make at these meetings by sending a letter or making a call? | — | — |
| 7. Are you willing to invest six months to a year to develop long-term relationships? | — | — |
| 8. Do you thank people who give you referrals or leads with a phone call or a letter? | — | — |
| 9. Do you pro-actively stick out your hand to meet new people at a business function? | — | — |
| 10. Do you believe in "word of mouth" referrals? | — | — |

YOUR SCORE: ____

80-100: Super Networker
50- 80: Excellent Networker
30- 50: You need some work

20-30: You're working too hard
0-20: You must be making a lot of cold calls

*Courtesy of TSBN —The Small Business Network*

# About Mary Maloney Cronin

Mary Maloney Cronin, speaker, author, and marketing/communications consultant is President of Cronin Communications, a firm dedicated to helping small businesses market and communicate more effectively through customized consulting and workshops.

Recognized as One of the Top 50 Women in Business in the State of Pennsylvania by the Commonwealth of Pennsylvania, Cronin is also one of Oldsmobile's prestigious National Athena Award recipients for outstanding women in business. Featured in *Successful Women*, the *Pittsburgh Tribune-Review,* and others for her unique, relationship-based approach to doing business, she is called upon frequently for marketing, public relations, and communications advice.

Cronin holds a Master's degree in Organizational Psychology from Villanova University, Villanova, Pennsylvania, and a Bachelor's degree in Communications/Marketing from Duquesne University, Pittsburgh, Pennsylvania.

# Company Profile

Cronin Communications helps businesses and professionals stand out in a crowd. Cronin Communications is a unique firm dedicated to helping small businesses market and communicate more effectively by providing customized consulting and workshops. Cronin Communications has earned its reputation for helping companies focus on what makes them unique, and capitalizing on that uniqueness in the marketplace and the media. Cronin Communications has a select group of private consulting clients plus a growing list of professionals including small business owners, entrepreneurs, medical practice administrators, and executives who consistently give high ratings to training programs.

Ms. Cronin offers keynotes, half-day programs and full-day workshops in three topic areas including marketing, communications and public relations. Titles include...

- *How to be a Standout Marketeer*
- *How to be a Top Communicator in a Changing Business World*
- *Everyone Remembers the Elephant in the Pink Tutu: How to Cash in on Thousands of Dollars of Free Publicity*

She has received exceptional reviews for her high energy, straightforward approach from small businesses as well as companies such as Mellon Bank, Smith Kline Beecham, and UPS. If you're looking for ways to change behavior and are ready to take your business to the next level, call Cronin Communications. We welcome the opportunity to work with you.

**CRONIN COMMUNICATIONS**
*...Helping small businesses*
*market & communicate more effectively*
709 Tally Drive • Pittsburgh, PA 15237 USA
Phone: (412) 366-2187, or toll-free 1-800-798-4702
Fax: (412) 367-2407, or toll-free 1-800-798-4703
E-mail: MMCronin@aol.com
Website: http://www.cyberscoreinc.com/cronin

## ❖ Chapter 4 ❖

# Thought Starbursts...
# A New Way of Thinking

*by*

*Debbie Gracey*

Thought Starbursts' non-linear formats
encourage ideas to be generated quickly
and allow a tremendous amount of significant
information to be put on one piece of paper.

*—Debbie Gracey*

# A Sea of Information

Imagine yourself swimming in a sea of information. Your goal is to make sense of the ideas in which you are submerged. You are struggling to grab each important thought and idea as it floats by. Vigorously, you attempt to arrange each thought in some kind of order. Waves swell and recede, jumbling the thoughts, requiring you to recapture and reorder them. Frustration grows. The sea begins to feel like molasses. More and more energy is required to keep your head above water. What's this? A helicopter! A long rope is dangling from the helicopter and it is coming directly toward you! Courageously, you snatch the rope and secure your footing on a large knot. Slowly the helicopter rises and as you look down on the tumultuous ocean you see the information taking shape. Not a usual shape. Something different. The shape is… flowing. You see a definite center with tentacles radiating from it, each representing a thought or idea. Very interesting—the center and tentacles represent the ideas you were struggling with in the sea. Rising higher, you see smaller outgrowths from the tentacles, each one also representing an idea. The octopus-like form you are witnessing from high in the air shows the relationship between the thoughts and ideas. The information is making sense! It is clear! Relief and enthusiasm wash over you. As the helicopter climbs, your attention now turns toward the sky in front of you and you know the name of this form—*Thought Starburst!*

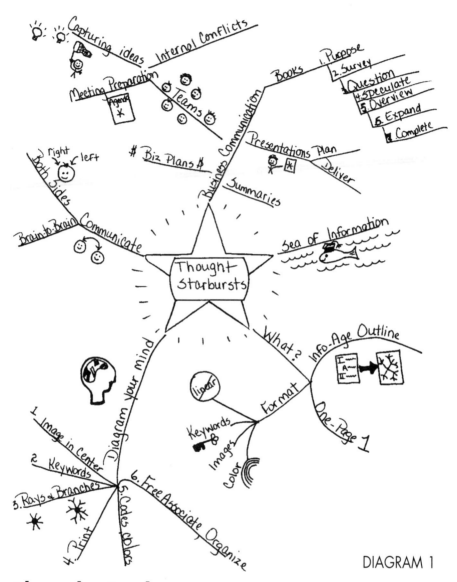

DIAGRAM 1

# Thought Starbursts

The diagram above is a *Thought Starburst:* a representation of ideas using key words, colors, imagery and connections. A *Starburst* is an "information age outline." Its non-linear format encourages ideas to be generated quickly and allows a tremendous amount of significant information to be put on one piece of paper. *Thought Starbursts* are superior to traditional outlines which slow thinking and limit creativity by prematurely imposing order on the thinking process, interfering with the speed and range of idea generation. *Starbursts* are an effective way to send and receive business communication. Think through the creation of presentations, articles, reports and memos using *Starbursts*. Take *Starburst* notes on books, videos and at meetings. Plan and problem solve with *Starbursts*.

# Diagram Your Mind

Human brains are remarkable. The neural circuitry of your brain is at least 1,400 times more complex than the entire world telephone system. According to Peter Russell in *The Brain Book*, psychologists estimate that most humans tap less than one percent of their brain's potential. *Thought Starbursts* encourage the brain's natural mode of thinking, opening the portal to latent brilliance. Six guidelines to maximize brainpower through *Starbursts* are:

1. **Start by drawing a picture of the topic in the center of the paper.** The center of the *Starburst* identifies the central theme—the beginning of the thought process. Pictures are important because they appeal to the eye and mind and are more easily recalled than words. Remember the old adage "a picture paints a thousand words?" It applies to *Starbursts*. Visual images also help the mind relax so that creativity flows. According to Dr. Jonathan Parker of Gateways Institute, people carry mental images all the time. By creating positive visual images, natural abilities to create, learn and remember are unleashed.

2. **Use key words.** Evidence suggests that brains store the memory of everything seen, heard, touched, smelled, or thought. Each time something new is experienced or learned, the mind looks for something it already knows, a mental hook, on which to hang the new piece of information. Associations are established in the mind. Key words, as found in *Thought Starbursts,* use associations to record ideas much more effectively and faster than complete sentences.

3. **Connect the key words with lines (rays) radiating from the central image and smaller lines (branches) radiating from the rays.** By linking key words with lines, the relationship between them is easy to see. The *Starburst* becomes a web of associations forming a diagram of the natural thought process. *Frank Schaffer's Teaching Club* calls a *Starburst* a web. Tony Buzan calls them mind maps. By any name, the connections are representative of the way people think.

4. **Print key words.** Printed words are much easier to read and remember.

5. **Use colors, pictures and codes.** Color stimulates the eyes. Sensory stimulation increases mental alertness, so lavishly apply colors to *Starbursts*. Color-code ideas that work together, use colors to show prioritization, and think of other fun ways to use colors. Codes, such as punctuation marks, shapes and letters are similar to pictures, producing positive effects as discussed in point number 1.

6. **Free associate, then organize.** Creating *Starbursts* is a two-step process. First, quickly generate as many ideas as possible in the free-association stage. Let words and images flow freely onto your paper. No limitations, please! The second step is to organize. Examine the *Starburst* more analytically, eliminating and consolidating concepts. Now give the ideas order and sequence by using numbers, additional colors or codes. The results: a creative and organized plan for communication.

# Create a Starburst

Creating a *Starburst* is easy. Joan is the president of the local legal administrators association. Sitting down to write an article on time management for the association newsletter, she wants to plan her communication. Starting with a big, clean sheet of white paper and eight colored markers, Joan is ready to let her imagination go to work. In the middle of her paper she draws a clock and prints the word "management" which is her central theme.

Now comes the fun! Joan allows her thoughts to flow freely onto the paper. For every idea she has about time management, she quickly draws a "ray" and labels each with a key word or image. She also draws branches, labeling them as well. Feeling no limitations, she free associates everything she can related to time management. She just goes for it! After recording every thought, Joan steps back and takes a look at her work.

Joan's creative brain has had its shot at the problem. Now it is time for her analytical brain to go to work. Looking at her *Starburst*, she determines which main ideas to use for her article and which ones to change or delete. Creating a new *Starburst*, she represents the chosen main ideas with rays drawn directly out of the center. Then branches, representing details, are drawn from the rays. Finally, numbers, colors and codes are used to organize. Take a look at the elements of Joan's finished *Starburst* (diagram 2).

- A clearly-defined central theme in the center of her *Thought Starburst*.

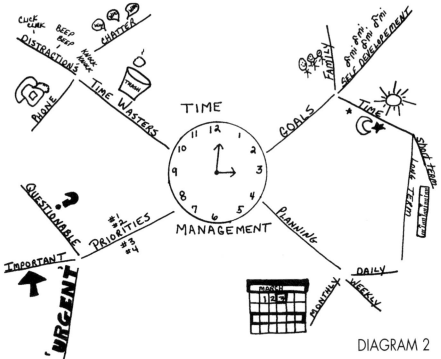

DIAGRAM 2

- The most important ideas are close to the center and less important ideas are closer to the edge.
- The links between key concepts and supporting details are recognizable because of their connections.
- All of her ideas are on one appealing page as opposed to lines and lines of words.
- Additional information is easily inserted into the *Starburst* via rays and branches.

Joan now has a plan for her time management article. With ease, she transforms the *Starburst* into an article by translating key words and images into sentences, using information on the rays as headings and main topics of paragraphs and filling in details from her branches. Joan may choose to include the *Starburst* itself as part of the article.

# Brain-to-Brain Communication

Communicating is about people connecting brain-to-brain. *Starbursts* use both sides of the brain. Partnering the right brain's rhythm, color, imagination, humor, and spatial relationships with the left brain's logic, analysis, mathematical reasoning, and detail is very powerful! According to Tony Buzan in *Use Both Sides Of Your Brain,* people do not perceive the world in linear fashion. Top-to-bottom, left-to-right and black-on-white is simply the format in which western society has printed and read the written word for several hundred years. The habit of using a top-to-bottom format prevents people from achieving their optimum mental performance when sending and receiving communication. *Starbursts* promote superior communication. Keep reading for practical examples of *Starbursts* in action.

# Business Plans

*Starbursts* enhance the ability to think through issues and develop plans.

Jack and Janet are thinking about becoming business partners. He is a professional speaker. She has a background in corporate training and development. Together they intend to launch a training and development firm. The company will market training packages to be used by aspiring speakers who have no experience in developing lesson plans and class materials. Train-the-trainer classes will be offered to the novice speakers. Class materials will be purchased by each student of the new trainers. Jack and Janet believe the venture has great potential.

Janet decides that a business plan is in order. Her goal is to document an overview of the issues affecting the potential partnership that need to be addressed. In the center of a large sheet of paper she writes the proposed name of the company. Thinking back to all of her discussions with Jack and the action items that have been swimming in her mind, Janet draws rays and branches as ideas come to her, labeling them with images and key words. Looking at the *Starburst* (diagram 3), Janet's rays include "participants," "speakers," "train-the-trainer," "sales and marketing," "administration," "costs," and "partnership." Each ray has several branches depicting details.

Janet takes a step back and analyzes the *Starburst*. She decides that the main issues are covered in the rays, therefore, no changes are needed. She rearranges several branches from the "speaker" ray to the "train-the-trainer" ray. Order is added by numbering the rays.

At their next meeting, Janet proposes the business plan to Jack. He enjoys the colorful, one-page format. The content is particularly impressive. Janet's plan is comprehensive and concise. The proposal does, indeed, become the plan to create the partnership. The *Starburst* is also used as a discussion document which can be easily updated by adding additional rays and branches.

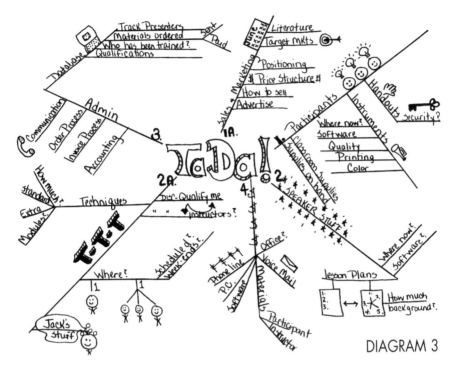

Track Presenters
Materials ordered
Who has been trained?
Qualifications
Database
Communication
Admin
Order Process
Invoice Process
Accounting
Literature
Target mkts
Positioning
Price Structure
How to sell
Advertise
Marketing
Sales
Participants
Where now?
Software
Quality
Printing
Color
Instruments
Handouts
security?

**TaDa!**

How much?
Standard
Extra
Modules
Techniques
TTT
Where?
Schedule d?
week ends?
Phone line
PC.
Software
Voice Mail
Office?
Materials
Participant
Instructor
Speaker Stuff
Where now?
Software
lesson Plans
How much background?
Jack's Stuff

DIAGRAM 3

# Team Meetings

Teams are becoming the mainstay of contemporary organizations. Organizations that use teams accomplish improvements 30 to 50 percent better than non-team-based organizations. Cross-functional teams are the current trend and create a new and exciting communication challenge. Team meetings are quickly becoming a part of day-to-day business communication.

Team leaders, who typically facilitate team meetings, play a key role in the successful combination of people and ideas from a variety of disciplines, departments and cultures. With effective communication, teams are likely to develop innovative products, processes and solutions. With poor communication, meetings are no less than nightmarish and the results of the team's work is marginal. Two areas in which *Starbursts* are tremendously effective are meeting preparation and capturing everyone's ideas during a meeting.

Barbara is the leader of an eight-person, cross-functional team at the headquarters of a large hotel firm. Team members include a bubbly woman who works the front desk at a local property, a cynical director of sales, an analytical information technology guy, and a corporate marketing

65

manager, among others. Barbara recognizes the importance of giving the team the opportunity to prepare for meetings in advance. For each meeting, Barbara creates a *Starburst* agenda. When several agenda items are planned, the central theme of the meeting is in the center and each ray is labeled with an agenda item. When the meeting has one large agenda item, she puts that in the center and includes main issues to be discussed on each ray. Agendas are printed on colored paper as an attention-grabber. Handwritten notes from Barbara request that each member come prepared. Team members receive their agenda several days before the meeting. The results? Barbara's meetings are fast-paced, invigorating and productive because people come prepared to discuss the issues, with preliminary legwork completed.

*Starbursts* also help Barbara to capture everyone's ideas during meetings. She knows from experience that some meetings are reduced to situations where each person listens to the others only long enough to form a rebuttal. Often, the strongest, loudest or highest ranking person's ideas are the ones remembered and used even if they are not the best. *Thought Starbursts* help to insure that all ideas are recorded so the best ideas can be employed.

During meetings, Barbara has several flip charts available. She draws a picture in the center of a page indicating the central theme to be discussed. As each member expresses ideas and opinions, Barbara draws and labels rays and branches on the *Starburst* (or *Starbursts*). She checks with the contributor to insure the idea is correctly represented. As the meeting progresses, the *Starburst(s)* reflect all thoughts, ideas and opinions discussed. At the end of the day, the team reviews their *Starburst(s)* to determine the most effective and innovative solutions. *Starbursts* help to accomplish a number of positives for the team:

- Each person's contribution is recorded, regardless of how articulate or low-ranking the contributor is.
- The team is able to look at the "big picture," a diagram of all the ideas together, in context, and decide which ones have the most merit based on the ideas themselves, not on who gave them.
- The team has a record of the meeting which can be a reference in the future.
- Minutes from the meeting are easily transcribed into a linear outline for distribution.
- As the team uses *Starbursts* for their meetings, members become more open and enthusiastic because they are truly being heard.
- As the team becomes comfortable with *Starbursts*, different members volunteer to be the "*Starburst* Scribe." At each meeting, the scribe incorporates their own personality and sense of humor to the *Starburst* with images, colors and key words. Also, members take

turns facilitating segments of the meetings. Enthusiasm and participation are heightened.

*Starbursts* help teams to build an effective and efficient communication platform, making work more fun for the leader and the team!

# Resolving Internal Team Conflicts

When a team is having internal conflicts, the time is crucial for honest, open communication. The discord, in fact, may have a root that is linked to miscommunication. Faltering at the onset of internal conflict results in delays, loss of momentum, decreased team energy, distracted players, lack of motivation—a host of potential negatives that contribute to the disintegration of the final results.

Team discussions, skillfully facilitated, are essential to keep the team cohesive, positive and moving in the right direction. An easy trap for teams to fall into when engaged in a discussion is blaming individuals for things gone wrong and attacking people instead of problems. The adept facilitator will help participants *Starburst* the discussion by recording issues, as opposed to personal affronts, on the rays and branches. The facilitator will ask clarifying questions that keep the discussion focused on identifying problems and root causes.

Every team member needs the opportunity to be truly heard during the discussion. The facilitator insures that each individual is given the chance to express himself, uninterrupted, and records all contributions to the *Starburst*. The facilitator keeps the entire meeting on a professional versus a personal level.

Once all issues, problems and root causes have been identified, a second *Starburst* is created with possible solutions, again, with everyone's points carefully listened to and noted. The team reviews the possible solutions together and determines the best way to heal itself.

The good news is that by rising to the occasion and committing to honest and open communication during difficult and painful times, the team will rise to greater levels of communication and effectiveness.

# Taking Notes on Books and Articles

The information age is famous for producing tidal waves of reading material. Books, trade magazines, newsletters, computer-based training, E-mails and communiqués—it never stops! Competing in business and professional career pursuits require staying abreast of changing technology, business practices, management techniques and a variety of specialized subjects. Taking notes on books and articles is a requisite when the reader needs to retain or refer back to valuable nuggets of information. *Starbursts* provide a quick, easy, fun, effective and easily referenced method of taking notes.

When reading books or articles, the best approach is:

- **Think about the purpose for reading the book.** Ask yourself what you expect to gain from reading a selection. Are you looking for new notions on a familiar subject? Do you need answers to precise questions? Is learning about a brand new subject your order of the day? Establishing a purpose helps readers determine if a particular book or article will be useful.

- **Survey the entire book or article.** Read the title, subtitle and jacket summaries. Review the author, dates of publication and copyright. Examine the table of contents and index. Read the preface, forward, introduction, recommendations and conclusions. Scan the maps, graphs, illustrations, charts, bold headings and questions. Read a paragraph or two. Now review what you've learned about the book's content and format and decide whether or not to read it.

- **Formulate questions.** Formulating what, who, when, where, how, and why questions creates a mental framework that makes reading more meaningful because the reading is now a search for what you want to know. "Mental hooks" are installed in the mind, ready to receive new information.

- **Speculate.** Take an educated guess at the answers to your questions. Mentally recall what you already know about the subject and what was learned by surveying. Find this difficult? According to Margaret Morgan Bynum and Debra Giffen in *Speed Learning*, schools train students **not** to predict, being fearful that a wrong guess will interfere with learning. Just the opposite is true! Learning from mistakes is very effective. Alternatively, if the speculation is right, then the reading simply reinforces what was already known or guessed.

- *Starburst* **an overview.** Create a *Starburst* with the framework of the book using the table of contents, major headings and summaries. Diagram the central theme and rays labeled with key ideas.

- **Expand your *Starburst*.** Now chapter by chapter, read the headings again along with the first paragraph under each heading and the first sentence of each paragraph after that. Review pictures, graphs and other visuals again along with summaries and anything set apart or italicized that indicate important information. At the end of each chapter, fill in the branches of the *Starburst* with important details.

- **Complete your *Starburst*.** By now a majority of the book has been read, understood and recorded. The reading completed to this point may well be enough. If every detail is needed, quickly read all the words in each chapter, adding as much detail to the *Starburst* as you deem necessary.
- **The final product.** The finished product is a one-page diagram of the entire book organized by main topic with the most important ideas toward the center and details closer to the edge. The mind finds it much more appealing and easier to remember than boring, linear notes. The *Starburst* can be used for future reference or a study guide, like traditional notes. If your goal is maximum retention of the material, review the *Starburst* a few hours, a few days, a few weeks, and a few months after the initial reading. Time-spaced reviews are the best route to long-term retention of information. See Diagram 4 for an example of *Starburst* notes on a book about building a successful small business.

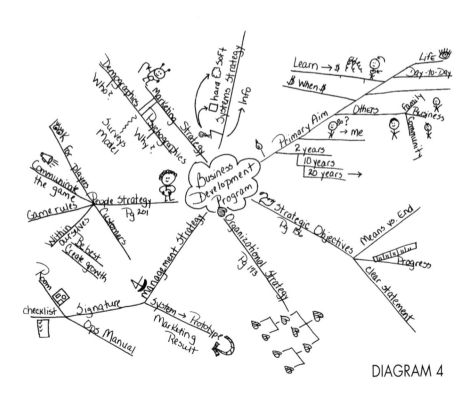

DIAGRAM 4

# Summaries

A truly daunting task is communicating to masses of people in many locations. To condense information into bite-size nuggets that a variety of people can understand, use summary *Starbursts*.

Gary is the Director of Marketing at a regional airline. His mission is to champion the company's shift toward a customer focus from its current operational focus. Tracking customer reactions to recent changes in service was the first step in Gary's master plan. The one-million dollar price tag was hefty for a two-hundred million dollar company but Gary achieved board approval for the project. The next critical step was winning middle management support and communicating the plan to the front line. Gary's strategy was to present the plan to as many managers as possible by traveling to each of the airline's locations, then asking managers to relay the plan to their direct reports. The presentation consisted of 20 slides and took about an hour to deliver. Audiences seemed receptive. Gary felt positive until he began receiving phone calls from front-line personnel challenging the huge expenditure. Gary could tell by the nature of the callers' questions that they had received only part of his message. Concern was his reaction because buy-in at all levels was important to the success of the plan. Gary knew from experience that giving copies of a 20-page presentation to front-line people was not an effective communication tool. They didn't have time to read it on their own and they needed to see a demonstration of their mangers' support. Delivering the full one-hour presentation to the front line was impractical. Gary needed a solution! He summarized the plan in a *Starburst* which took about 20 minutes to create (diagram 5). Managers conducted 15-minute briefings using the *Starburst* as handouts. Gary knew the *Starburst* briefings worked because he started receiving significantly fewer negative calls, and even a few positive calls. He felt much more secure that everyone received an overview of the entire plan.

# Planning and Delivering Presentations

Presentations are the scariest type of business communication. Three-by-five inch index cards are clutched protectively. The mind reviews once again the word-for-word memorization of the entire presentation. Perspiration forms on the brow and prayers that the mind will not go blank are said at warp speed. *Thought Starbursts* aid tremendously in the planning and delivery of presentations.

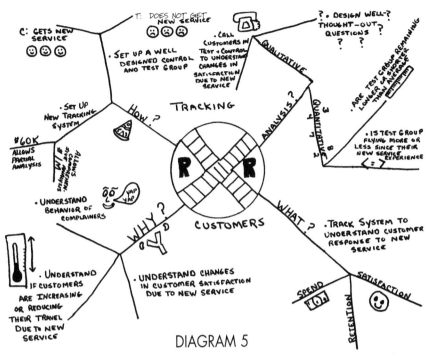

DIAGRAM 5

According to Michael Gelb in *Present Yourself*, the average executive spends the equivalent of three days preparing a 45-minute presentation—a period full of frustration, discarded ideas and crumpled worksheets. *Starbursts* can help.

John is developing a two-hour seminar on listening skills for a group of nurses. He is a stickler for customizing the presentation for the audience. After devouring seven books and articles on the topic of listening, he scans another fifteen magazine and newspaper articles addressing health care challenges faced by nurses. A *Starburst* is created for each book and article. To complete his investigation, John interviews three nurses and two recent hospital patients. He records each conversation in a *Starburst*.

Now comes the challenge of transforming research into a memorable seminar. John's goal is to determine the most important, interesting and relevant main topics for the seminar using all of his research, then to develop convincing support and examples for each main topic.

John spreads out all of his *Starbursts* on a large table. In the center of a big sheet of clean, white paper he draws an image and labels it "listening." Perusing the research *Starbursts*, he looks for key words that appear again and again. "Techniques" appears multiple times so he draws a ray on the "listening" *Starburst* and labels it "techniques." Next, branches are drawn representing the many thoughts that John finds on a variety of *Starbursts* related to techniques. John continues the process of integrating ideas onto one *Starburst* until he has all of the main ideas and branches he wants to address in two hours. Next, he revises the "listening" *Starburst* by adding numbers and other sequence indicators.

Balance between the spontaneity of natural talk and the structure of well-thought-out ideas is the formula for a dazzling delivery. To capture the balance, prepare presentation notes in *Starbursts*. John planned to give the nurses a set of handouts which corresponded with the seminar's overheads. On his copy of the handouts, the talk points were planned in a mini-*Starburst* on each page. John rehearsed using the *Starburst* talk points. He enjoyed the freedom of choosing his own words within a planned framework as opposed to memorizing the presentation verbatim.

John connected with his audience of nurses through plenty of eye contact, enthusiasm and animation. By glancing at meaningful key words and images that sparked his memory, he was free to share his knowledge with flexibility in his choice of words, sentences and, even in some cases, sequence. He managed the presentation based on the audience's needs, the questions they asked, concerns they expressed, how quickly they completed exercises and absorbed important points. John's own sense of freedom and enthusiasm projected confidence and credibility to the audience, keeping their enthusiasm high as well! See diagram 6 below for a modified

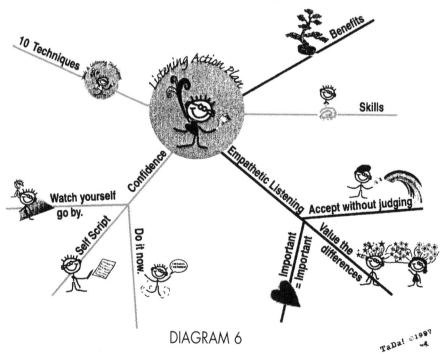

DIAGRAM 6

version of John's *Starburst* which he uses as an action plan for students to complete during class.

In the quest for quality communication, *Starbursts* are a priceless tool. Capture the power of the imaginative, artistic brain working in tandem with the logical, analytical brain to send and receive communication effectively and efficiently. Use *Starbursts* to think, plan, create, innovate, present, lead, facilitate, and learn. Fear not having colleagues look at you and your *Starbursts* with raised eyebrows. Believe in *Starbursts* and the people with whom you communicate will come to thank you!

# About Debbie Gracey

Debbie Gracey has 20 years of corporate experience in international and domestic management, customer relations, and training. As the manager of training for an international corporation, Gracey has trained professionals and staff from Europe, Canada, Mexico, Australia, the Caribbean, and the U.S.A. She has extensive experience in leading cross-functional, product development, and training teams.

Debbie lives in Imperial, Pennsylvania, with her husband and three wonderful children. She commutes between her offices in Pittsburgh and Washington, D.C.

For more information, contact:

**Gracey Global Training and Consulting**
12 Enlow Road
Imperial, PA 15126
(412) 695-7879

# Company Profile

Relationships are the key to successful business. Radiant relationships are people together accomplishing new thinking and fresh ideas. Gracey Global Training and Consulting works with people to form radiant business relationships so they can be more successful, enjoy their business and have a positive influence on their world. Organizations and individuals become relationship experts through our four most popular programs.

## Most Requested Programs

### Thought Starbursts... A New Way of Thinking

*Thought Starbursts* are a way of thinking that will help you develop ideas, solve problems, plan and learn. Turn time-consuming, tedious work into fun bursts of brilliance that will delight you and those with whom you work.

- Think through tough challenges and design creative solutions.
- Express yourself effectively through reports, summaries and presentations.
- Actively receive and retain information through note-taking, facilitation and book summaries.

### Listening from the Inside Out

If you want to manage people better—understand the customer's needs and seize opportunities that may have otherwise been missed—enhancing your listening skills is the key. Learn how to use listening to establish and maintain radiant business relationships with customers, subordinates and superiors.

- Gain knowledge and skills to listen more effectively, more often.
- Design a practical, creative action plan to become a better listener.
- Sense a new self-confidence to implement new skills immediately.

### Building Creative Teams

Teams are rapidly becoming the mainstay of contemporary organizations, accomplishing improvements 30 to 50 percent better than non-team-based organizations. This program helps you to achieve top performance, creativity and results through your team. Topics include:

- Relationships and results within the team.
- Bridge-building to the outside world.

Have you been given a team with little training on how to lead it effectively? Arm yourself with practical, creative ideas to become the leader you want to be.

# Most Requested Programs (continued)

## *Radiant Well-being*

To build radiant relationships with others, your own well-being must be achieved first. Taking responsibility for yourself is an art and a science.

- You are what you eat. Learn nutritional techniques that provide energy and vitality.
- Exercise your body, mind and spirit. Find practical ways to tone every aspect of your being.
- Alternative medicine. Western medicine only scratches the surface. Learn new sources of treatments that are non-invasive, gentle and natural.

❖ **Chapter 5** ❖

# Communication Comes from the Inside Out

*by*
*Deb Haggerty*

That part of us which makes us uniquely us
is our personality, or as some refer to it,
temperament. Personality is part of
our genetic makeup and, as such,
is unique to each individual.

—*Deb Haggerty*

C ommunication—the buzzword of the 90s. In over fifteen years of consulting, I have found that most business problems can be traced to communication: miscommunication, lack of communication, misunderstood communication. Most of us think that by talking we are communicating. Talking isn't communicating, though, because each individual listens, learns, and understands in a unique way. Understanding our own communication style is a requirement before we can hope to understand and communicate with others. Once we know our style of communication, we can begin to learn to modify it to match the style of someone else. For us to ensure communication occurs, we must speak in a manner that the other person understands. As Don Weiss, president of Self-Management Communications, Inc., states, "Definitions, context values, and attitudes affect what people perceive when you communicate, often creating a difference between intent and effect." Communication is the sum of what we do in an interaction with another—the words we use, our tone of voice, and body language. Peter Drucker has said, "Communication is understanding what is not said." The entire conversation, verbal and nonverbal, must be decoded in order to truly communicate.

The art of communication necessitates knowledge of the mechanics of communication. Webster defines communication as "a process by which information is exchanged between individuals through a common system of symbols, signs, or behavior; a technique for expressing ideas effectively." The thesaurus gives several choices of words for communication: *interaction, transmission, contact, connection, touch, interchange.* Communication requires us to interact, transmit, and connect with the proper message.

Many barriers to effective communication exist. Figure 1 illustrates how communication is supposed to flow.

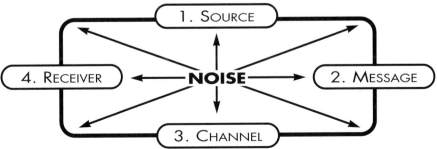

## Communication Comes from the Inside Out

If communication is critical, feedback should be sought to ensure the message received was the same as that which was sent. Ask the recipient to repeat back the statement, or rephrase, what was said to demonstrate the message was properly received.

Unfortunately, as we can see in Figure 1, many times "noise" gets in the way of proper communication. "Noise" refers to any of the distractions that can get in the way of the correct sending or receiving of messages. Anything from actual outside sounds, other people in the area, or the sender/receiver's own perceptions are "noise." Keeping "noise" from interfering with the intent of the communication is a constant effort.

One of the biggest generators of "noise" is personality. Personality largely governs how an individual will listen, learn and understand. In order to communicate well, each of us must discover who we are from a personality standpoint and recognize that our communication style is largely due to that particular personality type.

What is personality? Personality is the essence of who we are. That part of us which makes us uniquely us is our personality, or as some refer to it, temperament. Personality is part of our genetic makeup and, as such, is unique to each individual. Oswald Chambers, well-known philosopher-theologian, professes, "Personality is that peculiar, incalculable thing that is meant when we speak of ourselves as distinct from everyone else." Personality is what makes us who we are and governs why we act and react the way we do.

Studies of identical twins conducted by the University of Minnesota indicate that heredity is responsible for approximately two-thirds of our personality make-up. Our parents and grandparents have passed down to us personality characteristics much as they have eye or hair color. The remaining one-third of our personality is shaped by the environmental effects of birth order, the locale in which we grew up, the kinds of experiences we had in school, college, and work, and any significant or traumatic events in our lives. Personality type, that "incalculable thing" as Chambers calls it, which makes us uniquely us and determines communication style is determined before we are born and honed by life experiences.

The study of personalities is not new. The first documented study of personalities was done by Hippocrates, the father of modern medicine, in about 400 BC. Hippocrates, wandering around ancient Greece, noticed that there were people who seemed to have very different styles of acting and talking and being. A curious individual, Hippocrates decided to study the matter and see if a rationale for what caused variations in behavior could be discovered. His hypothesis, after much study, was that the reason for the differences could be ascribed to the prevalence of various kinds of bodily fluids that coursed through each person's body. He identified four basic types of fluids that influenced the personality traits of individuals. The names of these four fluids or "humors" are still utilized by some systems of personality study today.

## Sanguine

Hippocrates felt that those people who were very flamboyant, talked loudly and gestured widely had a great deal of rich, red blood running through their arteries, so he designated them by the Greek word for blood—*Sanguine*. People who are outgoing, like approval and need to be the center of attention fit this personality type. The word remains in use today to describe someone who is sturdy and cheerful.

## Choleric

The second type of personality studied was that of individuals who seemed to very determined, very work oriented, very much in charge: those people who took control of events and ran things. He decided that these people had a great deal of yellow bile, or *cholera* running through their systems. So Hippocrates called them **Choleric**. Today we refer to people who feel they are always correct and are easily moved to unreasonable or excessive anger when challenged as choleric in nature; i.e., hot-tempered.

## Melancholy

The third personality type was that of the sensitive artists and writers, those people who seemed to really be in touch with the feelings of nature and the world around them. These individuals often had another side to their personality: they were frequently very organized, very detailed, did well with numbers, and liked precision and order in their lives. These people, Hippocrates decided, had a great deal of black bile or *melan*, running through their systems and therefore he called them **Melancholy**. Today people of a sensitive nature who are easily depressed by events surrounding them are called melancholy or "blue."

## Phlegmatic

The last type of personality observed by Hippocrates was the Phlegmatic. *Phlegma* was the one of the four humors in early physiology that was considered to be cold and moist and to cause sluggishness. People with a prevalence of phlegm in their systems were quiet, slow-paced, and liked the very easygoing, placid life. A word coined to describe this type of personality is "stolid"—a combination of steady and solid.

Studies of the personalities have continued from Hippocrates' time until the present. There are over twenty-five of the so-called "four quadrant" systems in use today. Three examples are the DISC^plusTM developed by Profiles International, Inc., the "Personality Puzzle" system developed by Florence and Fred Littauer, and the "Platinum Rule" system developed by Dr. Tony Alessandra. Interestingly enough, Hippocrates may have been right. Recent scientific studies have shown that chemicals or drugs in the bloodstream actually do impact and even change personalities. Hippocrates may have been fairly accurate with his "scientific method" some 2400 years ago!

The best way to determine your personality is to take a simple test. Following are two of the most popular four quadrant systems, the Littauer's "Personality Puzzle," and Dr. Tony Alessandra's "Platinum Rule."

# Personality Puzzle Profile

*Created by Florence and Fred Littauer*

## Directions:

In **each of the following rows** of four words across, place an "X" in front of the **one word that most often applies to you.** Continue through all forty lines. **Be sure each number is marked.** If you are not sure of which word most applies, ask a spouse or a friend, or think of what your answer would have been when you were a child. (Note: Definitions of test words to follow.)

### STRENGTHS

| | | | | |
|---|---|---|---|---|
| 1. | __Adventurous | __Adaptable | __Animated | __Analytical |
| 2. | __Persistent | __Playful | __Persuasive | __Peaceful |
| 3. | __Submissive | __Self-sacrificing | __Sociable | __Strong-willed |
| 4. | __Considerate | __Controlled | __Competitive | __Convincing |
| 5. | __Refreshing | __Respectful | __Reserved | __Resourceful |
| 6. | __Satisfied | __Sensitive | __Self-reliant | __Spirited |
| 7. | __Planner | __Patient | __Positive | __Promoter |
| 8. | __Sure | __Spontaneous | __Scheduled | __Shy |
| 9. | __Orderly | __Obliging | __Outspoken | __Optimistic |
| 10. | __Friendly | __Faithful | __Funny | __Forceful |

| 11. | __Daring | __Delightful | __Diplomatic | __Detailed |
| 12. | __Cheerful | __Consistent | __Cultured | __Confident |
| 13. | __Idealistic | __Independent | __Inoffensive | __Inspiring |
| 14. | __Demonstrative | __Decisive | __Dry humor | __Deep |
| 15. | __Mediator | __Musical | __Mover | __Mixes easily |
| 16. | __Thoughtful | __Tenacious | __Talker | __Tolerant |
| 17. | __Listener | __Loyal | __Leader | __Lively |
| 18. | __Contented | __Chief | __Chartmaker | __Cute |
| 19. | __Perfectionist | __Pleasant | __Productive | __Popular |
| 20. | __Bouncy | __Bold | __Behaved | __Balanced |

## WEAKNESSES

| 21. | __Blank | __Bashful | __Brassy | __Bossy |
| 22. | __Undisciplined | __Unsympathetic | __Unenthusiastic | __Unforgiving |
| 23. | __Reticent | __Resentful | __Resistant | __Repetitious |
| 24. | __Fussy | __Fearful | __Forgetful | __Frank |
| 25. | __Impatient | __Insecure | __Indecisive | __Interrupts |
| 26. | __Unpopular | __Uninvolved | __Unpredictable | __Unaffectionate |
| 27. | __Headstrong | __Haphazard | __Hard to please | __Hesitant |
| 28. | __Plain | __Pessimistic | __Proud | __Permissive |
| 29. | __Angered easily | __Aimless | __Argumentative | __Alienated |
| 30. | __Naive | __Negative attitude | __Nervy | __Nonchalant |
| 31. | __Worrier | __Withdrawn | __Workaholic | __Wants credit |
| 32. | __Too sensitive | __Tactless | __Timid | __Talkative |
| 33. | __Doubtful | __Disorganized | __Domineering | __Depressed |
| 34. | __Inconsistent | __Introvert | __Intolerant | __Indifferent |
| 35. | __Messy | __Moody | __Mumbles | __Manipulative |
| 36. | __Slow | __Stubborn | __Show-off | __Skeptical |
| 37. | __Loner | __Lord over | __Lazy | __Loud |
| 38. | __Sluggish | __Suspicious | __Short-tempered | __Scatterbrained |
| 39. | __Revengeful | __Restless | __Reluctant | __Rash |
| 40. | __Compromising | __Critical | __Crafty | __Changeable |

Now transfer all your "X's" to the corresponding words on the personality scoring sheet and add up your totals.

# Personality Profile Word Definitions

(Adapted from Personality Patterns by Lana Bateman)

---

## STRENGTHS

---

1. ADVENTUROUS .....one who will take on new and daring enterprises with a
      determination to master them.
   ADAPTABLE............easily fits and is comfortable in any situation.
   ANIMATED ............full of life, lively use of hand, arm, and face gestures.
   ANALYTICAL..........likes to examine the parts for their logical and proper
      relationships.

2. PERSISTENT ...........sees one project through to its completion before starting
      another.
   PLAYFUL.................full of fun and good humor.
   PERSUASIVE ..........convinces through logic and fact rather than charm or power.
   PEACEFUL..............seems undisturbed and tranquil and retreats from any form of
      strife.

3. SUBMISSIVE ..........easily accepts any other's point of view or desire with little
      need to assert his own opinion.
   SELF-SACRIFICING .willingly gives up their own personal being for the sake of, or
      to meet the needs of others.
   SOCIABLE .............one who sees being with others as an opportunity to be cute
      and entertaining rather than as a challenge or business
      opportunity.
   STRONG-WILLED....one who is determined to have their own way.

4. CONSIDERATE.......having regard for the needs and feelings of others.
   CONTROLLED........has emotional feelings but rarely displays them.
   COMPETITIVE ........turns every situation, happening, or game into a contest and
      always plays to win!
   CONVINCING ......can win you over to anything through the sheer charm of their
      personality.

5. REFRESHING .........renews and stimulates or makes others feel good.
   RESPECTFUL...........treats others with deference, honor, and esteem.
   RESERVED..............self restraint in expression of emotion or enthusiasm.
   RESOURCEFUL .......able to act quickly and effectively in virtually all situations.

6. SATISFIED ..............a person who easily accepts any circumstance or situation.
   SENSITIVE .............intensively cares about others, and what happens.
   SELF-RELIANT .........an independent person who can fully rely on their own
      capabilities, judgment, and resources.
   SPIRITED ................full of life and excitement.

7. PLANNER ..............prefers to work out a detailed arrangement beforehand, for the accomplishment of project or goal, and prefers involvement with the planning stages and the finished product rather than the carrying out of the task.
   PATIENT.................unmoved by delay, remains calm and tolerant.
   POSITIVE ...............knows it will turn out right if they're in charge.
   PROMOTER ...........urges or compels others to go along, join, or invest through the charm of his own personality.

8. SURE.....................confident, rarely hesitates or wavers.
   SPONTANEOUS ....prefers all of life to be impulsive, unpremeditated activity, not restricted by plans.
   SCHEDULED ..........makes, and lives, according to a daily plan—dislikes their plan to be interrupted.
   SHY .....................quiet, doesn't easily instigate a conversation.

9. ORDERLY ..............a person who has a methodical, systematic arrangement of things.
   OBLIGING.............accommodating—one who is quick to do it another's way.
   OUTSPOKEN .........speaks frankly and without reserve.
   OPTIMISTIC ...........sunny disposition who convinces themselves and others that everything will turn out all right.

10. FRIENDLY...............a responder rather than an initiator, seldom starts a conversation.
    FAITHFUL ...............consistently reliable, steadfast, loyal, and devoted sometimes beyond reason.
    FUNNY .................sparkling sense of humor that can make virtually any story into an hilarious event.
    FORCEFUL .............a commanding personality, against whom others would hesitate to take a stand.

11. DARING.................willing to take risks; fearless, bold.
    DELIGHTFUL...........a person who is upbeat and fun to be with.
    DIPLOMATIC ..........deals with people tactfully, sensitively, and patiently.
    DETAILED ...............does everything in proper order with a clear memory of all the things that happened.

12. CHEERFUL .............consistently in good spirits and promoting happiness in others.
    CONSISTENT ........stays emotionally on an even keel, responding as one might expect.
    CULTURED ..............one whose interests involve both intellectual and artistic pursuits, such as theatre, symphony, ballet.
    CONFIDENT ..........self-assured and certain of own ability and success.

# Personality Profile Word Definitions
## (Continued)

13. IDEALISTIC.............visualizes things in their perfect form, and has a need to measure up to that standard themselves.

    INDEPENDENT.......self-sufficient, self-supporting, self-confident and seems to have little need of help.

    INOFFENSIVE........a person who never says or causes anything unpleasant or objectionable.

    INSPIRING.............encourages others to work, join, or be involved and makes the whole thing fun.

14. DEMONSTRATIVE...openly expresses emotion, especially affection and doesn't hesitate to touch others while speaking to them.

    DECISIVE...............a person with quick, conclusive, judgment-making ability.

    DRY HUMOR.........exhibits "dry wit", usually humorous one-liners which can be sarcastic in nature.

    DEEP.....................intense and often introspective with a distaste for surface conversation and pursuits.

15. MEDIATOR.............consistently finds themselves in the role of reconciling differences in order to avoid conflict.

    MUSICAL...............participates in or has a deep appreciation for music, is committed to music as an artform, rather than the fun of performance.

    MOVER.................driven by a need to be productive, is a leader whom others follow, finds it difficult to sit still.

    MIXES EASILY.........loves a party and can't wait to meet everyone in the room—never meets a stranger.

16. THOUGHTFUL........a considerate person who remembers special occasions and is quick to make a kind gesture.

    TENACIOUS..........holds on firmly, stubbornly, and won't let go until the goal is accomplished.

    TALKER.................constantly talking, generally telling funny stories and entertaining everyone around, feeling the need to fill the silence in order to make others comfortable.

    TOLERANT.............easily accepts the thoughts and ways of others without the need to disagree with or change them.

17. LISTENER...............always seems willing to hear what you have to say.

    LOYAL...................faithful to a person, ideal, or job, sometimes beyond reason.

    LEADER.................a natural born director, who is driven to be in charge, and often finds it difficult to believe that anyone else can do the job as well.

    LIVELY...................full of life, vigorous, energetic.

18. CONTENTED .........easily satisfied with what they have, rarely envious.
    CHIEF....................commands leadership and expects people to follow.
    CHARTMAKER .......organizes life, tasks, and problem solving by making lists, forms or graphs.
    CUTE ....................precious, adorable, center of attention.

19. PERFECTIONIST......places high standards on themselves, and often on others, desiring that everything be in proper order at all times.
    PLEASANT .............easy going, easy to be around, easy to talk with.
    PRODUCTIVE .........must constantly be working or achieving, often finds it very difficult to rest.
    POPULAR...............life of the party and therefore much desired as a party guest.

20. BOUNCY ..............a bubbly, lively personality, full of energy.
    BOLD ....................fearless, daring, forward, unafraid of risk.
    BEHAVED ..............consistently desire to conduct themselves within the realm of what they feel is proper.
    BALANCED............stable, middle of the road personality, not subject to sharp highs or lows.

---

## WEAKNESSES

---

21. BLANK ..................a person who shows little facial expression or emotion.
    BASHFUL...............shrinks from getting attention, resulting from self consciousness.
    BRASSY.................showy, flashy, comes on strong, too loud.
    BOSSY ..................commanding, domineering, sometimes overbearing in adult relationships.

22. UNDISCIPLINED .....a person whose lack of order permeates most every area of their life.
    UNSYMPATHETIC ...finds it difficult to relate to the problems or hurts of others.
    UNENTHUSIASTIC .tends not to get excited, often feeling it won't work anyway.
    UNFORGIVING......one who has difficulty releasing or forgetting a hurt or injustice done to them, apt to hold onto a grudge.

23. RETICENT ..............unwilling or struggles against getting involved, especially when complex.
    RESENTFUL............often holds ill feelings as a result of real or imagined offenses.
    RESISTANT.............strives, works against, or hesitates to accept any other way but their own.
    REPETITIOUS ..........retells stories and incidents to entertain you without realizing they have already told the story several times before, is constantly needing something to say.

# Personality Profile Word Definitions

## (Continued)

24. FUSSY ..................insistent over petty matters or details, calling for great attention to trivial details.

    FEARFUL ...............often experiences feelings of deep concern, apprehension or anxiousness.

    FORGETFUL ...........lack of memory which is usually tied to a lack of discipline and not bothering to mentally record things that aren't fun.

    FRANK .................straightforward, outspoken, and doesn't mind telling you exactly what they think.

25. IMPATIENT .............a person who finds it difficult to endure irritation or wait for others.

    INSECURE .............one who is apprehensive or lacks confidence.

    INDECISIVE ...........the person who finds it difficult to make any decision at all (not the personality that labors long over each decision in order to make the perfect one).

    INTERRUPTS...........a person who is more of a talker than a listener, who starts speaking without even realizing someone else is already speaking.

26. UNPOPULAR..........a person whose intensity and demand for perfection can push others away.

    UNINVOLVED ........has no desire to listen or become interested in clubs, groups, activities, or other people's lives.

    UNPREDICTABLE.....may be ecstatic one moment and down the next, or willing to help but then disappears, or promises to come but forgets to show up.

    UNAFFECTIONATE.finds it difficult to verbally or physically demonstrate tenderness openly.

27. HEADSTRONG ......insists on having their own way.

    HAPHAZARD .........has no consistent way of doing things.

    HARD TO PLEASE...a person whose standards are set so high that it is difficult to ever satisfy them.

    HESITANT..............slow to get moving and hard to get involved.

28. PLAIN...................a middle-of-the-road personality without highs or lows and showing little, if any, emotion.

    PESSIMISTIC ..........while hoping for the best, this person generally sees the down side of a situation first.

    PROUD..................one with great self-esteem who see themselves as always right and the best person for the job.

    PERMISSIVE ...........allows others (including children) to do as they please in order to keep from being disliked.

29. ANGERED EASILY...one who has a childlike flash-in-the-pan temper that expresses itself in tantrum style and is over and forgotten almost instantly.

    AIMLESS................not a goal-setter with little desire to be one.

    ARGUMENTIVE......incites arguments generally because they are certain that they are right no matter what the situation may be.

    ALIENATED............easily feels estranged from others often because of insecurity or fear that others don't really enjoy their company.

30. NAIVE...................simple and child-like perspective, lacking sophistication or comprehension of what the deeper levels of life are really about.

    NEGATIVE.............one whose attitude is seldom positive and is often able to see only the down or dark side of each situation.

    NERVY..................full of confidence, fortitude, and sheer guts, often in a negative sense.

    NONCHALANT.....easy-going, unconcerned, indifferent.

31. WORRIER..............consistently feels uncertain, troubled, or anxious.

    WITHDRAWN........a person who pulls back to themselves and needs a great deal of alone or isolation time.

    WORKAHOLIC......an aggressive goal-setter who must be constantly productive and feels very guilty when resting, is not drive by a need for perfection or completion but by a need for accomplishment and reward.

    WANTS CREDIT.....thrives on the credit or approval of others. As an entertainer, this person feeds on the applause, laughter, and/or acceptance of an audience.

32. TOO SENSITIVE.....overly introspective and easily offended when misunderstood.

    TACTLESS..............sometimes express themselves in a somewhat offensive and inconsiderate way.

    TIMID....................shrinks from difficult situations.

    TALKATIVE.............an entertaining, compulsive talker who finds it difficult to listen.

33. DOUBTFUL.............characterized by uncertainty and lack of confidence that it will ever work out.

    DISORGANIZED.....lack of ability to ever get life in order.

    DOMINEERING.....compulsively takes control of situations and/or people, usually telling others what to do.

    DEPRESSED............a person who feels down much of the time.

# Personality Profile Word Definitions
*(Continued)*

34. INCONSISTENT .....erratic, contradictory, with actions and emotions not based on logic.

    INTROVERT............a person whose thoughts and interests are directed inward, live within themselves.

    INTOLERANT .........appears unable to withstand or accept another's attitudes, point of view or way of doing things.

    INDIFFERENT .........a person to whom most things don't matter one way or the other.

35. MESSY ..................living in a state of disorder, unable to find things.

    MOODY................doesn't get very high emotionally, but easily slips into low lows, often when feeling unappreciated.

    MUMBLES..............will talk quietly under the breath when pushed, doesn't bother to speak clearly.

    MANIPULATIVE ......influence or manage    shrewdly or deviously for their own advantage, WILL get their way somehow.

36. SLOW...................doesn't often act or think quickly, too much of a bother.

    STUBBORN............determined to exert their own will, not easily persuaded, obstinate.

    SHOW-OFF ...........need to be the center of attention, wants to be watched.

    SKEPTICAL.............disbelieving, questioning the motive behind the words.

37. LONER..................requires a lot of private time and tends to avoid other people.

    LORD OVER...........doesn't hesitate to let you know that they are right or are in control.

    LAZY....................evaluates work or activity in terms of how much energy it will take.

    LOUD...................a person whose laugh or voice can be heard above others in the room.

38. SLUGGISH.............slow to get started, needs push to be motivated.

    SUSPICIOUS ..........tends to suspect or distrust others or ideas.

    SHORT-TEMPERED ..has a demanding impatience-based anger and a short fuse. Anger is expressed when others are not moving fast enough or have not completed what they have been asked to do.

    SCATTER-BRAINED..lacks the power of concentration, or attention, flighty.

39. REVENGEFUL.........knowingly or otherwise holds a grudge and punishes the offender, often by subtly withholding friendship or affection.

    RESTLESS...............likes constant new activity because it isn't fun to do the same things all the time.

    RELUCTANT ...........unwilling or struggles against getting involved.

    RASH ...................may act hastily, without thinking things through, generally because of impatience.

40. COMPROMISING ..will often relax their position, even when right, in order to avoid conflict.
    CRITICAL ..............constantly evaluating and making judgments, frequently thinking or expressing negative reactions.
    CRAFTY.................shrewd, one who can always find a way to get to the desired end.
    CHANGEABLE .......a child-like short attention span that needs a lot of change and variety to keep from getting bored.

# Personality Profile Scoring Sheet

## STRENGTHS

| | SANGUINE POPULAR | CHOLERIC POWERFUL | MELANCHOLY PERFECT | PHLEGMATIC PEACEFUL |
|---|---|---|---|---|
| 1. | Animated | Adventurous | Analytical | Adaptable |
| 2. | Playful | Persuasive | Persistent | Peaceful |
| 3. | Sociable | Strong-willed | Self-sacrificing | Submissive |
| 4. | Convincing | Competitive | Considerate | Controlled |
| 5. | Refreshing | Resourceful | Respectful | Reserved |
| 6. | Spirited | Self-reliant | Sensitive | Satisfied |
| 7. | Promoter | Positive | Planner | Patient |
| 8. | Spontaneous | Sure | Scheduled | Shy |
| 9. | Optimistic | Outspoken | Orderly | Obliging |
| 10. | Funny | Forceful | Faithful | Friendly |
| 11. | Delightful | Daring | Detailed | Diplomatic |
| 12. | Cheerful | Confident | Cultured | Consistent |
| 13. | Inspiring | Independent | Idealistic | Inoffensive |
| 14. | Demonstrative | Decisive | Deep | Dry humor |
| 15. | Mixes easily | Mover | Musical | Mediator |
| 16. | Talker | Tenacious | Thoughtful | Tolerant |
| 17. | Lively | Leader | Loyal | Listener |
| 18. | Cute | Chief | Chartmaker | Contented |
| 19. | Popular | Productive | Perfectionist | Pleasant |
| 20. | Bouncy | Bold | Behaved | Balanced |

SUB-TOTALS ____     ____     ____     ____

# Personality Profile Scoring Sheet

### (Continued)

## WEAKNESSES

| | SANGUINE POPULAR | CHOLERIC POWERFUL | MELANCHOLY PERFECT | PHLEGMATIC PEACEFUL |
|---|---|---|---|---|
| 21. | __Brassy | __Bossy | __Bashful | __Blank |
| 22. | __Undisciplined | __Unsympathetic | __Unforgiving | __Unenthusiastic |
| 23. | __Repetitious | __Resistant | __Resentful | __Reticent |
| 24. | __Forgetful | __Frank | __Fussy | __Fearful |
| 25. | __Interrupts | __Impatient | __Insecure | __Indecisive |
| 26. | __Unpredictable | __Unaffectionate | __Unpopular | __Uninvolved |
| 27. | __Haphazard | __Headstrong | __Hard to please | __Hesitant |
| 28. | __Permissive | __Proud | __Pessimistic | __Plain |
| 29. | __Angered easily | __Argumentative | __Alienated | __Aimless |
| 30. | __Naive | __Nervy | __Negative attitude | __Nonchalant |
| 31. | __Wants credit | __Workaholic | __Withdrawn | __Worrier |
| 32. | __Talkative | __Tactless | __Too sensitive | __Timid |
| 33. | __Disorganized | __Domineering | __Depressed | __Doubtful |
| 34. | __Inconsistent | __Intolerant | __Introvert | __Indifferent |
| 35. | __Messy | __Manipulative | __Moody | __Mumbles |
| 36. | __Show-off | __Stubborn | __Skeptical | __Slow |
| 37. | __Loud | __Lord over others | __Loner | __Lazy |
| 38. | __Scatterbrained | __Short-tempered | __Suspicious | __Sluggish |
| 39. | __Restless | __Rash | __Revengeful | __Reluctant |
| 40. | __Changeable | __Crafty | __Critical | __Compromising |

**SUB-TOTALS** ____   ____   ____   ____

**GRAND TOTALS** ══   ══   ══   ══

# Personality Analysis

## SANGUINE
### (POPULAR/Socializer)

| | |
|---|---|
| Profile: | Creative person |
| Best at: | Making initial contact with people |
| | Creating enthusiasm and excitement |
| | Encouraging and uplifting others |
| | Insuring that the group has fun |

| | |
|---|---|
| Is apt to be: | Too easily distracted and forgetful |
| Style: | Humorous and with a light touch |
| Warning: | Can come on too happy or cute |
| | Not considered serious or believable |
| | Don't let them handle money |

**Realize they need fun and adventure!**

## STRENGTHS

| EMOTIONS | WORK | FRIENDS |
|---|---|---|
| Appealing personality | Volunteers for jobs | Makes friends easily |
| Talkative, storyteller | Thinks up new activities | Loves people |
| Life of the party | Looks great on the surface | Thrives on compliments |
| Good sense of humor | Creative and colorful | Seems exciting |
| Memory for color | Has energy and enthusiasm | Envied by others |
| Physically holds on to listener | Starts in a flashy way | Doesn't hold grudges |
| Emotional and demonstrative | Inspires others to join | Apologizes quickly |
| Enthusiastic and expressive | Charms others to work | Prevents dull moments |
| Cheerful and bubbling over | | Likes spontaneous activities |
| Curious | | |
| Good on stage | | |
| Wide-eyed and innocent | | |
| Lives in the present | | |
| Changeable disposition | | |
| Sincere at heart | | |
| Always a child | | |

## WEAKNESSES

| EMOTIONS | WORK | FRIENDS |
|---|---|---|
| Compulsive talker | Would rather talk | Hates to be alone |
| Exaggerates and elaborates | Forgets obligations | Needs to be center stage |
| Dwells on trivia | Doesn't follow through | Wants to be popular |
| Can't remember names | Confidence fades fast | Looks for credit |
| Scares others off | Undisciplined | Dominates conversations |
| Too happy for some | Priorities out of order | Interrupts and doesn't listen |
| Has restless energy | Decides by feelings | Answers for others |
| Egotistical | Easily distracted | Fickle and forgetful |
| Blusters and complains | Wastes time talking | Makes excuses |
| Naive, gets taken in | | Repeats stories |
| Has loud voice and laugh | | |
| Controlled by circumstances | | |
| Gets angry easily | | |
| Seems phony to some | | |
| Never grows up | | |

# Personality Analysis

## (Continued)

**CHOLERIC (POWERFUL/Director)**
  *Profile:* Leadership person
  *Best at:* Motivating people to action
    Controlling the plans and productivity
    Giving quick and clear instructions
    Making sure the group sees the
    immediate gain

*Is apt to be:* Too impulsive and intimidating
*Style:* Authoritative and convincing
*Warning:* May come on too overpowering
  Seems to look down on others
  Often intimidates less confident
  people

**Realize they need action and excitement!**

---

### STRENGTHS

| **EMOTIONS** | **WORK** | **FRIENDS** |
|---|---|---|
| Born leader | Goal oriented | Has little need for friends |
| Dynamic and active | Sees the whole picture | Will work for group activity |
| Compulsive need for change | Organizes well | Will lead and organize |
| Must correct wrongs | Seeks practical solutions | Is usually right |
| Strong-willed and decisive | Moves quickly to action | Excels in emergencies |
| Unemotional | Delegates work | |
| Not easily discouraged | Insists on production | |
| Independent and self-sufficient | Makes the goal | |
| Exudes confidence | Stimulates activity | |
| Can run anything | Thrives on opposition | |

---

### WEAKNESSES

| **EMOTIONS** | **WORK** | **FRIENDS** |
|---|---|---|
| Bossy | Little tolerance for mistakes | Tend to use people |
| Impatient | Doesn't analyze details | Dominates others |
| Quick-tempered | Bored by trivia | Decides for others |
| Can't relax | May make rash decisions | Knows everything |
| Too impetuous | May be rude or tactless | Can do everything better |
| Enjoys controversy and | Manipulates people | Is too independent |
|     arguments | Demanding of others | Possessive of friends and mate |
| Won't give up when losing | End justifies the means | Can't say, "I'm sorry" |
| Comes on too strong | Work may become their god | May be right, but unpopular |
| Inflexible | Demands loyalty in the ranks | |
| Is not complimentary | | |
| Dislikes tears and emotions | | |
| Is unsympathetic | | |

## MELANCHOLY *(PERFECT/Thinker)*

Profile: Detail person
Best at: Planning and explaining the details
Keeping the financial records straight
Being sensitive to the needs of others
Making sure the group sees the long-range goal
Is apt to be: Too easily distracted and critical

Style: Accurate and sincere
Warning: Might come across too intellectual and remote
May make others feel less intelligent
Can get lost in the details
***Realize they need order and understanding!***

### STRENGTHS

| EMOTIONS | WORK | FRIENDS |
|---|---|---|
| Deep and thoughtful | Schedule oriented | Makes friends cautiously |
| Analytical | Perfectionist, high standards | Content to stay in background |
| Serious and purposeful | Detail conscious | Avoids causing attention |
| Genius prone | Persistent and thorough | Faithful and devoted |
| Talented and creative | Orderly and organized | Will listen to complaints |
| Artistic or musical | Neat and tidy | Can solve other's problems |
| Philosophical and poetic | Economical | Deep concern for other people |
| Appreciative of beauty | Sees the problems | Moved to tears with |
| Sensitive to others | Finds creative solutions | compassion |
| Self-sacrificing | Need to finish what they start | Seeks ideal mate |
| Conscientious | Likes charts, graphs, figures, | |
| Idealistic | lists | |

### WEAKNESSES

| EMOTIONS | WORK | FRIENDS |
|---|---|---|
| Remembers the negatives | Not people oriented | Lives through others |
| Moody and depressed | Depressed over imperfections | Insecure socially |
| Frequently feels hurt | Choose difficult work | Withdrawn and remote |
| Has false humility | Hesitant to start projects | Critical of others |
| Off in another world | Spends too much time | Holds back affection |
| Low self-image | planning | Dislikes those in opposition |
| Has selective hearing | Prefers analysis to work | Suspicious of people |
| Self-centered | Self-deprecating | Antagonistic and vengeful |
| Too introspective | Hard to please | Unforgiving |
| Guilt feelings | Standards often too high | Full of contradictions |
| Persecution complex | Deep need for approval | Skeptical of compliments |
| Tendency toward | | |
| hypochondria | | |

# Personality Analysis
### (Continued)

**PHLEGMATIC** *(PEACEFUL/Relator)*

Profile: Support person

Best at: Making sure the group is relaxed and comfortable

Always finding a middle ground

Staying calm and functional amidst chaos

Not overreacting to a negative situation

Is apt to be: Too undisciplined and indecisive

Style: Believable

Warning: May come across as too low-key, dull or lazy

Appears too unenthusiastic and unconvinced

Don't count on them for motivation

***Realize they need rest and some quiet time!***

---

## STRENGTHS

| **EMOTIONS** | **WORK** | **FRIENDS** |
|---|---|---|
| Low-key personality | Competent and steady | Easy to get along with |
| Easygoing and relaxed | Peaceful and agreeable | Pleasant and enjoyable |
| Calm, cool, and collected | Has administrative ability | Inoffensive |
| Patient, well balanced | Mediates problems | Good listener |
| Consistent life | Avoids conflicts | Dry sense of humor |
| Quiet, but witty | Good under pressure | Enjoys watching people |
| Sympathetic and kind | Finds the easy way | Has many friends |
| Keeps emotions hidden | | Has compassion and concern |
| Happily reconciled to life | | |
| All-purpose person | | |

---

## WEAKNESSES

| **EMOTIONS** | **WORK** | **FRIENDS** |
|---|---|---|
| Unenthusiastic | Not goal oriented | Dampens enthusiasm |
| Fearful and worried | Lacks self-motivation | Stays uninvolved |
| Indecisive | Hard to get moving | Is not exciting |
| Avoids responsibility | Resents being pushed | Indifferent to plans |
| Quiet will of iron | Lazy and careless | Judges others |
| Selfish | Discourages others | Sarcastic and teasing |
| Too shy and reticent | Would rather watch | Resists change |
| Too compromising | | |
| Self-righteous | | |

# The Platinum Rule:
# Finding Your Own Behavior Style Survey
*by Tony Alessandra*

## Directions:

This is an informal survey, designed to determine how you usually interact with others in everyday situations. The purpose of this questionnaire is to get a clear description of how you see yourself.

For each question, select the statement that describes you better. Base your answers on how you actually behave, not on how you think you should behave. Although some pairs of statements may seem equally true for you, select the one that is most representative of your behavior most of the time.

| QUESTION # | BEHAVIOR A | BEHAVIOR B |
|---|---|---|
| 1 | ◯ I am usually open to getting to know people personally and establishing relationships with them. | ◯ I am usually not open to getting to know people personally and establishing relationships with them. |
| 2 | ◯ I usually react slowly and deliberately. | ◯ I usually react quickly and spontaneously. |
| 3 | ◯ I am usually guarded about other people's use of my time. | ◯ I am usually open to other people's use of my time. |
| 4 | ◯ I usually introduce myself at social gatherings. | ◯ I usually wait for others to introduce themselves to me at social gatherings. |
| 5 | ◯ I usually focus my conversations on the interests of the parties involved, even if this means that the conversations stray from the business or subject at hand. | ◯ I usually focus my conversations on the tasks, issues, business, or subject at hand. |
| 6 | ◯ I am usually not assertive, and I can be patient with a slow pace. | ◯ I am usually assertive, and at times I can be impatient with a slow pace. |
| 7 | ◯ I usually make decisions based on facts or evidence. | ◯ I usually make decisions based on feelings, experiences, or relationships. |
| 8 | ◯ I usually contribute frequently to group conversations. | ◯ I usually contribute infrequently to group conversations. |
| 9 | ◯ I usually prefer to work with and through others, providing support when possible. | ◯ I usually prefer to work independently or dictate the conditions in terms of how others are involved. |
| 10 | ◯ I usually ask questions or speak more tentatively and indirectly. | ◯ I usually make emphatic statements or directly express opinions. |

| QUESTION # | BEHAVIOR A | BEHAVIOR B |
|---|---|---|
| 11 | ○ I usually focus primarily on the idea, concept, or results. | ○ I usually focus primarily on the person, interaction, and feelings. |
| 12 | ○ I usually use gestures, facial expressions, and voice intonation to emphasize points. | ○ I usually do not use gestures, facial expressions, and voice intonation to emphasize points. |
| 13 | ○ I usually accept others' points of view (ideas, feelings, and concerns). | ○ I usually do not accept others' points of view (ideas, feelings, and concerns). |
| 14 | ○ I usually respond to risk and change in a cautious or predictable manner. | ○ I usually respond to risk and change in a dynamic or unpredictable manner. |
| 15 | ○ I usually prefer to keep my personal feelings and thoughts to myself, sharing only when I wish to do so. | ○ I usually find it natural and easy to share and discuss my feelings with others. |
| 16 | ○ I usually seek out new or different experiences and situations. | ○ I usually choose known or similar situations and relationships. |
| 17 | ○ I usually am responsive to others' agendas, interests, and concerns. | ○ I usually am directed toward my own agendas, interests, and concerns. |
| 18 | ○ I usually respond to conflict slowly and indirectly. | ○ I usually respond to conflict quickly and directly. |

# Behavioral Profiles Scoring Sheet

Transfer your scores from each of the blanks on the Behavior Survey to the following table. *Note that sometimes the "A" response appears first and other times the "B" response appears first.* When you are finished, total each column.

| O | S | D | I |
|---|---|---|---|
| 1A | 1B | 2B | 2A |
| 3B | 3A | 4A | 4B |
| 5A | 5B | 6B | 6A |
| 7B | 7A | 8A | 8B |
| 9A | 9B | 10B | 10A |
| 11B | 11A | 12A | 12B |
| 13A | 13B | 14B | 14A |
| 15B | 15A | 16A | 16B |
| 17A | 17B | 18B | 18A |
| **O Total** | **S Total** | **D Total** | **I Total** |

*Compare the O to the S scores.* Write the higher score in the blank below and circle the corresponding letter: _____ **O S**

*Compare the D to the I scores.* Write the higher score in the blank below and circle the corresponding letter. _____ **D I**

*Find the combination that best describes your behavioral style. See the summary on page 102.*

☐ **O + D = Socializer**
(Popular / Sanguine)

☐ **O + I = Relater**
(Peaceful / Phlegmatic)

☐ **S + D = Director**
(Powerful / Choleric)

☐ **S + I = Thinker**
(Perfect / Melancholy)

*Alessandra & Associates, Inc.*
*Box 2767, La Jolla CA 92038*
*(619) 459-4515  (619) 459-0435 Fax*
*http://www.platinumrule.com*

# Summary of Behavioral Styles

## Relater Style

Slow at taking action and making decisions

Likes close, personal relationships

Dislikes interpersonal conflict

Supports and "actively" listens to others

Weak at goal setting and self-direction

Has excellent ability to gain support from others

Works slowly and cohesively with others

Seeks security and belongingness

Good counseling skills

## Socializer Style

Spontaneous actions and decisions

Likes involvement

Dislikes being alone

Exaggerates and generalizes

Tends to dream and get others caught up in his dreams

Jumps from one activity to another

Works quickly and excitedly with others

Seeks esteem and acknowledgment

Good persuasive skills

## Thinker Style

Cautious actions and decisions

Likes organization and structure

Dislikes involvement

Asks many questions about specific details

Prefers objective, task-oriented, intellectual work environment

Wants to be right, so can be overly reliant on data collection

Works slowly and precisely alone

Good problem solving skills

## Director Style

Decisive actions and decisions

Likes control, dislikes inaction

Prefers maximum freedom to manage himself and others

Cool, independent, and competitive

Low tolerance for feelings, attitudes, and advice of others

Works quickly and impressively alone

Good administrative skills

Personality survey systems use different words to describe the same or similar personality styles. The Littauer's system uses Hippocrates' original words while Dr. Alessandra uses socializer for Sanguine, director for Choleric, thinker for Melancholy, and relater for Phlegmatic. How do different personalities communicate?

☛ Let's look first at the **SANGUINE.** Another word for sanguine is *popular,* or in other systems, the *expressive,* or *socializer.* People who are the center of attention at a party, who like to tell jokes, who like to be around people and are very outgoing fit in this category. They love to tell stories, but sometimes these stories only bear a faint resemblance to the truth. However, the Sanguine feels that if it makes a good story better, embellishing is okay. They tend to gesture widely—huge gestures, lots of gestures—in fact, if you tell a Sanguine not to use their hands to talk, they're truly at a loss for words.

When I first started working for a large communications company, I had a sales job and was visiting a customer with my manager, Joe. The manager was not exactly pleased that the company had allowed females into the sales position. At this time in the early 1970s, the women's rights era was just beginning. Joe was trying to train me to be the same kind of salesperson he was. He was a very quiet individual, very reserved, and my outgoing style clashed with his. As we were travelling to the customer's premises, he told me that I needed to get more serious about my job and that I was not allowed to use my hands to make a point while speaking with the customer. The worst sales call I have ever been on in my life, before or since, followed! I could not talk. I was so self-conscious about my hands I just could not seem to find the verbal words I needed to illustrate my points.

A Sanguine very much likes to be the center of attention. They also communicate non-verbally by the kinds of clothes they wear. These individuals tend to dress in the latest fads. Female Sanguines like to wear bright colors and interesting fabrics and somewhat fashionable or out-of-the-ordinary styles and combinations of accessories. The males wear bright pocket handkerchiefs, patterned socks and the fashionable Rush Limbaugh or Loony Tunes ties. Sanguines dress to stand out in a crowd.

At a party, you will find the Sanguine in the center of a group of people gesturing and telling stories, and yet, at the same time, looking outside of the crowd that surrounds them to see if there is perhaps something more interesting going on elsewhere. The Sanguine, above all curious, may look past you or around at other people while they are talking with you.

They are interested in you, but they just want to make sure that no one else is there that needs them a bit more. Sanguines are easily distracted so if you are talking to one, they may wander off in mid-sentence. They are very touchy, affectionate people, too, given to hugs and effusive gestures of welcome. To ensure you have the attention of a Sanguine, touching their arm and reestablishing eye contact before making a specific point to them is advisable.

☞ The second personality style in Hippocrates' system is that of the **CHOLERIC.** The Choleric is the typical "type-A" personality. Cholerics are *the drivers, the directors, the powerful people* of the world. They are workaholics—counted on to get something done if a job needs to be done. They come to the point very quickly when they're communicating. Almost abrupt in style because for them you need to "cut to the chase," "get to the bottom line," "get to your point!". They want to cut through all superfluous communication and just get to work!

Cholerics use very precise, very abrupt, very emphatic gestures when they want to make a point. Someone who pounds on the table, like Nikita Krushchev and his "shoe on the desk" at the United Nations in the 1950s, is most likely a Choleric. If someone is pointing a finger, "Uncle Sam wants YOU! style," a Choleric is talking. If someone is gesturing "in your face," this person is most likely a Choleric.

Because the Choleric is so driven by goals, they will do whatever it takes to get the job done. A popular bumper sticker reads, "Those of you who think that you are always right are very irritating to those of us who really are!" This is what the Choleric thinks. Unfortunately, (or fortunately from their point of view) the Choleric usually is right. Because Cholerics are usually correct, impatience with people who don't see their point of view or don't come around to their way of thinking is a hallmark trait. Goal-oriented Cholerics drive hard to get that goal accomplished, sometimes steamrolling over the people around them who are perceived to be in the way. If they are thwarted, manipulation of others, through any means possible, will be used to accomplish the goal.

Cholerics are the people normally in charge of things because of their skills in accomplishment. When someone is organizing people, is getting things done, has shirtsleeves rolled up and has just plunged in to the task at hand, that person is indubitably a Choleric. In communicating with Cholerics, get to the point, get to the bottom line and use no conversational niceties.

In their choice of clothing styles, Cholerics are a cross between the Sanguine and the Melancholy. You will tend to see Choleric men wearing red power ties and short-sleeved shirts—very practical attire. Cholerics begin the day with a professional image and the attitude of total control. However, when there's work to be done, the tie gets loosened, the jacket comes off, the sleeves get rolled up, and the task at hand is all that matters.

☛ The **MELANCHOLY** personality is almost the direct opposite of the Sanguine. These are the *analytical-thinker-perfectionist* types. The Melancholy is very *quiet* and *reserved*, more *self-contained*. They tend to talk slowly, choose their words with care, use very few gestures, and if gestures are used, they occur very close to the body as opposed to the flung out, flamboyant gestures of the Sanguine. Melancholy people are very, very orderly. They speak in an orderly, logical fashion and, in fact, logical is one of the words often used to describe a Melancholy person. Having things in order, being perfect, is one of the driving forces for a Melancholy. A Melancholy may pause before answering you during a conversation. This pause is not because they don't know the answer to your question or they do not understand your question, rather they are very carefully processing the information to try and determine what was really said to ensure their response expresses their true opinion.

Melancholies are very methodical, like things to go in a logical flow, and are absolutely driven to distraction by the way a Sanguine personality jumps from one subject to another. In contrast, Melancholies will talk one subject through until they are sure their point has been communicated. They will give infinite details about a subject, sometimes much more detail than necessary, but Melancholies want to make sure their listeners have been presented the entire picture that a Melancholy would need to hear. They want to make sure you have all the facts that are necessary in order to make a decision, or respond, or continue the conversation.

Melancholies are easy to recognize by their attire and demeanor as well. Their style of dress is very conservative. They will tend to wear very simple, plain, elegant clothing because Melancholies want to look perfect at all times to convey that perfect, orderly, organized image. They will wear classical clothing of high quality that will not go out of style, muted colors, such as gray, navy and black. The Melancholy style is to be precisely put together—all pressed and polished.

Melancholies are very much into numbers, charts and graphs. Where the Sanguine uses word pictures and gestures to communicate, the Melancholy likes to have back-up data, information, charts, flow charts, outlines, and detailed methodologies to show you what it is that they are trying to communicate. This detail can be very irritating to others.

Because part of their personality is very sensitive, they will tend to reflect the moods of those around them. The Melancholy's moods are usually evenly balanced. If they are upset, they will easily become depressed.

They may be pensive, quiet and withdrawn. If someone around them is sad, they'll reflect that sadness. Also, the Melancholy is very thoughtful and observant of what goes on around them. Many great artists, musicians and writers come from a Melancholy personality because they wish to communicate the beauty, wonder, or emotion of what they see and feel around them to the rest of the world.

☛ The final personality type is the **PHLEGMATIC.** Easygoing and relaxed describes them. Phlegmatics do not like conflict, so they are the *mediators, the peaceful ones, the relaters*—the people who, faced with loud voices and apparent anger, will attempt to make people comfortable, mediate the argument, and calm the situation down. Phlegmatics are very good at diplomacy, listening to all points of view, and helping others to see differing opinions.

Phlegmatics are nice people, not terribly outgoing, but they're very content to talk with you if you come to them. They won't seek you out in a conversational situation nor at a party, yet are delightful to converse with when so engaged. The most relaxed of all the personality types, their speech is little bit slower, and they have an extremely dry sense of humor. Listening carefully to a Phlegmatic is required behavior because their tongue-in-cheek sense of humor will take you unawares, and then you flinch, "Oh, no! I should have seen that coming!"—an event which amuses them to no end.

A Phlegmatic's relaxed, "the world's okay," "let's just keep rolling along" manner fits with their style of dress. A Phlegmatic can be recognized by clothing style, as they will be the individuals who are the most casually dressed for the situation. They'll be appropriately dressed, yet it will be as casual as possible while still proper for the occasion.

Phlegmatics are good workers, steady and reliable. They will continue to work despite chaos around them. However, if a task is given to them that is not desirable, they are masters of procrastination. "Oh, you mean you wanted it today?" Phlegmatics work well in a variety of positions, usually those where tact and diplomacy are required. Some of our best diplomats have been Phlegmatics because of their ability to see both sides of a question and to mediate an amiable solution for all concerned.

~

While there are four distinct personality types, most people are a blend of two of the four, although some are strongly one type. Most of us have some of the characteristics of each type, but one or two predominate. My husband, Roy, is a strong Choleric and exhibits the characteristics of a Choleric in his conversational style, his dress and in his involvement with others. Roy has just enough of the Melancholy to insist on detail and time to process information before making a decision. Most pure Cholerics make snap decisions, but because there's a bit of the Melancholy moderating his personality, he will take time to consider the outcomes before making a decision.

I'm a blend of Choleric and Sanguine, so where I may be task-oriented and focused on getting the job done, I make quick decisions. I also like to talk to people, I gesture a lot and wear wild and crazy-colored clothing. Also I like receiving approval, applause for what I'm doing, as well as the recognition for a job well done. Because Roy and I are both Cholerics, occasionally there are conflicts. The Choleric, you see, wants control more than anything else. When there are two people wanting to control the same issue, there's conflict! When two Cholerics converse, they need to be able to recognize these personality traits to determine whether there is indeed conflict about the issue or whether there is conflict because of the need to be in charge driven by the individual's personality. Once clarified, communication can occur.

One of my clients is a very strong Choleric. He is very bright, very energetic, very task oriented, and has wonderful ideas on how to run his business. He makes very quick decisions about what would be good ideas to implement. To implement these decisions, he says to his staff, "I have a great idea! This is what we're going to do! Let me have your plans for accomplishing it by tomorrow at 5:00 P.M.!" Because he is such a strong personality and flashes with anger if they do, his employees tend not to ask questions or challenge him. Remember, a Choleric will try and control with threat of anger: they just roll right over people. Since the decisions originated quickly, were spur of the moment and not terribly well thought out, his company had no focus and no stability. People were unhappy because they couldn't depend on what the direction was going to be from one day to next. I can still remember the day I walked into one of his departments—the gloom hanging in the air could be cut with a knife. I talked to Ted, the manager of the department.

"What happened?" I asked.

"Well, Charlie just came through here again," Ted grimaced.

"Oh! What happened?"

He shrugged, "Well, apparently one of our customers called in with what turned out to be a minor complaint, but all Charlie heard was the complaint. He came down here roaring with anger and jumped all over the technician who had worked at this customer's premises. Charlie chewed him up one side and down the other and told him he never wanted it to happen again. Unfortunately," Ted continued, "the whole group was here. The technician was embarrassed and had no chance to explain to Charlie what the situation was. Charlie just dumped and left. Morale is really in the pits!"

Now what did Charlie intend to communicate and what message was perceived by the employees? For Charlie, customer service is the hallmark of his business. If he does not provide excellent customer service to his clients, he feels there will be nothing to differentiate his company from others and his clients will go elsewhere. Providing excellent customer service is of paramount importance to him. Unfortunately, in his attempt to convey his beliefs to his technicians, he did not communicate the importance of customer service. In true Choleric fashion, he just jumps all over anyone who does not meet his standards of customer service, and because he thinks he's always right, he criticizes individuals before giving them a chance to explain what the situation truly is. Charlie is totally unaware of the sensitivities of the people working for him. Instead, what he communicated to the entire department was that mistakes were intolerable, original thinking was forbidden, and the only correct way was Charlie's way or they would be criticized and thoroughly embarrassed in front of their peers.

As a result, customer service was *not* good. Customer complaints continued to increase. Why? There were several problems. 1) Charlie never bothered to listen to what his technicians were telling him. 2) He never bothered to hear that additional training was necessary. 3) He never bothered to understand that the products they were selling had a major fault in them. 4) The fault needed to be fixed in order to improve the level of service for his clients. Charlie took a long time to see that his problem was not this department, that his problem was himself and his style of communicating. After becoming familiar with personalities and their different means of communication, he discovered he needed to make sure that he was conveying his ideas in the right tone of voice and in the appropriate manner so that communication would take place. He needed to ensure his employees could understand why what he was telling them was so critically important. On the other hand, Charlie also learned that he needed to listen because others in his company also had good ideas. Others, because of their jobs, had the expertise necessary to provide sound, accurate information and to make better decisions for the company and for the employees. Once Charlie understood the communications process, the atmosphere smoothed out in his company, he stopped having high technician turnover, and "miraculously," his customers stopped complaining.

Communication is critical! A recognition of personalities and how communication occurs as well as how that communication style appears to other people is imperative if we're going to work successfully, communicate successfully today. To illustrate this point further, another client is a classic Melancholy-Phlegmatic blend. Jim is very quiet, shy almost, and yet he is the president of a company. During his tenure with the company, he had performed most of the jobs in the company. Because he was a Melancholy, he knew how to do them all correctly. The company grew and he was promoted to the presidency. In his new position, he continued to be involved in each function and insisted that he approve every decision. All work had to be rechecked before any proposals were sent out. All of the data had to be reevaluated before a decision was approved. However, if the decision was not the one his people recommended, Jim didn't want to hurt anybody's feelings (the Phlegmatic side of him). He would not tell them exactly what was required to correct the situation, just "maybe, well, you should try this again," "this isn't exactly right," "I need a little more information," "go back to the drawing board." His employees were tremendously frustrated.

I asked him once how he had learned his job and what happened if a mistake occurred. Jim pondered, "Well, when I was coming up the ranks if I made a mistake my boss would chew me out."

I queried, "Then what happened?"

He continued, "Well, I wouldn't make the mistake again because I learned that's not how you do it."

I replied, "Jim, don't your people deserve the same opportunity to learn what you have learned?"

Jim challenged me, "The risks are so much higher. The dollar volume is so much greater. The numbers are so much bigger."

I responded, "While that's true, the thought processes are still the same. You need to give your people the opportunity to learn on their own. Set an arbitrary number, let them make some decisions on their own and don't check every thing before it goes out, just check those things that are critical."

Jim's other problem was he was so detail-oriented (a Melancholy trait). He needed to verify all the aspects of his business. As a result, he was failing in his job. The president needed to be the prime sales person. Jim needed to be out talking to clients, making sure his customers were happy. He needed to be networking, introducing himself to new and potential clients and bringing in business. That's not a Melancholy-Phlegmatic's usual personality style. A method of communicating had to be developed for Jim that allowed him to be comfortable going out and talking to people without turning him into a "stereotypical sales personality." The style of communication Jim used was very different from Charlie's, but caused equally negative problems in his company. Communication was not occurring with those in the lower echelons of the business in either instance. Both men needed to learn to moderate their personality styles. Another component was to examine their modes of communication and recognize how it was impacting those around them. Change was required for success in the jobs they held and to make their companies successful.

Stuart was a Sanguine-Phlegmatic manager. Stuart had problems communicating, too, because Stu loved to be the center of attention. As do most Sanguines, he loved to tell stories. Employees hated being summoned to Stu's office. At least an hour would pass before they could escape and return to work because Stu loved to talk. According to the office grapevine, Stu loved to hear himself talk. He loved to tell stories about the good old days and the way things were. Stu loved people, loved having people to talk to, and loved to be the center of attention. He never wanted to hurt anyone's feelings. He always tried to say nice things and to create happiness and contentment. Stu wanted an upbeat, happy office. Instead, he irritated the employees who needed to get the job done. When direction was needed on how to do the job, Stu just couldn't give it to them… "Well, whatever you think is best," "We'll go and run it up the flag pole and see if anybody salutes," or "Well, give it your best shot." Superficial as some Sanguines can be, Stu didn't know the answers, didn't want the details: he just wanted to talk. His managers were very frustrated because they couldn't get the direction they needed. In Stu's case, most of the time his employees weren't completely convinced of his truthfulness. If they wanted to tell stories and not work, Stu's office was the place to go. Obviously, telling jokes and having fun didn't get the work accomplished. His employees were very frustrated because he didn't give them what they needed to accomplish their tasks.

If you were talking to him, you'd think his people walked on water. When he was talking to his boss and his boss' boss, Stu sang the praises of his employees. Praise was no help for his people with their day-to-day jobs, though. When they struggled and had to learn everything on their own, when they had to go to other people for help because they couldn't get it from their happy-go-lucky manager, praise had little value. What did he communicate? Just the opposite of what he wanted to. Did he create a happy and healthy atmosphere? No, because he didn't realize that not all people were like him and that he needed to moderate his behavior to create a structure that would allow them to perform their assignments effectively and in a timely manner.

We've now seen examples of how very different personality types communicate and how each style can negatively impact communications. How can we understand who we are, our style of communication, then take that a step further and truly communicate with others whose styles are different?

Tony Alessandra, Ph.D., the author of *The Platinum Rule*, espouses a theory of communication that is very relevant. Most of us grew up with the *Golden Rule*—"Do unto others as you would have OTHERS do unto YOU." Tony advocates an enhancement. The essence of this chapter affirms his theory. We should carry the *Golden Rule* one step further. Practicing the *Platinum Rule* should be our goal. The *Platinum Rule* says, "Do unto others as they would have YOU do unto THEM." In other words, if we truly want to communicate, to translate, to facilitate communication—to interact, transmit and connect with the proper message, we need to determine the needs of others and their preferences of communication. Once it is understood that communication comes from the inside out, our behavior can be moderated so that our conversation is on an equal level with someone else's style—not from out of our own. Joanne Cole, president of J. Cole Communications, writes, "Being a good communicator is a natural skill for very few people. Most of us have to work at being good communicators and learn to observe not only how we speak and listen but also what kinds of unspoken messages we send...."

**"Communication truly comes from within us, from our basic personality style. Once we learn who we are, and how we communicate, we can begin to understand and truly communicate with others."**

# About Deb Haggerty

Deb Haggerty is President of The Haggerty Group, a management consulting firm she founded in 1985. While most of her clients are located in her local region, she has served companies from coast to coast. Deb's unique management approach, **P**eople, **O**rganization, and **S**trategy **I**ntegrated **T**ogether **I**n **V**ital **E**nterprise, is known as **"POSITIVE."** Prior to forming her own company, Deb was with Southern Bell and AT&T for thirteen years.

Deb holds a BA in English and an MBA in Personnel and Human Resources Management and has earned the designation of Certified Management Consultant. Recognized nationally as a professional speaker, she is a member of staff for Florence Littauer's CLASSeminar and the Personality Plus Training Workshop.

Memberships include the National Association of Women Business Owners, the Institute of Management Consultants, the Society of Human Resource Managers, the American Subcontractors Association, the Pennsylvania Society of Association Executives, Toastmasters International and the National Speakers Association.

# Company Profile

Deb Haggerty is President of The Haggerty Group, a management consulting firm founded in 1985. Deb's unique management philosophy, **P**eople, **O**rganization, and **S**trategy **I**ntegrated **T**ogether **I**n **V**ital **E**nterprise, is known as **"POSITIVE."** Prior to forming her own company, Deb was with Southern Bell and AT&T for thirteen years.

Deb's presentations include:

### Help! My Computer is Driving Me Crazy!
What do all those numbers mean? What do I do now? A basic introduction to computers and technology.

### The Personality Puzzle
Knowing who you are helps you make sense of others to solve the "puzzle" of personalities.

### Preparing a Powerhouse Presentation
Teaches effective communications skills while building confidence in presenting to audiences of any size.

### Captivating Customer Service
Learn the concepts of practicing customer servant-hood, not merely providing customer service.

### Team-Building for the 21st Century
"No man is an island…" How to function as a team to achieve company goals and objectives.

### Strategies for Success
What is success? How do we know when we're successful? A non- traditional look at success.

### The Time Game
Prioritizing your time the right way!

870 Clubhouse Road
York, PA 17403
Toll-free: 1-888-DebSpkr (332-7757)
Fax:  (717) 854-0776
E-mail:  deb@debhaggerty.com

❖ **Chapter 6** ❖

# Speakerskills®: Selling Your Ideas

*by*

*Cyndi Maxey*

...there is a sense of power that comes with
continued success in front of groups.
People give added credibility to a speaker,
simply because the individual has the courage
to be standing in front of the room
and the audience is not!

—*Cyndi Maxey*

T he scenario: you're in a typical board room in a typical organization's headquarters. You've gathered the right people. The appropriate management staff is there, as well as the decision makers for every aspect of the plan. You're next on the agenda. All eyes turn to you as you push back your chair and rise to walk to the head of the table where your laptop awaits. You have center stage. Now it's your turn to sell YOUR idea.

How are you feeling at this moment? Perhaps a few goosebumps have erupted along your arms. Your heart may be responding with some rapid poundings, even as you read this page. Do you face your listeners with excitement, or is it fear? Are you feeling regret for what could have been, had you just taken the time to plan? Perhaps you're wondering why you ever signed up to be a salesperson—the art of persuasion not being your forté.

Some of you who are reading this book *are* full-time salespeople; selling to external customers is what you do everyday. For others, selling to external customers is only part of your job. Many more of you don't sell products or services at all, but do sell ideas and projects internally every day.

Whatever the position, everyone is a salesperson in one respect or another. Individuals are selling products, services, and ideas every day. Recently, the American Management Association surveyed 2,800 executives, asking them, "What is the number one need for success in business today?" Their answer: "…to be able to persuade others of your value and the value of your ideas." Indeed, to persuade others is the general purpose of most business presentations.

## Getting People to Listen

Perhaps as a child, you played "school." You could round up the neighborhood children and talk to a captive audience. You could gather all the kids and stand on the driveway with the chalkboard and talk and talk until they got bored and ran away.

Today, fewer and fewer audiences are truly captive. People have more choices, especially about who they will listen to, when they will listen, and for how long. Business audiences are typically better informed than they were a generation ago. As presenters, you're competing with increasing sophisticated technological communications for attention. Consequently, when you're lucky enough to have the right people in the room, you'd better be prepared.

# Overview

In this chapter, your communications coach will guide you through a process for being better prepared to persuade others of your value and the value of your ideas. You'll assess your persuasive ability. You'll discover how to "mind your P's and Q's" and how to borrow from the art of improvisation to handle unexpected occurrences. Finally, you'll be asked to complete an action plan for selling your ideas to others in the future.

## Your natural best

Let's start by looking at when you're naturally at your best persuading others. Take your thoughts outside of work for a moment, and remember the last time you convinced someone to do something that was really important to you. Perhaps you convinced your child to persist with violin lessons or persuaded your roommate to start a grocery list when food items run low. How did you plan to communicate your feelings to the other person? What was it that you said or did that made it work?

You have a natural persuasive ability. Think of how you get what you want. You do it somehow! Some individuals are more people/interaction oriented, getting results through getting to know people really well. Others get results through careful, logical planning by building an argument that can't be resisted.

To help you determine when you're at your persuasive best, take a moment to list the last few work-related situations when you successfully sold an idea, a plan, or a product. Next, assess why it worked. Was it your careful planning? Did a thorough understanding of the buyer figure in? What emotional buy-in was involved? Was it situational? Was it your sense of conviction? An assessment of your feelings about your past successes will help you benchmark and visualize positive outcomes from your future presentations.

## The benefits for you

What are the benefits for you in selling your ideas effectively? First, successful idea selling is good for the psyche—for the soul, the self and the mind. Your hours of creative thought time and research are finally rewarded. After a winning presentation, your self-esteem is high and your ego is nourished. Second, persuasive people who are effective in front of a group are often first in line for promotion within an organization, due to their visibility. Professional ability is often determined by the impression a brief presentation makes. Finally, there is a sense of power that comes with continued success in front of groups. Believe it or not, people give added credibility to a speaker, simply because the individual has the courage to be standing in front of the room and the audience is not!

# Mind your P's and Q's

Have you ever heard the expression, "Mind your P's and Q's"? Perhaps your mother reminded you to do just that as you left with your friends for a Friday night out. The translation meant, "Be careful," or "Watch what you're doing." Historically, the phrase stems from the era of Renaissance printing, when type was set manually letter by letter. The P and the Q were similar, and the typographer was cautioned to "mind the P and Q" so that each was placed correctly in the press.

In this chapter, you'll follow a format of P's and Q's to help you sell ideas. The format will also help you to "be careful and watch what you're doing" as you plan your presentations. The P's to mind are purpose, personalize, perspective, price, and payoff. The Q's to watch out for are quality and quantity.

## Purpose: The result you want

When an opportunity to speak occurs, your first question should be, "Why am I speaking?" Too often, presenters focus instead on "What should I say?" The focus on *why* instead of *what* will encourage you to design the talk for the needs of the audience. Ask yourself these questions:

- What is it that you would like them to walk away with?
- What is your objective?
- What does your client want?
- What do you want to happen as a result of your idea?

If you are clear about why you are speaking, you will be able to write a clear objective as well as better measure your success.

Writing a clear purpose statement is an essential first step. Though the typical business presenter's overall purpose is usually to persuade, there are many specific purposes for persuasion in a work environment. Here are a few to consider as you formulate a specific purpose statement.

- To generate or increase business.
- To solve a problem.
- To improve the quality of a product, service, or process.
- To change a system for increased effectiveness.
- To improve work performance.

All of these purposes will ask for a call to action. A persuasive presentation always tries to influence or change the beliefs of an audience. Your specific purpose statement might be "…to convince office managers that the Friendly Phone training program is the right choice for administrative personnel who use the telephone daily," or "…to encourage senior citizens to get yearly checkups provided at the outpatient clinic of City Hospital." Note that both purpose statements call for an action that can be measured.

## Personalize: How to relate to the audience's needs

Basically, an argument will persuade an audience for one of three reasons: (1) your character, (2) your reasoning, or (3) your emotional appeal to their needs. Though the strongest argument results from a combination, one of the three may have greater impact for particular individuals.

When Aristotle wrote about rhetoric and coached Grecian citizens in public speaking in 336 B.C., he emphasized that of the three dimensions of speaking—you, the talk, and the audience—the audience was, by far, the most important. You begin to think about your audience composition when you ask, "Why am I speaking?" and to formulate your purpose statement based on the answer.

The next step is to think further about the audience's self-interests. The key is to personalize the idea for the people in the room. Personalizing starts very early in the planning process. Develop a healthy list of questions to ask both your planning partner and yourself to help you personalize the presentation. An audience analysis keeps the focus where Aristotle said it should be—on the audience. The obvious questions are "Who will be there?" and "What are their jobs and responsibilities?" Here are some additional questions that will help personalize your presentation:

1. With whom should you speak weeks or even months before the presentation to gather information about the audience's viewpoint?
2. What preconceived ideas will they have about you and your topic?
3. What references to their work experience will be effective?
4. What experiences can be shared that will help them identify with you?

5. Are there any words, hot buttons, or situations that would be helpful to know about?
6. How do individual levels of industry knowledge differ?
7. What will be the two or three most important benefits that the decision makers are looking for?

# Perspective: How to share your unique viewpoint

Audiences are also persuaded by the character of the presenter. Consider the results of this study on ethos by researchers K. Andersen and T. Cleavenger. A persuasive talk was taped and played to three groups. Each group was given a different identity for the speaker. The three identities were: Surgeon General of the U.S.; Secretary General of the Communist Party in America; and a university student. When asked to rate the speaker, the group who thought the speaker was the Surgeon General rated the presenter significantly more competent than the other groups. The study illustrates that factors other than clear purpose, excellent reasoning, and emotional appeal are related to credibility. For example, titles may have an innate credibility in themselves.

As you contemplate what to say, keep in mind that audiences are more likely to be persuaded by someone whom they feel is one of them. This is called "the assimilation/contrast effect." Basically, audiences who perceive a presenter as similar to themselves will tend to exaggerate the similarity. For example, salespeople will assimilate with another experienced salesperson. However, audiences who perceive a presenter as having different values will exaggerate the dissimilarity. Community leaders and politicians must learn to communicate values similar to those who live in their communities. Achieve the assimilation effect by telling stories that emphasize the importance of an idea in a framework that the audience can relate to. Your persona is very much a part of the presentation, influencing your credibility.

# Price: What if the audience doesn't buy the idea now

Emphasizing the consequences of taking no action, this step provides an opportunity to appeal to the audience's fears. In order to clarify the "price to be paid" for not buying the idea now, you need to engage the buyer's fears—loss of future profit, loss of growth, loss of morale, loss of opportunity, loss of dignity, or loss of customers. A good attention-getter, this tactic asks the audience to view your idea from a new angle—one that directly influences their welfare. Again, the focus should be on the audience's needs. The ultimate strength of the appeal comes from the strength of the supporting research; the audience must be able to see the contrasting results of your idea for the future versus the status quo, or other, less effective choices.

For example, a financial planner speaking to parents of elementary school children would alert the audience to invest in college savings plans now, rather than regret the lack of funding in twenty years. Few parents would want to be left without funds for a college-bound child. As another example, an organizational consultant addressing human resource planners about future needs may want them to begin English as a Second Language training now, rather than pay the price: being caught with severe communication difficulties caused by increased future immigration.

To determine what price or loss to emphasize, consider the feelings your audience might have if one of the following happens:
- The competition reaches the goal first.
- Public perception changes.
- Quality standards change.
- Resources become more scarce.
- Personnel issues take a new precedent.
- Crisis management may result.
- A moment of opportunity is lost.

If the audience has been thoroughly polled, the element of fear with the greatest impact will strike hardest. A common adage to consultants and salespeople is to "find the prospect's pain and then offer a solution." That's what price is about—the pain that comes with realizing the consequences of not taking an action sooner.

## Pay-off: What if the audience buys your idea now

Audience benefits should be the easiest aspect of your idea to plan and talk about. A benefit is what the idea buyer gains from the idea. The benefit results from the features and facts you present. If you've approached a sales presentation without thinking about buyer benefits, you're wasting your time and theirs. For example, when a furniture designer is selling a particular chair design idea complete with facts, drawings and research, the audience is really listening for WII-FM. They are thinking, "**What's In It For Me**?" The designer must consider the people in the room. What do these buyers want most... value for the cost... unsurpassed comfort... long-lasting investment... another means for impressing clients? The correct answer to these questions will persuade customers to buy.

Imagine a little boy trying to convince his friends to be a part of a chain letter which involves writing copies of the letter to five other friends. To his chagrin, he discovers that his fellow ball players and bike riders won't take action because they fail to see the benefit in that much writing. After many attempted tries and failures, he finally thinks of the benefit: he asks them if they want to be a part of a world's record for the world's longest chain letter! This outcome appeals to the eight-year-old mind and sells the idea. The boy has learned to position the idea.

Positioning benefits correctly is a skill that comes with knowing the audience thoroughly. It goes beyond listing facts and features. Just as the little boy discovered how to persuade his ball-playing friends, you can learn which benefits are most important to the audience. For example, if you are selling an idea on how to change a procedure, you're really selling the benefits that the change will bring; e.g., more time spent with customers. Too many presenters get stuck at the features level, failing to reach the all-important benefit level of idea selling. With well-positioned benefit statements, the presenter can build to a winning conclusion, asking the audience to visualize a better future with all the new ideas in place.

## Quality of support

Aristotle wrote about ethos, logos, and pathos as important facets of persuasion. Logos is the ability to persuade with reasoning. The quality of the supporting evidence is tantamount to your emotional appeal. While considering options for support, again keep in mind the type of audience being addressed. For example, engineers will often appreciate facts, statistics, and data. Human resource professionals may respond favorably to survey results, trend analysis and personnel data. Almost everyone responds to stories of some kind. Stories can illustrate the success of a product or your personal involvement with an issue. Stories can often be easier to remember than lists of data, while appealing to the heart rather than the head. Emotional appeal is a major reason people buy ideas and products, and stories are a way to reach the emotions.

Classic persuasive supports include facts, statistics, examples, testimonials, visuals, analogies, and illustrations. Use a variety. Try to remain true to the adage, "If you can't give an example, then don't make the point." Examples clarify and give added credibility. For instance, if an idea worked well in a certain situation, you should be able to illustrate that situation specifically for the audience.

Be cautious, however, with comparisons as to how the idea worked with others; sometimes this can work to your benefit and sometimes it can backfire. If audience members feel that your comparison is incompatible to their situation, they'll let you know. For example, if you're presenting to attorneys and you attempt to show how your idea worked well for health-care supervisors, expect several very pointed questions regarding its applicability in their arena.

# Quality of sincerity

Aristotle wrote that ethos, involving the character of the speaker, is "the most potent of all the means to persuasion." Especially where knowledge is inexact, your listeners are prone to believe you, a trusted personality. For example, studies have shown that children can be persuaded to eat foods they normally wouldn't eat if the food is endorsed by a superhero. Also, people have accepted false personality information about themselves when it's presented by a respected psychologist. Obviously, the character of the speaker impacts peoples' judgment as to what is right or wrong.

What factors help you establish ethos, that is, make you credible? The primary qualities associated with ethos are competence, trustworthiness, and dynamism. A competent presenter is perceived as trained, experienced, qualified, skilled, informed, able, and intelligent. Trustworthiness is established with kindness, congeniality, friendliness, and hospitality. A dynamic presenter is frank, emphatic, bold, forceful, energetic, and active. Ethos is the sum of the audience's assessment of your character.

Be cautious in assuming competence. The strength of your character is most likely related to some topics more than others. For example, a well-published writer may be seen as an expert in certain areas of academic research but lacking perspective in certain on-the-job applications. Focus on your unique experiences and qualifications. Then, assess your abilities and your background to determine your natural areas of credibility.

You also must be seen as trustworthy. To audiences, trust is found in the sincerity and congeniality that you convey. You've probably heard the saying, "It's not what you say, but how you say it." This statement applies to establishing trust. Find a way to communicate your credentials that will convince the audience of your expertise. For example, people respond better to warmth and a lesson learned than to ego-centered boasting. You can smile, use caring vocal tones and practice an open stance. You can pause frequently and establish direct eye contact. Direct eye contact and pause, especially, are two rapport-building skills of the established professional speaker. Use them to your benefit to establish trust.

Dynamism is conveyed when your body and vocal energy demonstrate enthusiasm. Dynamism is particularly important in your opening remarks. Volume should be appropriate: when presenting, the volume should be louder than you speak one-on-one. Dynamic body energy should be conveyed in your alert posture, your carefully selected movement choices, and your upbeat facial expressions. Dynamism doesn't just happen. As the persuasive presenter, you should plan and practice your approach. As your talk progresses, you can continue to be dynamic in the manner in which you use your visuals, emphasize key points, refer to handout materials, and handle questions.

# Quantity: Less is more

The quantity of your presentation will affect its quality. Most executives and business audiences today want their information delivered in a short and simple format that's easy to remember and to pass along to others. A classic persuasive format is pretty simple: their need, your idea, the benefits of your idea, your call to action. In other words—purpose, personalize, perspective, price, and pay-off work together! The important thing is to stay with your format. Provide a brief set-up, and get to the heart of the matter quickly.

Select your words carefully, especially in the opening, closing, and at key points in your appeal. Reinforce a theme or a phrase that you'd like audiences to remember. Put on your marketing hat. Do you want them to "…invest now and smile later"? Or perhaps you are selling "…people—our most important resource." Most people listen poorly and remember less than 50 percent of what you say. Make it easy for them to walk away remembering your purpose, theme, and a few key points.

Writers and journalists know about the "law of three." It's easier for people to remember three points rather than seven or fifteen. The most memorable information placements are first and last. The middle gets forgotten. You're probably going to remember the opening and closing of this chapter better than all of the details in the middle. In selling an idea, start with a strong piece of evidence and end with one. Keep details in groups of three. Build in internal reviews to help the listener remember what you want to sell.

Mark Twain once wrote, "I'm sorry I wrote you such a long letter; I didn't have time to write a short one." If you've ever had to shorten a talk to fit a time frame or an article to fit editorial requirements, you have gained respect for the skills of a good editor. Words go easily on paper; editing them is harder. Words can hide ideas. Why not get rid of excess words? The goal is to have your ideas stand out.

One way to shorten your presentation is to force yourself to cut it back five or even ten minutes. After you write it, practice it with a stopwatch, and then edit it. Chances are, no one will notice. You'll probably have cut unneeded detail or repetitious remarks. Keep in mind that somewhere in the gap between writing, practice, and final delivery, most presentations get longer. In the actual setting, you will repeat things unintentionally, handle unexpected questions, and take longer with visuals and handouts than you planned. Before you know it, those five or ten minutes return anyway!

# Expecting the Unexpected

You've given your presentation. You've personalized, added your perspective, clarified the price, and stressed the payoff. You've been as dynamic as possible in communicating your purpose. And then, you get questions. At this point, crowd control is up to you. Prepare by writing questions you think you'll get and what your answers could be. To prepare the audience before you begin your talk, tell them your plan for questions. Stick to the plan.

You may also need to handle impromptu questions throughout your presentation. Set the tone by answering the first one quickly and honestly, and then move on. You want to avoid getting bogged down in questions, unless you really want them. Keep questions on track. Don't be afraid to say, "I appreciate that thought, Joe, and we'll see it coming up with my next slide." Always save the questioner's self-esteem in such a situation. Answer an individual's question for the entire group by looking at everyone as you answer. This technique will keep you from getting entangled in one person's cause.

A formal question-answer period can be your most challenging hurdle in selling an idea. You may need to begin the session yourself. You can lead into it by saying, "One question that you might have is…" or "Some people have asked me about…." Also, you can select a friendly audience member beforehand, ask for permission to refer to them, and later say something like, "Joan, I know you're often concerned about how this fits in with recruitment…." These comments will hopefully encourage involvement from others.

On the other hand, you may be bombarded with questions that are unfriendly. Here are a few keys to help you through this situation, which most presenters will face at some time. First, keep a calm demeanor and a neutral expression. Convey an open body posture and a positive facial expression and vocal tone. Second, rephrase or restate the question to remove any hostility. For example, if the question is, "Why couldn't you see this problem coming sooner?" the rephrase could be, "What is the reason for the current timing of this proposal?" or "Your question concerns timing…." Third, keep your answer simple. Chances are that the questioner doesn't really want a lengthy explanation. Fourth, be honest. If you don't know, say so. Offer to respond later.

# Borrow from Improvisation

To help you think on your feet, you can borrow techniques from improvisation artists. Improvisation is based in the art of listening and relying on intuition to make decisions. As the questioner is asking the question, you can be mentally reviewing the intent of the question. Because you're thinking faster than the questioner can speak, the art of active listening helps you use thought time to your advantage. When it's your turn to respond, keep in mind these pointers:

- *Think or say, "yes, and…."*

  This technique instills a positive attitude towards an objection. You might say, "Yes, this is an important issue, and I know that it will continue to be," rather than, "But, I did address that issue in my first point…" which makes you sound defensive.

- *Use silence.*

  Silence allows for everyone to think—not just you, but the audience as well. Begin your answer. Pause. Think. Continue.

- *Find agreement.*

  Improvisation artists are taught that conflict is not as interesting as agreement. The "yes, and…" technique supports this. When handling an objection, find the agreement. There is always a degree of agreement somewhere. For example, if the questioner asks, "Where is the extra money supposed to come from?" you might answer, "Extra resources? It's true that resource allocation has been a challenge this quarter, and I've got a few ideas that could help us."

- *Don't force connection.*

  An improvisational skit that is forced is not as effective as one that evolves naturally. As a presenter, you should not feel that you have to force an answer.

# The Idea Selling You Will Always Do

Earlier, you read about some benefits of presenting: presenting energizes your psyche, encourages your promotion and develops your personal power. You'll notice the absence of a fourth "P" word: perfection. Selling ideas will probably never be perfected. Perfection and presentations somehow don't go together. You can bake the perfect cake; you can shoot the perfect photograph. However, anything as interactive and situational as a persuasive talk probably will never be perfect. Practicing your talk will help make it permanent in your mind; it will not make it perfect. Relieve your stress and forget perfection!

One well-known professional speaker doesn't look at audience evaluations anymore because he feels that he gives them the best he can at that time. He prepares, he presents, and he learns from whatever happened. What a stress-free way of looking at presenting! Perhaps you're not in a position to ignore the appraisal of your presentations. However, you can always put them in perspective. Look at trends; be honest with yourself.

The most important appraisal is your honest self-appraisal. Are you using your natural persuasive ability? Did you practice? Did you personalize? Were your stories appropriate? Did you really do the planning you needed to do? Did the questions sound familiar because you already had prepared for them?

Perhaps your self-appraisal will uncover that you need further training and development in some related skill. There are many related skill areas including writing, storytelling, sales, improvisation, acting, movement, and computer technology that can help you as a presenter. Most people who are serious about building presentations skills, take continual classes, read books and listen to tapes.

Look in your geographic area for coaching help. Many of the contributors to this book are members of the National Speakers Association (NSA), an organization dedicated to the enhancement and growth of professional speaking, welcoming guests to meetings and special events such as Speakers' Schools. There are Toastmasters groups in most major cities, and community colleges and universities offer continuing education programs that include speaking courses. You have already used this book as your coach; there are live presentations coaches out there, too! Call NSA for additional recommendations.

There is an old story of a man watching his son trying to lift a fallen tree from his bicycle. The boy struggled until the father asked, "Why can't you lift it, son?" The boy replied, "I'm using all my strength, but it won't move." The father answered wisely, "Son, you're not using all your strength. You haven't asked me to help." As this story illustrates, your strength lies not only within you, but also within those around you. Ask your coworkers and friends to critique your presentation or videotape you. If you can't afford to hire a private coach, join together and hire one. Most consultants would love to oblige, and everyone wins.

# Instant Replay

The scenario: you're in a typical board room in a typical organization's headquarters. You've gathered the right people. The appropriate management staff is there, as well as the decision makers for every aspect of the plan. You're next on the agenda. All eyes turn to you as you push back your chair and rise to walk to the head of the table where your laptop awaits. You have center stage. It's your turn to sell YOUR idea. And you CAN'T WAIT!!!

# About Cyndi Maxey

Cyndi Maxey (MA, Northwestern University—Communication Studies) is a speaker, trainer, and consultant helping people to build business relationships through speaking and listening skills. For the past 16 years, she has developed training materials, presented workshops, and coached others throughout the nation—most recently for Novus Services, Inc., Kimball International, Zenith Data Systems, Ameritech, Unichema International, and Andersen Consulting.

A leader in the Professional Speakers of Illinois, Chicago Chapter NAWBO and Chicago and Regional ASTD, she has received awards for outstanding service to the training field. She has earned the CSP (Certified Speaking Professional) Candidacy, a National Speakers Association professional designation. Her article, "Energizing Groups," recently appeared in *Training & Development* magazine, ASTD's national publication.

Cyndi lives and works in Chicago, Illinois, in the historic Lakewood-Balmoral neighborhood where block parties still reign each summer. Her actor/writer husband, Rob, and her two active children provide both balance and chaos in her life.

# Company Profile

**M**axey Creative, Inc. is a communication skills consulting firm providing training programs, materials, and one-on-one coaching for all employee levels—from front-line service representatives to executive speakers.

Speaking & Listening Programs are Speakerskills®, Interpersonal Insight, Serviceskills, and the "Catch the Wave" Employee Development Series: Interpersonal Excellence, Positive Change, Constructive Conflict, and Coaching for Excellence. Other popular topics include *Telephone Service Excellence, Margin Notes: What Experienced Trainers Know, The Service Professional,* and *Giving and Receiving Feedback.*

The Speaking & Listening programs range from a half day to two days in length, and can be tailored to meet specific organizational concerns and learning objectives. Full training program materials—Leader's and Participant's Guides and visuals—are available for all programs. Cyndi's keynote topics include "Putting it in Perspective," and "Fine Tuning Your Communication Skills."

For more information, contact Cyndi Maxey at:

*Speaking & Listening Programs*

**Maxey Creative Inc.**

**Maxey Creative Inc.**
5407 North Lakewood Avenue
Chicago, Illinois  60640
Phone:  (773) 561-6252
Fax:  (773) 275-5417
E-mail:  cyndimaxey@aol.com

❖ **Chapter 7** ❖

# Negotiation

# IS

# Communication

*by*
*Laurel Bellows*

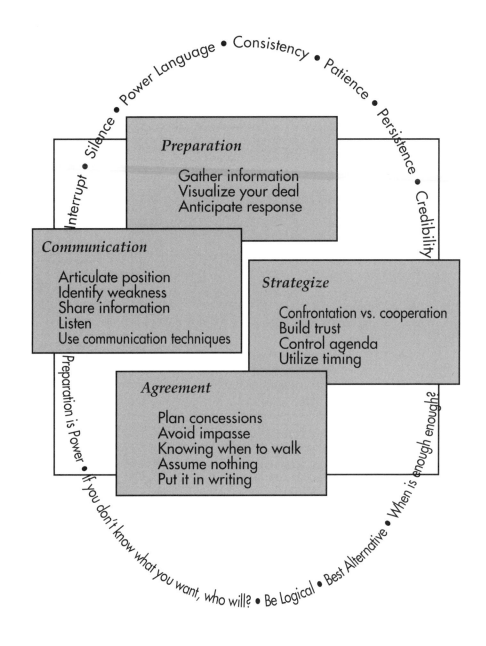

Negotiation is simply the use

of specialized communication techniques

to get something you want from other people.

—*Laurel Bellows*

# A Beginning

Say the word negotiation and you picture an enormous conference table surrounded by unsmiling people, usually men wearing dark suits, white shirts, conservative ties, engaged in a power dance. You feel the tension build as the scene begins to decompose. Papers and half-filled coffee mugs are strewn everywhere, smoke fills the room, jackets are tossed aside, ties are loosened, shirts are wrinkled and polite inquiry turns terse and accusatory. You envision high stakes and complex documents. You imagine a hot dispute over the acquisition of a multi-million dollar subsidiary.

Or, you visualize an imposing conference table surrounded by negotiators with perfect posture, shirts buttoned, ties straight, an undercurrent of tension masked by formality… an intricate international trade agreement discussed with diplomatic restraint.

You are right. Fortune 500 companies are always at the bargaining table and diplomats are endlessly resolving international disputes. Unions face management to hammer out contract renewals and all of baseball goes on strike. At the other end of the scale, you negotiate personal items (dinner plans and bedtime) and less important professional decisions. Where will the office party take place? Should employees receive Presidents' Day as a paid holiday? *By envisioning only the most dramatic scenarios, you lose sight of the routine nature of negotiation and its practical goals.* The tendency is to place too much stock in the process and insufficient emphasis on the purpose.

**Negotiation is simply the use of specialized communication techniques to get something you want from other people.** If you are a salesperson, negotiation is your life. If you are a lawyer, your trade is to negotiate the settlement of divorce or personal injury cases or to work out a business deal for your client. If you are a business person, you negotiate employee salaries, the lease of your space, the price of your product. Obvious? Absolutely.

**Negotiation is an everyday, every moment skill used by everyone.** Planning the next vacation requires negotiation with family, travel agents and hotels. The price of the antique chair found during last year's trip might have been lower had you applied expert negotiation skills. Focus on your actions. You will find yourself surrounded by negotiating opportunities all day, from the simple decision to return a call or discount a price... to the more complex, improving your skills as you lease a car, contract with a new advertising agency, plan a business conference, discuss commission structure with your stock broker or negotiate a manufacturing and distribution agreement.

**Every negotiation has several points in common.** First, negotiation is always between people, even when the biggest corporations or countries are involved. People make the deals. Next, at the outset, every negotiation involves disagreement or, at least, differing viewpoints. Otherwise, there would be nothing to discuss. The tone of the encounter can range from confrontive to constructive, but the focus of each negotiation will be on coming to terms.

**Not surprisingly, people who dislike confrontation fear negotiation.** In anticipation of an unpleasant conversation with a landlord, many would rather agree to an increase in rent just to avoid a face-to-face dispute. Before rationalizing that the increase is small compared to the cost of moving, remember that even giving in is a form of negotiation, although unsuccessful. By keeping in mind that the goal of negotiation is to resolve problems, not to create them, your natural concern about losing, appearing incompetent or being bullied, diminishes.

# Keep the Goals in Mind

**The goal is to arrive at a wise, durable and efficient agreement that will improve, or at least not damage, any future relationship.** If the resolution is roughly acceptable to both sides, there will be sufficient incentive to assure that everyone benefits from living by the terms of the agreement. A one-sided deal will provide temporary satisfaction to the "winner," but is more likely to breakdown or result in long-term conflict.

**You can look at negotiation as a game if it makes the process more inviting.** As games go, negotiation is more like playing competition chess than family Monopoly. The goal of both games is to win, but playing Monopoly does not require a serious game plan. You win by buying and building wherever chance dictates, relying on the dice to land a player on Boardwalk after you've built three hotels.

In chess, of course, the path to winning is full of options, bound by rules. The game requires pinpoint focus on a step-by-step game plan. Each player can and must visualize the goal—checkmate—along with every move that leads up to it. Chess and negotiation are games of strategy, planning and preparation.

The difference between chess and negotiation is that at the end of the chess game winner takes all. Negotiation is the attempt to arrive at an agreement that benefits both sides. You can never assume that everyone shares the same objectives. The fun begins when everyone's objectives are as different as the number of creative solutions presented. After all, no other game provides an infinitely stimulating variety of personalities, agendas, options, and solutions. As you prepare to play, just be sure to remember the results *you* seek and the importance of measuring progress through an ongoing comparison to real alternatives.

*Keeping the ultimate goal of negotiation in mind—reaching a lasting, mutually beneficial agreement—will positively influence the tenor of the entire negotiation process.*

In the negotiation game, there are no rules, simply acceptable and unacceptable tactics all of which you must be prepared to experience. Instead of memorizing rules, absorb simple communication guidelines for developing your own negotiating style, as you learn to recognize and respond to the techniques employed by those seated at the same negotiating table.

Master these guidelines, and you will leave every negotiation knowing that you either maximized the opportunities available to you and arrived at the most efficient, profitable agreement possible, or walked away from a bad deal before it got worse.

# Preparation is Power

Although preparation is the single most important key to the success of any negotiation, few negotiators perform the investigation or engage in the soul searching required to complete the preparation process. A negotiator cannot communicate a position or hope to persuade the opposition without meticulous preparation.

Hard work is the key. Preparation is a time-intensive process that requires discipline and attention to detail. Without adequate preparation, the negotiation will be unstructured at best. At worst, the negotiation will proceed according to someone else's strategy.

## Strategy and preparation are inseparable

What is your vision of the perfect deal?

**If you don't know what you want, who will?** Your first job is to identify your needs and force yourself to detail your objectives. Outline what you want and why. Force yourself to picture the day-to-day results of the final business arrangement you envision. What are the details that must be incorporated into the deal before your vision becomes reality? If you are buying and renovating a building, force yourself to walk through every step from the moment you sign the contract until the day you sit at your new desk.

The easiest way to be sure that you don't gloss over important considerations but rather maintain the discipline of determining exactly what scenario will make this deal work for you, is to draft a rough agreement—nothing fancy, nothing legal—just a written version of the business deal in your mind.

## Brainstorm—it's time to strategize

**Thoroughly prepare your own agenda.** Anticipate the specific points that need to be negotiated and note the supporting facts and your reasonable demands.

**What facts support your position?** Evaluate your strengths. Push aside insecurities which may tempt you to overemphasize potential weaknesses and sidetrack you from making a strong case. Speculate systematically. What do I know? What don't I know? What are the assumptions I might make? How can I confirm the validity of those assumptions?

**Anticipate your response to each counterargument** you expect to hear. Discover the facts which support your opponent's point of view. Identify the objectives of the opposition. Anticipate your opponent's assumptions and arguments. Develop the facts necessary to refute the other side's demands. Ascertain the abilities, limits, needs, expectations, and priorities of each party to the negotiation.

**Consider the differences between the viewpoints of each party.** Differing needs, timetables, capabilities, and alliances result in different priorities. These priorities, in turn, affect the value which each negotiator places on various options or the deal as a whole. The way each party perceives the future of their business will have a dramatic effect on the options at each stage of the negotiation. The extent of each side's appetite for risk might well determine the outcome.

Other "off the table" considerations can play a major role in the discussions. Does this negotiation contemplate a continuing relationship or is this a one-time deal? Will the negotiated agreement be satisfied immediately with cash or carried over time? The likelihood of future dealings will influence the tactics you and your opponents choose. Whether the negotiators have personal interests on the line, such as money, reputation, or advancement within a company might determine the pace and attitude of the discussions.

## Utilize all available resources

Don't procrastinate and don't get lazy. Research the seniority, authority, past track record, and credibility of the other side. Discover everything you can about the individuals who will be handling and overseeing the negotiation for your opposition. Learn about the particular business entity with which you are dealing and the general business climate in your counterpart's industry.

What is the reputation for delivery, quality and service of the company on the other side of the table? Is money desperately needed? If so, is it to expand because business is great or is it to cover debt? Who owns the business and who sits on the board? Are they favorable to the type of deal you are proposing? What has been the experience of others who have sold them a similar product or entered into a similar joint venture? Would they do it again? With what adjustments?

Use friends, bankers, stock brokers, competitors, suppliers, Chamber of Commerce, the Internet, and participants in business associations to gain information about the industry generally. Specifics as to the condition and reputation of the company with whom you are negotiating are available from customers, suppliers, newspapers, trade publications, television, receptionists, and secretaries. Does the company have an annual report? Use your public library's business section for names of officers, information or products and latest earnings. Remember that the most powerful tool in any negotiation is information.

## Strategize communications

Determine the order in which issues will be discussed and resolved. Sometimes you may choose to handle smaller issues like delivery requirements, financing, plant scheduling, who will keep oversight responsibility, or accept responsibility for defective merchandise—the details—early in the negotiation. Smaller preliminary agreements often build consensus and set the tone.

Addressing the deal breaker early is equally appropriate, even if you set aside the discussion for final decision later. By making an initial effort to resolve the most controversial issues, you may find a way of breaking a large disagreement into smaller, more workable parts. Initial discussion of big issues sets its own forthright, no-nonsense tone. Perhaps you will discover that there are no creative options available to make further discussion worthwhile, considering the attractive alternatives available to the parties. Most importantly, be prepared to change direction, addressing different issues at different times and returning later to issues left on the table.

**What are the options that could become components of a final agreement?** Brainstorm with friends and associates to develop options that may not be initially apparent but could reconfigure the proposal to the benefit of all the parties. Consult with experts, builders, doctors, educators, anyone who can see the deal from a different point of view. Divide the problem and solve the parts. Indicate a willingness to expand the available choices.

**What alternatives do you have to this deal?** Identify your alternatives to the deal being negotiated, weighing each alternative separately. Determine which of several choices is the best for you at the outset of negotiations. Take the time to obtain sufficient information on each alternative to permit consideration of the various choices available to you throughout different stages of negotiation.

**What information will you communicate and when?** Consider what information is harmless to divulge and what information should remain confidential. Determine what information the other side will need or demand before entering into an agreement.

*Decide what information you need before making a decision.* In addition to the information gleaned from pre-negotiation research, plan to ask open-ended questions throughout the negotiations to obtain new facts, to verify information you received from other sources, to check the credibility of the other side... or, simply to gauge the tenor of the reaction of the other side. How do you plan to get that equipment into the country? Who manufactures this product? Who are your competitors? What's your cost? Are you union? What's your wage scale? What arrangements do you have for packaging? What parts of your process do you outsource? What are your shipping/importing/exporting arrangements and related costs?

*In response to opponent's inquiries, keep your answers short and truthful.* Attention to communication skills allow business people to plan in advance to use specific *blocking* techniques. Anticipate requests for information your opposition is certain to try to elicit from you. Decide when to answer questions about your pricing, profit margin, distribution network, what you paid for the property, finance charges, quickest delivery dates, preferential customers or contract terms.

*Be prepared to vary the following blocks:* Ignore the question entirely or answer only the favorable part. Choose to answer a question with a question and take control of the conversation. Sometimes, give a more general answer than requested. Other times, provide a very specific response to a very general inquiry, giving one example only. Or, be direct and declare the question "out of bounds" for the moment or forever.

## Above all, choose your communication tactics

**Determine the overt tone of the negotiation and your role in advance.** The decision to take control over the timing and pace of negotiations should be made early. Do you have a deadline or is the other side under time pressure? Is it to your benefit to create a deadline, an artificial delivery requirement, or to slow down the negotiations until the other side faces a time crunch? Given that 80 percent of concessions occur in the last 20 percent of the process, some form of timetable is certain to make negotiations more efficient. Sometimes the timing is controlled by travel plans. Your plans should always be flexible so that no one can use your schedule against you.

**Will the talks be hard or soft?** Will this be a highly competitive negotiation, characterized by an arrogant, belligerent attitude? Or, will the approach be factually oriented, open to options and creative strategizing? Will you choose to use a hard, dominant approach or a soft, relationship-building strategy?

Whether or not you choose to create a cooperative atmosphere, *personalize the negotiations.* Exchange personal and professional information to establish the unspoken ground rules. Regardless of the initial formality, make an attempt at small talk, first names, shoulder and arm touching, a warm smile and a friendly, firm handshake. You can learn from the reaction to your overture. If the atmosphere has been made intentionally formal or uncomfortable, identify and cure the problem either directly or indirectly. If your chair is uncomfortable or the sun is in your eyes... move.

*A Word to Women:* Negotiation is a game that *most* women don't want to play. Because negotiation implies disagreement, women shy away. Believing that the goal of conversation is to make or maintain friendships, women see the pull and tug of negotiation as destructive to future relationships. This is short-sighted. Negotiation is about resolving disagreements and *building* relationships. Women are talented at finding creative solutions and developing common ground.

Along with these relationship-building skills, comes women's frequent impatience with the indirection and timing of the negotiation game. Women, intent on avoiding confrontation, tend to seek an immediate solution. Working women, engulfed with the details of balancing home and office lives, are not interested in a protracted negotiation dance. The temptation is to become a "bottom-line" negotiator, given to quick compromise. The objective may be to cut through the process, place the best offer on the table, measure it against the best alternatives of both parties, explore a few creative options and move on to the next deal, but the result will be disastrous. Impatience makes women negotiators vulnerable.

To compensate for this Achilles Heel, women are champion chameleons. A negotiator practiced in the art of reading people and situations who makes full use of the wide range of colors, styles, dress, emotions, plus talks both sports and children is a devastating adversary. Instead of imitating the pinstriped uniform men feel constrained to wear, why not choose the color of your dress, bright or pastel, to coincide with the personality of the individual you need to convince? Consider dressing to coordinate with the tone you choose to set for the meeting, bold fast-paced colors and style or simple, conservative dark with or without a splash of the unexpected colored shirt. Similarly, take the opportunity to vary your mood, just like a clothing accessory, ranging from gregarious to strait-laced or from open to recalcitrant. Women are as capable as men in the use of anger, silence, and a belligerent attitude. They are also capable of making a convincing plea for mercy or help, successfully obtaining concessions or information which might be otherwise denied.

Tough and unpredictable, women should welcome participation in a game in which they can so easily excel.

*A Word to Men:* Often men believe that the only negotiation tactic needed is to choose an attitude somewhere between aggressive and belligerent. Some people can outshout the opposition and accomplish something, but men with this attitude risk making an enemy of a woman opponent. In a man's world of team sports, all it takes is the final buzzer to turn cut-throat competitors back to locker room chums. In the woman's world, forgive but never forget is often the watchword. In short, take into account the gender of your opponent.

As for man-to-man negotiations, the old "take no prisoners" demeanor is no longer admired in an era of team management and consensus building. Tough stands based on objective criteria and identified goals work, so long as your mind remains open to innovative solutions which serve the needs of all parties. The ability to "temper tantrum" your way into a deal is no longer a valued skill.

**Watch out for stereotypes.** To assure a diverse workforce, the watchword is to identify and overcome unconscious prejudgments. Still, stereotypes are based on generalizations which, when accurate, can be useful as well as misleading. As a general rule, women don't like confrontation, while men enjoy conversational sparring. Equally general, women are able to build the trust and rapport necessary to eventually reach an agreement. Accountants focus on the details; lawyers say "no" which tends to deal break instead of seeking the path to a creative "yes." As long as you recognize the pitfalls of these stereotypes, the use of generalities to speculate about how your opponents may act and react is essential to negotiation.

# Does your counterpart have authority... or, are you wasting your breath?

Be certain that you are spending the effort to influence the person with the authority to make a decision. Establish the extent of the authority of the other side from the outset. Are there monetary limits on their ability to reach an agreement? Suggest that your counterpart reduce the number of people involved in the decision-making process. Can you eliminate the late-game ploy of an appeal to higher authority, a supervisor, the president or a board of directors?

## Preparation results in confidence

When faced with a confident approach supported by facts and logical demands, opponents often reconsider their own valuation of the deal and question the viability of their own proposals. Your high expectations, if reasonable, cause the other side to rethink their demands.

# It's All About Communication

Communication strategy and negotiation techniques are inseparable. Skilled persuasion encourages the other side to see things your way. To obtain the best results from your negotiating efforts, you must be able to communicate your interests, needs, proposals, and awareness of the other side's objectives... effectively... to the person sitting on the other side of the table. Think about what's at work in a conversation, and intentionally put what you know about communication into action.

## Conversational techniques

**Presenting and defending your position.** Present your case with supporting facts and no hint of compromise. People formulate opinions quickly and tend to stick to their first impression. So, make the most of your first presentation and be succinct. *Take control over your material* and you will *exude the confidence* which accompanies the person who can support a prepared and logical position. You do not need a loud voice or a six-foot wingspan. You *do* need the ability to think on your feet and a *methodical, fact-based approach* to your argument.

**Responding to their position.** Persistent, accurate, fact-based rebuttal is always the most effective response. Restating the opposing position avoids misunderstanding, summarizes progress and demonstrates empathy, even for a position with which you disagree. A grasp of back-up facts will magnify your ability to reveal the weaknesses of the case put forth by the other side. Once in a while, as a negotiating ploy, if you intentionally misunderstand details, you will elicit additional or more accurate information which the other side has been holding back.

**Sharing information.** The ability to share information and the timing of the decision to disclose important facts brings its own power. Imparting useful information is equated with expertise. With a wide range of pertinent facts at your disposal, your status in the negotiation will skyrocket, particularly if you are viewed as the expert on your team. Just be sure to draw the line between a confident presentation and outright arrogance.

**Interruption** is another communication technique which brings its own power. When judiciously used as an active listening device, interruption indicates interest and a willingness to understand the other side's point of view. But, interruption is also a technique for maintaining control of a conversation, or asserting dominance over the entire negotiation process. Overused, interruption is irritating, offensive and interferes with the free flow of creative ideas.

**Silence,** as a response to a particular proposal, results in control and frequently unexpected information. The purpose of silence is to force an adversary to feel uncomfortable and fill the gap with unnecessary explanations, hopefully negotiating against himself. Don't succumb. When your counterpart suggests that $100,000 is a reasonable annual consultancy fee, respond with silence. If the next words come from the would-be consultant, you will usually hear an explanation which will give you information, or may add value like an additional number of hours the consultant is willing to spend or his willingness to cover expenses. Sit silently and wait. You will always learn something.

**Powerless language.** Communication techniques such as interruption and silence improve negotiation posture. Beware of the opposite effect of powerless language which reduces both your status and your credibility. Apologies and indirection (beating around the bush to make a simple point) call your level of competency into question. Seeking reassurance by inserting questions, as part of an otherwise strong position statement, send the message that even you don't believe in your position. Questions like, "Don't you agree that… ?" or "It's important to remember… isn't it?" weaken your argument.

**Nonverbal communication techniques.** Anger, a frown, a sigh, eye contact or no eye contact, drumming fingers, closed arms, crossed legs, a nod, a smile, a squint of the eyes, or an outright flinch all carry meaning worthy of translation. If your opponent sits at the edge of her chair, she is interested. If she's leaning back, she's confident. A casual touch means she's probably sincere. Is he playing with his glasses? Label him thoughtful. And if he's looking at notes, give him time to think.

# Gender gap: are you communicating?

Pretending that men and women communicate in the same manner is detrimental to the development of successful negotiation techniques. Certainly, some women revel in confrontation, are direct, belligerent, bad tempered, given to interruption and bouts of silence. Similarly, some men are soft spoken, prefer settlement to battle, find it difficult to be indirect and favor a bottom line, lay-it-on-the-table approach.

Yet, for the most part, men use conversation to obtain and maintain the upper hand. Men are more comfortable when they control the floor, often using confrontation as a means to obtain this control. Men gather and impart information to preserve this control, holding center stage as they exhibit their expertise. In contrast, female conversation focuses on building or preserving relationships. Rather than confrontation, women seek consensus, preferring agreement to confrontation. Plus, reticent to be viewed as arrogant know-it-alls, women often hesitate to tout their opinion.

Negotiation is inherently adversarial and involves parties who disagree. Women, or anyone who compromises early to avoid discord, must work harder to avoid being run over by the savvy, affrontive adversary who spots the discomfort or fear and works to maximize the unpleasant atmosphere.

Perfecting both offensive and defensive conversational strategy will permit women to enjoy the pull and tug of the negotiation game.

# Secrets of the great persuaders

**Persuasion is not a trick.** Persuasion is a technique that can be learned by paying attention to communication realities that are often simple and obvious. Repetition is persuasive, so find several different ways of driving the same point home. Facts, particularly written factual materials, are persuasive. Information which is rare or obtained surreptitiously is persuasive. So is the appearance of trying to be even-handed and objective. Body language can be a great persuader, or signal deception. Consider these examples: The person who constantly jiggles pocket change is untrustworthy. Lack of eye contact destroys credibility. In contrast, an open, relaxed body is more likely to persuade.

**Be patient and be consistent.** These are the attributes of someone in no rush to sell the Brooklyn Bridge. Also, remember credibility increases with the perception of your status and authority. The authority comes from the expertise developed by thorough preparation. The status comes from your title, your résumé, and the professional credibility you have developed. Women, especially, should get used to emphasizing titles or status which connote authority and expertise. Be sure your opposition knows all about you, if they haven't taken the time to check you out on their own. Humility does not garner the confidence or respect which are prerequisites to successful negotiation.

An articulate, comprehensive, insightful approach presented with confidence will force the other party to reconsider their initial perceptions of the deal and the value of its component parts.

**Be an active listener.** To be a successful negotiator you must learn to absorb the information being communicated to you by the other parties. Permit the other side to clearly describe their position, acknowledging your understanding and support wherever possible. Remember the goal is to map common ground and to build upon it. You do not need to agree with your opposition in order to demonstrate your recognition of their problems and needs. You do not need to disagree about every nuance, either.

**Building trust: the chameleon's advantage.** Is there any doubt that you trust those who are most like yourself. Therefore, it should come as no surprise that the best negotiators have perfected the art of matching their behavior to that of the person they hope to persuade. Is your opposition gregarious or shy, thoughtful or decisive, formal in dress and language or casual? Does the other side speak with a Southern drawl or a New York clip? Is a pat on the back or a touch on the arm taken as a sign of camaraderie or does your opposite number take several steps back from every conversation, treating close proximity as an intrusion?

If you speak the same language, you impart a feeling of mutual understanding. First, determine the negotiating style of your opponent... then mimic her tempo, tone and mood. Is your counterpart direct, analytical, fact driven and detail oriented? Or, is the other side comfortable with building a personal relationship through small talk, willing to work in an atmosphere without time pressure and relatively low formality?

Talking like your opponent is the first step; you can look more like him, too. Dress to match the personality of the opposite party, being certain to opt for the dark formal suit rather than a sports jacket for those given to structure and principles; be wary of too much weekend

As soon as I saw you I knew we could talk.

informality unless you've checked in advance. Don't ignore choices of clothing colors, hair style or jewelry when attempting to match the flashy or simple style of your opponent.

Finally, reinforce your sameness in friends, upbringing, hometown, community affiliations, children, hobbies, sports, and education.

# Reaching Agreement

There is a lot to read about competitive, "hard," "positional" bargaining and its counterpart, cooperative, "soft" negotiation with a focus on mutual gain. The message is that emphasizing objective criteria, rather than individual personalities and positions, will lead to an optimal agreement apart from egos and posturing for defense and attack.

Somewhere in between lies reality. No deal which involves issues of personal importance to the negotiators or to the clients of the negotiators can be separated entirely into issues and people.

As soon as someone states a position, they own it. They are prepared to defend it. The push and pull is natural, but the extent to which the negotiation is driven by this first down strategy will determine the likelihood of success. You can ask questions to test a position without disputing it. "Are you suggesting that the sale of your business could be separated from the real estate?" Is it really your position that revenue will triple over the next five years?" "Do your projections anticipate downsizing your workforce?"

Relevant inquiries can determine a willingness to move in a different direction without using a frontal attack. Recognizing that the business for sale has been the lifelong focus of the seller adds an emotional component that may provide the key to creating ways other than purchase price to

Are we reaching agreement?

recognize the value of his "baby." A simple show of interest will go a long way toward negotiating issues, not yardage.

*Get in the habit of presenting your objectives and reasoning first, followed by your proposal.* Reverse it and the other side will focus on the proposal and ignore the needs which drive it. Be sufficiently confident to have and present high expectations. Your proposals should always be the furthest reaching which can be supported by objective criteria. Demands which are embarrassing to justify undermine your credibility. On the other hand, be wary that early use of the cooperative technique may be interpreted as weakness.

## Attend to the details:
## Don't be fooled by the simple deal

When someone insists on a rush to the finish line, don't be mislead by the assurance that because the transaction is routine, the details can be assumed or worked out later. Press for closure on all the issues.

When one side insists there is only one simple issue left to address, like price, proceed to the outline you prepared and beware. Omissions are as devastating as misunderstandings. Assure yourself that all other considerations important to the deal you envisioned as part of your preparation are all discussed and resolved.

**Who makes the first offer?** Before making an offer, be sure you have explored the interests of all parties and available options. Has all pertinent, non-confidential information been shared?

Occasionally, the initial offer will provide unanticipated information by valuing the matter higher or lower than expected. The first offer is generally followed by equal concessions. The party making the first offer often makes the first concession.

**Expand your options... but don't complicate the deal.** With all the talk about expanding options to find creative solutions, the ability to recognize the time for closure becomes all important. Too many choices can be just as detrimental as having no alternatives. Getting bogged down in evaluating a wide range of options for every detail under consideration will encourage procrastination in addressing the main issues of contention.

After exploring all the options, be prepared to present a well-timed offer which addresses the interests of both parties. Be firm. Be concrete. Be persuasive. "Here's what's going to work for both of us... "

**What's your response?** Instead of rejecting the offer, treat the offer as one of a number of plausible options. Rephrase their point of view and refute it with facts and convincing scenarios. Indicate the specific needs which are not met by their proposal. *Call on your communication skills.* To be convincing, your position must be consistent; you must be persistent in the presentation of the objective criteria, market value, law, and expert opinion which support your solution. Clarify your position and instead of setting up a defensive posture, ask the other side to explain what is wrong with it. Encourage your opposition to think of a better solution.

**Compromise: When is enough... enough?** The ultimate question is always "Which concession is my last?" The well-known book, *Getting to Yes* by Roger Fisher and William Ury, stresses the importance of using your *best alternative* in an ongoing comparison to the deal on the table. Constant comparison allows you to determine whether the proposal before you is beneficial, whether you should push for further concessions, make some additional concessions of your own... or walk. By maintaining a "best alternative" at your fingertips, you have a realistic standard against which to measure the most recent proposal. Instead of an inflexible "minimum-maximum" or "bottom-line" approach which may inhibit creativity, your best alternative forces you to come to grips with the value of each proposal.

**Remember only one "best" alternative exists at any one time.** If your apartment lease is up, other alternatives include moving to another rental building, finding a roommate to share a larger apartment in the same building, leasing with the option to buy, moving from city to suburbs, buying a condominium, or buying a house. Of all these alternatives, only one is the "best" at any given moment considering all the circumstances.

The choice of a *single* best alternative will provide an accurate measure against which the landlord's most recent proposal can be compared. If the landlord's offer is better than your best alternative, keep negotiating. On the other hand, if it is clear that no deal the landlord offers can surpass your best alternative, the decision is obvious. Move on. The same theory applies to all deals, large and small.

When preparing to negotiate a business transaction, don't forget to determine the other side's best alternative. The options available to your counterpart will drive the deal you must offer or accept.

**Closure.** Lack of patience results in excessive and unreciprocated concessions. As agreement appears imminent, people are tempted to offer larger concessions just to see the process end. Instead, use two or three smaller concessions when you are willing to make one large one. Never make a concession without obtaining something in return. And, be mindful of the law of diminishing concessions. Offering smaller and smaller concessions sends the signal that you're approaching your bottom line, and that the next concession, if there is one, will be even smaller. Remain disciplined. The closing phase is the most competitive portion of the nego-tiation. Avoid the temptation to move quickly.

Reaching agreement does not require a repertoire of complex tricks. Simple, methodical and thorough wins the day.

# What Agreement has been Reached?

**Having reached an agreement, get the details in writing.** Whether you obtain a letter of intent, an interim agreement, a detailed contract, or just initials on notes saying "agreed," written agreements prevent dis-agreements. When dealing with people who say "trust me, a handshake is all we need around here," get something signed. At the very least, send a pleasant letter thanking them for their hospitality, reiterate the terms of the agreement and request an acknowledgment. Failure to receive a response is a strong signal that no deal exists.

Most disputes arise from conflicting understandings of what's been decided. No deal benefits from ambiguity. Dot the "i's". Take notes along the way to remind you of which points you covered, and which you left for later. Notes permit you to recap your agreements at various stages of discussion to avoid misunderstanding. Keep your own record of the meet-ing, positioning yourself to control the drafting of the final agreement. In the event of a dispute as to what was and was not agreed, your notes may resolve the dispute and will certainly refresh your own recollection as to the credibility of the other side's most recent position or change of heart.

## Beware of the nibble

After the final agreement is reached, one side asks for just one small additional concession. Demand an extra for each nibble or the agreement will be eaten away as you allow everything to be renegotiated.

## Know when to walk

"I'm taking my marbles and going home," says the grown-up negotia-tor, after describing the final scenario. "If we agree, here's what happens. But, if we still disagree, I must opt for my best alternative." Having given the reason for leaving, make time to meet again, giving the other side the opportunity to live without the deal, and GO.

Walking away from the table is not just for when you don't want the deal. Sometimes it's the only way to entice the other side to close. Be aware, if you're under pressure to reach an agreement, all the other side may need to do is outwait you. Walking out in order to force a deal is a dangerous play—not to be used unless you're prepared to stick with no deal at all or negotiate from a weaker position if you appear at the table the next morning. Yet, despite the threats, deals seldom get worse when you walk away. But, be prepared to walk away from the table… and mean it.

*Remember:* just because something is negotiable, does not mean it *has* to be negotiated. Another deal will come your way.

# Back to Basics...
# It's a Small, Small World

Acknowledging the discipline of negotiation will be your greatest asset. Learning the timing, tricks, and thought processes of top negotiators will never be a substitute for methodical preparation. Know the people, your opposition both on the business end of the deal and at the negotiation table, their style, credibility, and authority. Your detailed inquiries will provide the information you need about their business and motivation. Remember to end each negotiation with a smile, a handshake and a few well-chosen words to convey your respect for the other side. For the agreement to work, everyone should feel like they walked away with an important advantage.

As parting words, let me remind you of the classic Disney song, "It's a small, small world." Your name provides a powerful key to successful negotiations in the future. *A victory at any cost today may make others unwilling to deal with you in the future.* On the other hand, if you conduct yourself as if the world is sitting at your table, you will earn a reputation for credibility and fair dealing, a reputation from which you will reap benefits far beyond the deal you have just concluded.

At the end of your negotiation, the players shake hands, stand back and examine their accomplishments. By using straight-forward communication strategies, opposing sides have come together, found common ground and forged an agreement. There is no greater satisfaction than melding two independent visions of the perfect deal into one lasting, efficient and mutually beneficial relationship… negotiated by YOU.

# Bullets by Bellows:
# 10 Pointers for Successful Negotiations

1. **Prepare, prepare, prepare.**
   Use personal contacts to evaluate your counterparts, their personality and their company.

2. **Determine the extent of your counterpart's authority.**
   Don't wait to find out that the other side needs approval from someone else.

3. **Set a precise goal and be able to justify and quantify your demands.**
   Articulate specific requirements. Use real numbers to support your position.

4. **Put your dream agreement in writing.**
   Writing it out keeps you focused during the actual negotiations.

5. **Keep your best alternative in mind.**
   Use it as a benchmark against which to compare other options.

6. **Anticipate the other party's main goal and best alternative.**
   Be flexible. Consider creative options that work for both sides.

7. **Practice your questions and anticipate the questions you will be asked.**
   Properly phrased questions elicit informative answers. Develop strategic answers to advance your agenda.

8. **Strategize timing.**
   Plan disclosures. Choose when and what to concede.

9. **Never loose sight of your reputation.**
   A victory at any cost will make others unwilling to deal with you later.

10. **Remember—not every negotiation ends in agreement.**
    Sometimes the best result is to agree to disagree.

# About Laurel Bellows

Laurel G. Bellows, a partner of the Chicago law firm of Bellows and Bellows, P.C., is widely recognized for the courtroom and negotiating skills she has honed through her commodity and securities litigation experience and her general business and employment law practice.

In 1991, she became only the second woman to ever be elected president of the 22,000-member Chicago Bar Association. In the year 2000, Laurel will be President of the National Conference of Bar Presidents.

*Crain's Chicago Business* magazine named her one of Chicago's 100 "Women of Influence" and *Chicago Magazine* has designated her as one of the city's 28 "Power Lawyers." In 1997, *Working Mother* magazine included her on its first list of the nation's 25 most influential working mothers.

Laurel speaks frequently to business groups on the topics of employment law, negotiation, and public speaking, and has authored or been interviewed for articles on these topics in publications such as *Your Money, Nation's Business, Chicago Life, Investment Dealer's Digest,* and *Working Woman.*

She founded the Alliance for Women to examine gender equality issues in the legal field. She has written for or appeared in articles in the *New York Times, The Chicago Tribune, Today's Chicago Woman, Registered Representative,* and many other national and local publications.

Laurel is a Vice-President of the International Women's Forum and Past Chair of The Chicago Network, a select group of 250 significant women of achievement.

Ms. Bellows graduated from the University of Pennsylvania. She received her law degree from Loyola University of Chicago School of Law.

# Company Profile

Bellows and Bellows is a business law firm with a strong emphasis on commercial litigation, business transactions, and employment law.

The firm has represented many public investors or brokerage firms in cases concerning improper or fraudulent investment transactions. These clients look to the firm to resolve these cases through negotiated settlement, arbitration, or courtroom litigation. The firm has participated in many precedent-setting cases. Bellows and Bellows also provides securities law counsel to companies planning public and private offerings, and represents companies and individuals involved in disputes related to employment discrimination.

Laurel Bellows works with corporations of all sizes and their executives to draft and negotiate employment agreements. Both individuals and businesses turn to her for counsel relating to employment contracts, termination agreements, change of control documents, and employment manuals.

## BELLOWS AND BELLOWS
### ATTORNEYS AT LAW
### 79 WEST MONROE STREET
### CHICAGO, ILLINOIS 60603

Laurel G. Bellows
79 West Monroe Street, Suite 800
Chicago, Illinois 60603
312.332.3340
Fax: 312.332.1190

❖ **Chapter 8** ❖

# Conflict
# Communications

*by*
*Vicki Niebrugge*

Be open to assessing your own style
of communicating during conflict situations
and how you might be able to
give yourself more options.

—*Vicki Niebrugge*

C onflict is an inevitable result of the relationships you have, the diversity of the workforce, and possibly a product of the assertiveness and open communications workshops that were so popular in past decades. Some conflicts are just small nuisances, others get in the way of allowing you to work up to your full potential, and still others result in irreparable harm to business relationships, completed projects, and organizational advancements.

About ten years ago, I had a boss who was a great mentor. He had the ability to zoom in on problems and discuss them in a way that people did not get defensive or resentful. One day a corporate vice president approached me about a decision that I had made with which he did not agree. My boss was also at this meeting, but said little. The vice president and I discussed the issue, his feelings about it, and the ramifications of the decision. At one point in the conversation his speech became louder, his face reddened, the veins in his neck stood out. His anger increased, then subsided. I said little, wanting to learn as much as possible about his thoughts on this issue.

After the discussion, my boss told me that he thought it would be beneficial for me to work on handling conflict more effectively. His observation was that even though I listened carefully to the VP and asked him questions so that I thoroughly understood his perspective, I should have been a more active participant in the conversation by explaining the information I had gathered and how I came to my decision.

I left that conversation thinking about conflict. Clearly, I was not born with conflict management skills. I had to admit that there were times when conflict frightened me. Research I conducted led me to explore the origins of fear, and what fears are inherent in humans at birth. I discovered most physicians and psychologists agreed that babies are born with only two fears: a fear of falling and a fear of loud noises. Which meant, if I was afraid of conflict it was because I *learned* to be afraid of conflict.

It is the same with you, too. The feelings and attitudes that affect your willingness to deal with conflict are often a direct result of how you learned to deal with it. From whom did you learn to deal with conflict? You may find, like many others, that it goes back to the first conflicts you saw being handled by family members—your parents, siblings, or whoever raised you. Take a few minutes to think about it. How did your parents handle conflict? Or, at your first job when you saw your boss or coworkers experience conflict with others, how was it handled? What did you learn? Who was your teacher? From whom did you pattern your conflict handling mode?

Go ahead—stop reading and think it over for a few minutes.

You probably have one basic approach to dealing with conflict—you ignore it and hope it will go away. Or, perhaps your preference is to see it as an opportunity for power and competition, jumping in with both feet and drawing more and more energy as the conflict heightens. Still others are able to approach it with a spirit of collaboration. Each approach is valid depending upon the situation and the people involved. As you read on, be honest with yourself about how you communicate when in conflict. Rarely do you want to admit you pout, avoid, ignore, manipulate, threaten or bully. If you are reading this chapter you must have an interest in improving your conflict communication skills, and the first step is to be honest with yourself about how you currently handle conflict. Forget what you think might be the right and wrong way to handle every situation. Release any grudges about how you think you learned to deal with conflict and from whom. Be open to assessing your own style of communicating during conflict situations and how you might be able to give yourself more options.

# Take a Look Inside

You may know the feeling—your boss calls you into his office, or maybe a coworker catches you in the hall and wants to talk. The person looks angry and upset with you. The words flow quickly, gaining speed and emotion. The face you are looking at rises in color, the eyes you see become intense and focused. The comments now sound like an attack. Your hands start to sweat; your heart races.

Another scenario may come to mind. Imagine you are at a weekly status meeting you have to attend. The boss presents an issue for consideration. Terry begins the discussion. Before the first sentence is completed, Lee interrupts loudly, ignoring Terry. Terry begins again, and is cut off by Lee a second time. Their nonverbal behavior becomes more and more exaggerated, looks are being thrown back and forth, arms waving, papers flying. Your mind goes back to a time when you witnessed another conflict that escalated, maybe even one that erupted in violence.

Feelings. In most professional settings, employees are told to leave their feelings at home and not to bring them into the office. That's impossible. How you feel about conflict, what goes on in your gut and your heart has a lot to do with how you approach communicating during a conflict—or if you even can begin to make sense of it. It is extremely rare to be able to be logical and emotional at the same time. One side of the brain always prevails, and the beginning of a conflict almost always triggers the emotional side.

For many years I volunteered at a 24-hour telephone crisis center. No matter who called in and what the issue was, when people were experiencing a conflict with a coworker, a boss, or a loved one, the first thing they did was to vent about the situation. Even if it was an issue with few choices and clear direction, a flood of emotions came flowing from the person. The emotional release cleared the air for logic and problem solving to prevail. Some theories say it relates to your inability to use both sides of your brain at once. Others give the credit to your emotions being stronger links to your brain than to your logic. Whatever the cause may be, your emotional reservoir needs to be flushed out before your logic can kick in.

Have you ever heard someone say "I can't talk about that right now. I'm just too angry." Have you had the experience of saying something out of emotion and then regretting it? I'm sure you have your own experiences that told you when it was wise to hold your tongue. Unfortunately, it's usually a lesson you probably wish you had learned in a less painful way.

When you're feeling like your emotions are overtaking your brain, and your mouth, it is time to postpone the discussion. If the other person appears very emotional, it may also be the time to postpone the discussion. How you introduce the concept of stalling a conversation is important. You're upset and the other person is upset, and often what is said sounds like this, "I think we should postpone the discussion. You're too emotional to continue this conversation now." No one ever wants to admit they are too upset or not in control enough to have a discussion. Taking the responsibility yourself by saying "I'd like to think about this a little before we discuss it. Can we meet in 30 minutes?" Or, "I have a telephone appointment I need to keep. Let's get together at 2:00 P.M." This will give you time to cool down and think through your approach.

Grounding yourself before your conversation will help you avoid those moments that you immediately wish you could replay. Be sure your mind is in the moment—not thinking about where you are going next, not anticipating who you will see at your meeting this afternoon, not jumping to the end of your conversation and imagining your closing comments, but hearing every comment and sensing every innuendo. Pause for a few seconds, take a few deep breaths, and exhale slowly. Think about where the conversation is right now. What is the goal you have for the next ten minutes of this conversation? If you have studied communication techniques in the past you are aware of these strategies. Do you use them? The difference between people who communicate effectively in conflict and those who don't, rarely has anything to do with what they know, but rather what they apply.

# Communication

Communication is the key to resolving most conflicts. Unfortunately, it also is often the cause of most conflicts. Dual meanings, misunderstandings, masked agendas—all these things get in the way of effective communication. Following are some keys to effective communication during times of conflict. When you're in the middle of a conflict probably is not the time you'll pick up this book, so now is the time to reflect on these keys. Think of examples when you've seen other people use these techniques and ways you could use them for yourself.

Communication is the ultimate skill of lifelong learning, studying how to communicate is a skill that needs to be never ending. Be a lifelong learner. Use additional techniques to communicate at a higher level as you talk to others, and as you talk with yourself.

# Be Aware of What You're Saying to Yourself

**"If you think you are or you think you aren't,**
you're right.**"**

—*Henry Ford*

You are always engaged in conversation with yourself. When you are quiet notice that you will start to pick up the discussion in your head—assessing, evaluating, comparing experiences with those you have lived in the past. Self-talk is one of the most powerful tools you have for altering your beliefs, changing your attitude and improving your actions. During times of conflict self-talk can help or hinder. Think about what conversation goes on in your head during conflict. "Oh no, here he goes again, bringing up that sale we lost five years ago. I can turn this lecture off." Or, "The last time she started this, no one in the office could take any vacation time for three months! Here we go again!" Even if you're trying to remain constructive and on track with your comments, your self-talk can derail you. You can convince yourself that the conflict will work out or it won't, and your prophesy will often fulfill itself.

Become more aware of your self-talk, particularly in these situations. You can change what you are saying to yourself. Telling yourself to pay attention, continue to work on seeing things from the other person's perspective, and to stay focused will alter the focal point of your attention. Look at the intensity of how you think about things and how you word them, especially when you are talking to yourself. "It's impossible to work with her" gives you an entirely different outlook from "She always finds a new twist on the topic to explore." Be "confused" instead of "totally at a loss," "irritated" instead of "livid," "challenged" instead of "giving up." Try this for a week and see what a difference it makes in your thinking and your results!

# Be Congruent in Your Verbal and Nonverbal Behavior

## "Hide not thyself from thine own self."
*—Isaiah 58:7*

The impact of the messages you interpret from the nonverbal behavior of others has been proclaimed strongly by thousands of articles and books on communication. I once gave a performance appraisal to a woman who repeatedly told me how open she was to feedback and suggestions for improvement, but sat across from me with her arms folded, her legs crossed, her left shoulder toward me, and her eyes glaring. It was obvious to me that she did not want anyone, even her boss, to review her performance, much less give her any suggestions for improvement.

What you are thinking during your conversation will come out in your nonverbal behavior, even when you aren't aware that it is happening. Becoming more aware of your posture, facial gestures, and movements also helps you be more cognizant of how you are really feeling. During some conflicts that awareness will help you get in touch with other concerns you are having that haven't yet hit your conscious mind. Explore them. If you realize during a conversation that you are physically pulling away from someone, or not meeting their eyes, take a minute to consider from where those behaviors are coming. You will get insights not before realized.

You may also be aware of incongruity in someone else's verbal and nonverbal behavior. That awareness usually starts with a feeling of mistrust, negativity or confusion. The confusion grows as you try frantically to figure out why you are feeling this way, while at the same time the conversation appears to be on a constructive path. Stop for a moment, look at the person's eyes, their facial expression, gestures, hands, movement, and posture. If it appears to be incongruent with what is being said, make a conscious decision whether or not to surface it and how. You may want to call the person's attention to it, or you may only want to ask a question that will surface the tension, i.e. "I wonder if you are feeling some anger around this issue." Be prepared, however, for the person to deny your interpretation and continue the discussion. Oftentimes people are trying to problem solve and their focus is on the anticipated solution, not on what is occurring at that moment. They may not be aware of or willing to discuss the feelings that are being displayed.

Think about the person's style in relationship to how they are expressing themselves. Just because people are sitting with arms crossed does not necessarily mean that they are defensive about the topic. Crossed arms may mean they are cold, or it may be a normal and comfortable posture for them.

# Express Yourself in the Positive Rather than in the Negative

## "Most of the shadows of this life are caused by standing in our own sunshine."

—*Ralph Waldo Emerson*

Sometimes just keeping the conversation focused on positives will contribute to lessening or avoiding the conflict entirely. Tell people what you can do, what you agree with, and what you would like to see happen rather than what you cannot do, where you have disagreements with them and what you do not want to see happen any more. "Here's what I can do for you," or "Let's talk about where your idea could fit in the project plan."

You may know that you disagree with someone before they know it. Beginning your response with "No" or "I disagree with you" may set you up for mental jujitsu. Ask questions. Be sure you understand the other person's point of view. Find the areas on which you agree—then you have a foundation from which to launch into a discussion of the other areas.

One of the hardest situations in which to stay positive occurs when criticism is directed your way. Not the kind of constructive criticism that comes with a corrective action plan, but criticism that contains only negative comments regarding your work. These eleven steps may help you in such a situation.

1. **Be centered and take in the comments.** Listen. Be careful that you are not listening to your self-talk over the conversation of the other person.

2. **Beware of becoming defensive.** Hold open the possibility that the criticizer may have valid information for you to consider. Have a heightened awareness of what you are saying to yourself. Stay constructive and focused on the present situation.

3. **Let the critic finish.** Encourage the person to give you all the information he or she has. Remain calm and objective. "Is there anything else?" said openly and without sarcasm, may help. Listen to them completely before formulating or delivering your response.

4. **Ask for evidence on which the criticism is based.** Probe for specific examples, times, and situations.

5. **Ask questions of yourself.** What is the constructive purpose here? What is the real issue? Could there be a hidden agenda here? Do I agree? How can I make this a constructive conversation? Am I feeling defensive? If so, why?

6. **Let the criticism be a source of learning.** Think about the new information you are gaining through this conversation. And, if nothing else, you are learning a perspective that your critic is holding, and perhaps one with which others would agree.

7. **Try to understand the needs of the critic.** Think about why this person has brought this up, and why now? Does the person need to vent, to talk, to explain?

8. **Explore why the critic has criticized.** Why did this person choose to talk about this with you now? And why are they expressing themselves in this way?

9. **Determine what the real problem is.** It may be related to the issue under discussion, or it may not. However, if you begin to lay blame on another person or situation be cautious about your assumptions.

10. **Respond carefully.** Double check your own motive in your response. Do you agree or disagree, and do you want to discuss it now? Are you hurt, and feeling like you want to hurt the person

back? Or, do you want to delay the conversation for a later time when you could have a more constructive conversation?

11. **Talk about it.** Discuss the situation with *one* confidant, not someone who will talk about it with others. Verbalizing it will help you clarify your thoughts and getting another perspective on the conversation will help you be objective. Be cautious who you choose as your confidant—you don't want the whole department discussing your issues. Have an understanding with your confidant about which conversations are confidential.

Criticism is never easy to take, but can be a great source of learning and growth. Just because someone shares information with you in a negative way does not mean the information is invalid. They may not know how to approach you in a way that is constructive and positive.

# Overcoming Resistance and the Quick Refusal

Picture this scenario. Charlie has been experiencing a conflict with another member of his team, Mike, for weeks. Suddenly, while taking a shower one morning, Charlie comes up with the perfect solution to both of their issues—one that will meet the needs of everyone on the team, be low cost and quick to implement. An hour later he bounds into Mike's office, enthusiastically explaining his idea, pushing Mike for quick agreement. Mike responds by looking at Charlie, accuses him of overreacting to his own idea, and gives him that "not in my lifetime" expression. Clearly, Mike has no intention of adopting this plan.

The above result may have been different if Charlie had thought about how he had seen Mike respond to suggestions or requests for quick answers in the past. Conflicts can often be avoided by thinking through the communication style of the person with whom you are going to be talking. One key piece of information that may have helped Charlie was to consider Mike's decision-making style in other situations.

How people process information has a direct effect on communicating in times of conflict. People process information internally or externally. Extroverted processors prefer to talk out issues, and make decisions during their conversations. Internal processors prefer to think through decisions, and their conversations weighing pros and cons usually occur internally before talking with others.

If you suspect the person processes information more internally than externally, giving them time to reflect will be to your advantage. "I'm not going to ask you to make up your mind right now about an idea I had this morning, but I'd like to tell you about it." Preparation that includes considering timing as well as content will pay off with less conflict and more cooperation. If you believe that you are an internal processor yourself, ask for time to consider issues and weigh out the alternatives prior to making a decision. Stay true to your most effective decision-making style.

# Allow People to Save Face

At the beginning of most conflicts, a turning point appears between benign discussion and conflict. Often in that space an accusation appears—very often an incorrect accusation. "You cut the budget last year the day before we launched the project. You made one quick decision, and the whole thing failed. Now I'm being blamed for the failure, and the cost overrun." The reply of "you're wrong," or "that's not the way it happened" usually comes back quickly. Decisions are made on the basis of the information that people have. Often it is not enough information, maybe not even the correct information. If you retort quickly, the conversation will escalate, and take you even further from the truth.

Allowing people to save face, especially if there are others in the room during the conversation, will contribute to diminishing the intensity and maybe even the existence of the conflict. "A lot of people think that's what happened. Let me tell you what really occurred with that budget." The head-to-head confrontation is gone, and it develops into an opportunity for information sharing. Discipline and patience are required to avoid responding with anger and a sharp response. Allow the other person to maintain their self-esteem and consider the possibility that they may have been given inaccurate information.

# Balance Advocacy with Inquiry

The normal position in conflict is to advocate for your position, sharing your judgments, your assumptions, and your views of the situation. As you inquire more, ask more questions, seek more data, and genuinely listen to the responses you get, you develop a better understanding of the other person's point of view. Occasionally, if you listen carefully, you find that they are both taking the same position and haven't listened or understood the other person's position enough to realize there is agreement. If you listen to children, you will be reminded of how many questions they ask on a daily basis. I recently spent a vacation with a friend from college and her family. From their two sons, I counted over 300 questions from each of the two boys on a daily basis. I did the same thing in the office one day during a day-long management meeting. I counted an average of seven questions from each adult in the room, during the same time period that I had been with the boys. The inquisitiveness and willingness of children to question and explore is fascinating. Children learn at such a rapid pace with their inquisitive nature. Conversely, as adults, our learning would be magnified if we were to ask more questions and listen to the answers.

As adults, we assume what others are thinking. We often take our own assumptions and project them on others. We fail to invite others to share how those conclusions were reached and on what they were based. Challenge yourself to ask five questions each hour and see what a difference it makes in the quality of your thinking and the decisions you make.

When I ask more questions I uncover another's assumptions, perspectives, and thoughts. The more I learn, the more I discover that, at times, I am not right in the conclusions I have drawn. What prevented me from hearing the other perspectives were the meanings I attached to the actions or to the words someone else used. True understanding comes from asking questions. Get the viewpoint of the person with whom you're talking. Ask, listen, ask, listen, ask, listen—then talk.

# Probe for Specifics

Conflict arises on the heels of generalizations. Someone makes a sweeping statement, another takes offense, people begin to justify their points, and soon it is the heat of battle. One of the most common places to see this scenario is during the once-a-year performance appraisal. Comments such as "You don't seem to understand the chain of command around here" is an example of such a statement.

Any time one of those generalizations arise, ask for examples so you know to what specifically the comment refers. "Can you give me an example of a time when I did not follow the chain of command?" As this question is asked, watch your body language and tone of voice. Asking this question with a true spirit of inquiry will give you practical information that you can respond to and base your actions upon.

# The Risk

Human beings are predictable. Your associates know how you respond to most situations, and from that will anticipate your reactions to future situations. That creates trust. Trust comes from consistency.

What that also means is that your colleagues know, or think they know, how you will respond in times of conflict. Because of your past behavior, an assumption will be made about whether you will avoid a conversation, disagree quickly, become defensive, or refuse to listen. They will act based on this assumption and will approach you hesitantly, boldly, or maybe not at all.

If you assessed your conflict style earlier in this chapter, and decided to make some changes based upon that assessment, you will respond in a different way than people expect you to respond. You may misuse some of the techniques. You may exaggerate them. Your coworkers may be confused. Some may appreciate the changes, some may not.

Changing your conflict management style brings with it some elements of risk. Try out a new strategy in a low-risk situation. Become comfortable with new techniques during a conversation with a work friend, or even a situation at home. Discussing an important issue on which your next career move hinges is not the time to experiment with a conflict management technique that is new to you.

# Time for Action

How many times do you seek information designed to help you increase a skill or to give you new strategies, and actually do something suggested in the reading or the workshop? This question reminds me of a comic I saw recently of a woman slouched down in an easy chair, hair in curlers, a hot cup of coffee in one hand and the remote in the other while the words "Good Morning, Exercise Lovers!" greeted her from the television.

My hope is that you will take at least of one of the topics discussed, and try something new as it relates to communicating in times of conflict. These suggestions may help you.

- Think about your conflict communication style. Ask for feedback from your coworkers, your boss, your colleagues in other departments. Understand how they view your communication style during times of conflict, and what led them to that conclusion. Use this information to determine where you need to improve.

- Become aware of your self-talk in all situations, not only in times of conflict.

- Check your nonverbal behavior. Strive to be congruent; be sure that your body language and your verbal language are giving the same message. Learn from the times that you aren't.

- Reduce the number of negative words in your conversation. Practice asking more questions in a true spirit of inquiry.

- Be honest with yourself about how you are feeling. Be aware of how you are asking questions. Work through any defensiveness you may be feeling before you inquire.

- Learn from your conversations during times of conflict. To strengthen your skills in the area of conflict communications, you must constantly reassess your ability to resolve conflicts and mediate disputes. Ask yourself these questions after every interaction:

    *How did I respond when the conflict began?*
    *Did my verbal and nonverbal behavior match?*
    *Am I pleased with the outcome?*
    *How could I have been more effective?*

# Good News and Bad News

There is good news bad news. The bad news is that even as you improve your skills in conflict communication, you cannot resolve every problem you have, nor can you manage every conflict. This book did not come with a magic wand, and I don't know how to get one for you. The good news is that you can improve the way that you communicate during times of conflict, and the issues that stay unresolved will diminish as you use these techniques.

**"You're going to spend the rest of your life getting up one more time** when you've been knocked down— so you'd better start getting used to it."

—*John Wayne in* The Train Robbers

# About Vicki Niebrugge

Vicki Niebrugge is a speaker, facilitator, and consultant whose clients consistently praise her insight, energy, humor, and ability to get to the core of their problems and assist in creatively solving them. She has worked with organizations in a variety of manufacturing, health care, educational, and service organizations.

Vicki brings a unique background to her work. With experience in human resources, training, law, and employee development, she has been featured in publications by Commerce Clearinghouse, nationally syndicated newspapers, and audio tapes by the American Society for Training and Development and the Society for Human Resource Management. She is a past president of the Michigan Chapter of the National Speakers Association and is the recipient of numerous professional and community awards.

Vicki's content-laden workshops and seminars are practical and professional, blending humor, warmth and concrete skills, giving participants high value and immediate application. She holds Bachelor's and Master's Degrees from Eastern Michigan University and a J.D. from the University of Toledo College of Law.

# Company Profile

The *NOVA* Group is a training and consulting firm focusing on issues that affect the overall performance of organizations. The *NOVA* Group helps corporations and associations meet objectives by facilitating employee communication and increasing productivity.

Workshops and seminars by the *NOVA* Group are custom designed and specifically tailored to meet individual needs. They are designed for the adult learner. The most requested programs include Conflict Resolution, numerous aspects of improving Communication Skills, Creating Learning Organizations, Eliminating Self-Sabotage, and a variety of supervisory and management skill development programs.

The consulting arm of the *NOVA* Group works in the areas of management retreats, human resource audits, organizational development, and strategic planning. Since 1989, organizations have been turning to the *NOVA* Group as a reliable source for sound business information and assistance with compliance on legal issues affecting human resource management and employee satisfaction and productivity.

For more information, contact:

*Vicki Niebrugge*
**NOVA Group**
P.O. Box 130327
Ann Arbor, MI   48113
(734) 662-7149
Fax:   (734) 662-8820
E-mail:  NVAGrp@aol.com

# Chapter 9

# Leading Your Team's Best Talents:

# Helping Others to Succeed Together

*by*

*Kevin E. O'Connor, CSP*

When a leader understands what a team
is, how to influence its members, and
how to protect the team's creativity,
the leader and the team
can then thrive together in a
productive atmosphere.

—*Kevin O'Connor*

**"Leaders are best when people barely know they exist, not so good when people obey and acclaim them, worse when people despise them. But of good leaders who talk little, when their work is finished and their aim fulfilled, the others will say, 'We did it ourselves.'"**

—*Lao Tzu*

Today's movement away from authoritarian leadership and toward team development was envisioned in this statement from a noted Chinese leader more than 2,000 years ago. Now, more and more people and organizations are beginning to experiment with a leadership that empowers others rather than a leadership that is, itself, powerful.

This chapter is devoted to leadership and teams. There are three key skills that distinguish successful leaders of teams: understanding the nature of team leadership, the ability to know how to influence others without manipulation and to increase one's own credibility, and knowing how to break through bureaucratic cycles and institutions in order to make measurable progress. Therefore, when a leader understands what a team is, how to influence its members and how to protect the team's creativity, the leader and the team can then thrive together in a productive atmosphere.

# Leader Skill #1: The Nature of Successful Team Leadership

Jim Meisenheimer, a former sales manager for Baxter International, advised his assistant about their team: "They don't have to like you; they just have to respect you." Many a leader has made the critical error of thinking that being liked is somehow synonymous with success. Effective leaders garner respect when others feel empowered and respected by the leader. By showing respect to them, the team leader consequently enables team members to understand how to treat one another with respect.

The writer Bernard Malamud wrote, "Respect is what you have to have in order to get." A leader cannot afford to forget this important advice. Especially today, because of an increased legislative and cultural awareness to the issue of respect, followers are very sensitive to how they are treated. Whether directly or indirectly, the leader must immediately convey respect to the others. When respect is evident, followers and leaders alike see it in the eyes of the other.

More than any other characteristic, respect bonds leaders to followers. This connective function of respect is most evident when the leader is in conflict with those who most need to be influenced. The famous Chicago psychiatrist, Rudolf Dreikurs, observed, "The real issue in all human conflict is never about things, but is always about respect." Dreikurs went on to say that all conflict can be overcome, even the most divisive, when there is respect. When respect is missing, the individual may consequently feel:

- a weakened ability to decide;
- relinquished of a right to control;
- a disregard for their judgment and ideas;
- their prestige and status are in question;
- their feelings or opinions are discounted;
- unfairly treated;
- defeated by this other person;
- powerless; and/or
- inferior.

Undoubtedly, these are deadly feelings for followers to have. Effective leaders are aware, with their attitude as well as with their actions, of the commanding role that respect plays in team communications.

If a leader suspects that followers are feeling irreverent, it is of crucial importance for the leader to address the issue. Some leaders are very specific: "I have the feeling that you may feel we haven't taken your idea into consideration, is that right?" Other leaders try to guess the other person's feelings: "I'm getting the impression that you feel you haven't had a chance to tell us what you think, is that correct?" Still other leaders decide to make a simple observation and invite a response by saying, "You seemed pretty quiet during the progress report section of the team meeting—want to tell me about it?" The specific language used is much less important than the recognition that something is wrong. When recognition is coupled with an understanding of the issue of respect, a productive discussion can then take place. The fact that the leader is willing to discuss these important but subtle issues can make an enormous difference to team members.

As a leader, make the respectful treatment of your peers, colleagues, team members, staff and customers your top priority. In doing so, you will gain enormous influence for yourself and help others feel vitally important to the work being accomplished.

In a *Harvard Business Review* article by Renato Tagiuri, the concept is stressed that the best leaders are "doers;" they are not simply a collection of certain personality traits. Leadership does not need to be a popularity contest, nor do leaders need to be charismatic. Good leaders act and help others accomplish more in the process.

Leaders also know when a decision is required. While the management function of work requires complexity and organization, the leadership role requires an ability to cope with change and to influence direction. Leaders may need to do both, but never substitute one for the other. Business leader T. Boone Pickens advises, "Be willing to make decisions. That's the most important quality in a good leader. Don't fall victim to what I call the 'ready—aim—aim—aim—aim' syndrome."

Often, leaders are in charge of educational programming, parliamentary procedure, reworking an executive committee's by-laws, and instituting clear standards for design, production or customer service. These duties are not always dynamic, urgent or interesting. Sometimes it is the mundane, but nonetheless important tasks, that bring clarity to the bigger picture. While leadership may not always be inspiring, it is *always* about making choices. Leaders must choose their focus coupled with respect for others and then move with decisive action. When leaders choose this direction, teams develop.

Effective leaders communicating with team members individually and in group settings have greater influence when they use leader skills that are genuine and most resemble who they really are on the inside. Authenticity with others begins by knowing oneself. Imitation may be the sincerest form of flattery, but it can also ensure failure if the leader does not understand the importance of being true to oneself.

Personality inventories, management retreats and performance reviews can aid an executive in discovering his or her natural talents. Another way is through critical incident debriefing—the daily identification of one or two incidents that went well. Requiring only a paper, pen and quiet time, this technique is a solitary activity of strategic reflection. The executive simply writes about a successful incident by answering the typical who, what, when and where questions. This procedure will give an outline for the most important question—the why question—which asks, "How can I account for this positive outcome? What did I do right?" A month or two of critical incident debriefing notes can reveal the successful, underlying patterns used by the leader to create an individual and innate style for success. When used in conjunction with a personal coach or mentor, this technique can be a powerful addition to an executive's learning laboratory.

Authenticity also develops a unique style and inspires trust in others. There are three necessary skills needed in order to accomplish authenticity: trusting, waiting and serving.

# Trusting

Trust is a virtue often associated with what one wants another person to do. In leadership, however, self-trust can be a skill that helps individuals to recognize their abilities, limitations and potential.

Harbans Dhindsa, educational administrator of the Tennessee School for the Blind in Nashville, Tennessee, has a sign above his door that reads, "Kindness is the language the blind can see and the deaf can hear." Firm and friendly could describe his personal and professional motto. This rare combination of people skills, substance and resolve make Dhindsa a trusted leader. When asked to take the superintendent's position, he declined. "This is what I like, this is where I belong, this is me." And, he added, "But I know just the right person for superintendent." The best leaders know where they need to be and who should be with them.

When you trust others, you encourage the gifts and talents they possess to flourish, even if those talents are unbeknownst to them. You, as the leader, must intuitively make a leap of faith to enhance the other's feeling of importance.

Leaders appeal to the heads *and* hearts of the followers, which builds a loyalty between the two parties. This loyalty—an emotional extension of trust—will sustain the relationship between leader and follower even during the toughest of times.

# Waiting

The second component to authenticity is the ability to wait. Jim Kellner, CEO and President of Applied Systems, uses a very common example to illustrate how he waits. "Plant your seeds, water them, tend the garden," he advises. "Let your people take their good ideas and run with them. If the ideas don't work out, you can always talk about it with them later." Kellner is speaking about the process of nurturing others within an environment of growth. Creativity thrives under such a system. Thinning and weeding can always be done before harvest, but waiting is the skill that helps others grow.

An age-old, but extremely effective technique, is to wait for a response once a statement or question has been voiced; incorporate some talk and some silence. Remember the last time you spoke with someone who acted as if they really needed your response in order to continue? The most effective leaders know when to wait and say nothing.

## Serving

Leaders serve the followers, which in turn makes it easy for the team members to create. At a recent conference, Dr. Gallo Torres, a dentist from Atlanta, assumed the position of host. Although clearly in charge, he became a welcomer, announcer, coffee server, relayer of messages and limousine driver all in one meeting! His role as part host, part concierge, part overseer freed everyone else to make the meeting a success. The best leaders are generally servant leaders.

Leaders who serve understand that their real wisdom is not in knowing, but in asking. Their wisdom resides in the group and it is their responsibility, through careful questioning and patient process, to help draw that wisdom forth. Leaders that believe they alone possess the truth are in danger of becoming a demagogue. On the other hand, leaders that believe they are without truth, reign with anarchy. But, when a leader believes that the truth is in the process of the leader-team interaction, then participating leadership exists.

One team leader at the largest telecommunications company in the Midwest takes a very effective strategy with her team. "They all know a lot more than I do and I tell them so," she explains. "What I do for them is work the bureaucracy, provide the resources, defend the budget and make sure there is plenty of coffee. Then, they are free to create."

Service also stems from the ability to change with each situation. When things aren't working, adaptable leaders change their approach, focus or pace to enable the group to move in another direction. Leaders serve, but not always in ways that others may expect. The nature of successful team leadership is a combination of respect, doing and being.

# Leader Skill #2: Influence Without Manipulation

Effective communication with team members will also extend the leader's influence and initiate real change within the team. Establishing good communication with others is a skill *and* an art. Skills can be learned; art comes from practice.

As adapting, waiting, initiating movement, and changing directions are all obvious skills for the leader, so is communicating. A well-written, timely memo or a discreet, well-timed nod of the head to encourage the contribution of a shy team member can be as effective as public kudos.

## The Essentials of Empathy

"To see with the eyes of the other, to hear with their ears, to feel with their heart" is how psychiatrist Alfred Adler defined empathy in the late 1800s. Today, empathy is described as tuning into the other, suspending judgment, accepting (even if you don't always agree), and responding in a way that confirms the best intention to be with the other person. Empathy produces a response in the other that says "this person knows how I feel." This type of empathy is the interpersonal equivalent of a solid handshake. Done well, empathy can be a real gift to the other. However, if poorly executed, it becomes an invasion.

Although there is no single, correct way to empathize, there are some simple guidelines that effective communicators use to consistently tune in to others' feelings.

- **Data.** Use others' behavior as your data. The more distant someone seems, the more likely they will feel distant as well. Tune in to their responses, verbal intonations and facial expressions to assess how they might feel.
- **Links and Hunches.** Look for links, patterns, incongruities and disparate components in what someone is saying. If they are complaining about their children, their employees and the consistency of the mustard in the cafeteria, there is a reason for it. This person may feel as if they are losing control of everything and may not even be aware of the pattern themselves.
- **Tentative Response.** After you have formulated your hunches, combine them with the data you have observed and respond accordingly. "I wonder if…" or "Could it be that…" or "I wonder if you are feeling as if…" are all very good ways to take a hunch and respectfully begin a conversation.
- **Listen Carefully.** Do not argue or try to make your point while attempting empathy. Your exclusive, singular goal is to have the other person feel that you really *do* understand. This recognition response from the other person is critical for you to continue. Continue the conversation in this manner until you perceive the

look in their eyes, tone in their voice, or the quiet nod of their head that says, "yes, you do understand."

- **Resist.** Avoid the temptation to set the record straight, help them get over the feeling, or remedy them. These are not only ineffective strategies, but useless and nearly impossible as well. Many times, a sincere "thank you for letting me know" is sufficient. Other times a "can we meet about this again soon?" or even a tentative suggestion or offer to help can provide the other person with direction.

## Important and Special

The competitive advantage of every leader is to make others feel important. When you make yourself the important one, only you are convinced of it. The best leaders make others, whoever they are, the most important priority.

This ability to recognize the other person is especially useful in working with teams. Individual recognition is not easily received on working teams, unless, of course, someone remembers. You, as the leader, can ensure that special recognition happens by making mental or written notes at meetings of specific incidents or individual contributions that you have noticed. Then, follow up with personal messages to reap big benefits for all concerned. The competitive advantage of every leader is to make others feel important. When others realize their importance and the regard that the leader has for them, belief in the leader, the team, and in their own abilities is born.

Contribution is enhanced when individual efforts are recognized. Modern psychology is clear in its teaching: What gets recognized gets repeated. Make it a habit to find the good in others, look for their positive contribution, accentuate their productivity, and ask for their input at the start of projects. Feelings—good or bad—are contagious among team members.

## Take Special Care

Be sure to acknowledge others specifically, genuinely and frequently. Find ways to commemorate victories or projects—even those that are incomplete—and your team will thrive. The CEO of a paper company in Wichita, Kansas, wanted to celebrate the timely delivery of a major project with his factory workers and unexpectedly ordered pizzas for everyone. His wife came to him and said, "Do you know that those pizzas cost $276 just for the first shift?" The CEO responded with a grin, "Did they enjoy them?" She winked at him and said, "They ate them all!" He turned back to his desk and said, "Great, that's what was supposed to happen. They did a great job for us. Let's make sure that the second and third shift get enough too." Recognition for and remembering to celebrate with employees is very important.

Your team members think and feel. These feelings influence their perceptions of reality. Leaders must understand that individual perception is reality for that person. A deaf and blind adult, Kerry Wadman from Vancouver, Canada, believes that, "After all, things aren't as they are, but as *we* are." When team members feel listened to, respected and understood, they are much more likely to consider your viewpoint.

## The Personal Focus is Lasting

The best leaders focus on individuals. Jack O'Malley, former Republican State Attorney for Cook County, Illinois, is a capable prosecutor and an astute politician. O'Malley knows the importance of eye contact. Like many busy leaders in one-on-one conversations, he could divert his gaze or attempt to make as much eye contact as possible with those around him, including the person with whom he is speaking. Instead, his focus is on the person right in front of him, and *only* that person.

In leadership, good, old-fashioned "people skills" are invaluable. Eye contact, smiles, remembering names, acting like a host or hostess, finding common ground, and showing interest are all essential skills that are easily forgotten by many professionals in their haste. Good leaders know the value of a smile.

## The Strong Leading the Strong

Harvard's Tagiuri noted that the best leaders understand that they must "accept a certain amount of hostility and resentment from their subordinates, which is an inevitable aspect of all human relationships, especially when there is an inequality of power." Tagiuri recommends that the leader help employees refocus their energies on the task at hand, on the job as a whole, or to divert their negative feelings toward the competition. This refocusing skill is vital, especially when you lead the strong-willed. Tactics, such as structured brainstorming, peer consultations, solution-focused questioning (as contrasted with questions that focus on the problem), and frequent references to previously agreed-upon goals in the past will help the strong-willed *want* to follow.

However, leading the strong-willed can be challenging. If the leader regards the team's strength as competition to their authority or position, it will work against goals. Many successful leaders prefer a room full of strong, direct personalities to a room full of quiet, agreeable types because they don't want "yes" people endorsing every whim. A room full of nods at a meeting often results in a company full of passive disagreement *after* the meeting. Good leaders retrieve the disagreements early and often, and strong team members are happy to oblige!

## Plan With a Plan

Mike Jenkins, Vice President of CM Products, Inc., Lake Zurich, Illinois, knows the value of detailed planning when working with highly technical groups. Mike has a degree in engineering; goals, purpose, specifications, control and precision are important hallmarks of his profession. The essential skills of good engineering do not, however, always translate to effective leadership or communication. Instead, it is a skill that needs to focus not only on the goal, but also on those who help achieve that goal.

Regardless of your professional training, an essential key to leadership and communication is to clearly know where you want to go and who is with you on that route. The best leaders thoughtfully map out a work plan in advance with the end result in mind. However, while too much planning stifles the participation of others, it is imperative for others to feel a part of the process. A good leader will build participation into every step.

## The Art and Science of Encouragement

Encouragement helps teams grow, move and progress efficiently, which is essential to morale and creativity. When a team or an individual is "stuck," it is essential that the leader take action.

Athletes who fall, get up and continue the race are often as admired as the winners because the spectators appreciate their struggle and emotion. People who have failed can come back with a victory that outshines their earlier failure. Some famous "failures" have proven themselves despite difficulties:

- Walt Disney went bankrupt twice before beginning Disneyland.
- Einstein was four years old before he could speak and seven before he could read.
- Thomas Edison's teachers told him he was too stupid to learn anything.

- Beethoven's teacher once said of him, "As a composer, he is hopeless."
- Oh yes, Walt Disney was also fired by a newspaper editor because he never had any good ideas!

Each of these famous "failures" moved beyond their errors and grew from the experience. Encouragement promotes growth. More importantly, for teams, encouragement helps individuals break away from peer pressure and move toward unique contributions.

The word "encouragement" comes from the French "cour," which means "heart." Think of your favorite encourager. Do they appeal to your head or work wonders deep in your heart? Psychologist and author, Michael Popkin, recommends the following steps of encouragement to help others find their heart:

1. *Show confidence in the person's ability.* Don't try to label their behavior or improve the person's performance with suggestions. At first, just work to understand. Once that is accomplished, be careful not to try to solve the problem *for* them.

2. *Build upon the strengths—subtle or obvious—of others.* Phrases such as "I admire…," "I'm impressed," or "May I tell you something that strikes me?" are all affirmations that enable people to see their strengths through others' eyes.

3. *Stimulate independence and interdependence among those you want to influence.* Never do for anyone else those things they could do or learn to do for themselves; it is disrespectful of their ability and potential. When independence is encouraged, then others are allowed to recognize their own power and self-worth.

# Leader Skill #3: Breaking the Bureaucratic Cycle

In his book, *The Empowered Manager*, Peter Block contends that many organizations "unintentionally encourage people to choose to maintain what they have, to be cautious and dependent." Block calls this the "bureaucratic cycle," in contrast to the "entrepreneurial cycle," which is a structure that encourages autonomy, authenticity and creativity. Team leaders that focus on breaking the bureaucratic cycle do so in an intentional way; they take risks, repeat what needs to be learned, and when trouble hits, act accordingly.

# Risky Decisions

Leadership is also about making decisions that involve risk. Responsible risk-taking is often an expected facet of leadership from superiors and subordinates. Follow any great leader who began with a single idea and what emerges is a story of great risk, courage and independent thinking. Ray Kroc of McDonald's had to pay his secretary in stock options in the early days of little or no cash. Fred Smith of Federal Express is said to have proposed his idea for on-time, overnight delivery of packages worldwide in a school term paper and had the idea labeled as preposterous. Any company traced back to its founder will reveal what Block calls "an instinctive act of greatness, courage and autonomy" and will be a measure of the risk that may now be needed for that organization.

In any community, the local dry cleaners, hot dog stand, plumbing supply store, church, or private school are all prime examples of someone who made risky decisions. And, although few will make national headlines, they will have important consequences on the organizations and people who depend on a leader with a vision and the courage to act.

Denise Perry, a meeting planner in British Columbia, Canada, recently hosted the largest international meeting of its kind in that area. On deadline day for registration, she and her team had only one-fifth of the required registrants. When asked why she did not cancel the event, she responded, "I decided we needed to do more work. I believed in the project. We just had to kick a little bit more!" Her team worked harder under her leadership. Each, in their own way, brought in the remaining 80 percent for an overflow crowd. The best leaders have the courage to say, "We need to do more!"

In leading teams, what is seen is sometimes more important than what is documented, what is heard more important than what is read, and what is felt more important than what is researched. In short, leaders are viewed by their actions in moments of great need and pressure. Team leaders need to be sensitive to the perceptions of others but not dependent on them; teams look to the leader to take the risk and direction.

# Broken Records Aren't Always Bad

A standard colloquial expression in North America that indicates a person is repeating the same message over and over again is that they sound "like a broken record." In teams, however, repetition frequently has positive results.

Professional educators have demonstrated that humans learn in a variety of ways. The most important part of the learning process is readiness, that stage of development when a person is ready to learn. A baby, ready to take its first steps, can walk one day and yet did not take that step the day before. The same is true with teams in business. Each team member is at a different stage of development. What makes sense to them today might have been a jumble of information the day before.

A solid message repeated in various ways also gives people breathing and learning room for the future. Breathing room is accomplished by an absence of threat, and no fear of job loss or pressure to perform differently prior to training. Learning room is acquired through an active educational department that permits advanced training of all kinds. The best leaders know it is difficult for people to change and therefore give them sufficient time and training to do so.

Psychiatrist Alfred Adler said that "everything worthwhile is about movement." Making progress from one place to another is a primary expectation of team members regardless of their task or mission. When that expectation is not fulfilled, the leader becomes the scapegoat. This can be prevented by marking progress along the way, in even the smallest of increments. Noting progression whenever and wherever it is found can be a very useful leader skill.

Energy, attention, dialogue, disagreement and questions should be verbally noted at regular intervals. To become a better leader, observe what is going on around as well as within the team. At a recent leadership training workshop, one manager's role in a simulation exercise was to simply observe his peers and take notes on anything he noticed. At the end of the exercise, the observing manager had two insights. First, his ability to see what was going on without having to be a team member gave him a unique perspective that the team valued. Secondly, he recognized how much more he needed to "just observe" his team back home. "I can do more for them by using this one technique, as long as I give them the feedback," he commented.

Although the role of the observer is chiefly a mindset, the leader must have an attitude that focuses on efforts as well as specific behavioral attributes. Leaders write notes to themselves, even innocuous notes, that comment on ordinary activities in the group or other seemingly ordinary details that, when put together, may reveal important dynamic situations. Leaders also take a few minutes before and after each meeting to prepare goals, remind themselves of their role, pinpoint activities to be used during the meeting and record their observations. This provides the leader with a written record for reference in the next meeting or future consultations.

## The Compliment

An easily accessible and highly personable skill is the compliment, which is the formal act of courtesy and respect. One very effective way to give individual attention is through the use of strategic complimenting. To use this technique effectively, the leader must ask two very important questions: "What is it I want to acknowledge in a very specific way?" and "How will that help this person move forward in the right direction?" More than merely being nice, this type of complimenting is used to encourage change or movement.

## Act "As if"

Modern psychology, management theory and the philosophy of positive thinking subscribe to the hypothesis that reality follows belief. What a person believes to be true is often more powerful than what is true:  an objective reality. The 19th century philosopher, Vahniger, called it the "as if" principle. He asserted that if one acts "as if" life is this way or that way, then *their* reality will agree with the believer. More importantly, the believer will act "as if" this is true. Think of the last time you tried to convince someone to try a food that they had previously avoided. You knew that if they would try this food prepared in a different or special way that they would change their mind. Belief is difficult to shake; it is reality.

However, belief does not need to have a negative connotation to it. You can act "as if" in a positive way and shape your destiny. Harry was comfortable as a faculty member at a large university. Like many other institutions, this school encouraged faculty to apply for tenure. It was explicitly stated that those candidates rejected for tenure status would probably not be teaching there within the next five years. Harry applied and was rejected unanimously. Most professors in his position would have started a job search immediately.

Instead, Harry took a bold step and decided to make the committee *his* team; he would act as if they were teammates and *he* was the leader. Over the next few months, he took each of them out to lunch with just two questions in mind. "What were your reasons for denying me tenure?" he would ask, and "What can I do next time in order to gain the appointment?" One year later, Harry was a full professor with a tenured position. "I had partners on that committee," he quips, "who I thought were above me. I didn't have to change their thinking, I had to change mine!" The best leaders act, and they act "as if."

Another way that leaders act "as if" is within themselves. Many times, leaders have absolutely no control over who becomes a member of a given team. Leaders are not obliged to like everyone on the team, only to work effectively with them. When confronted with persons who pose problems, leaders can opt to act "as if." Rather than see the difficult person as disruptive, leaders might act "as if" this team member was exercising firmly held convictions. Rather than see a team member as negative to new product ideas, the leader can act "as if" this person was representing a consumer objection that needed to be factored into the new marketing strategy. Acting "as if" is an attitude of leadership and communication.

## Attitude

The attitude of communication means that the ability for two people to work together effectively is in harmony with the expectations that both have. Leaders who are willing to take chances for the good of the group and the project, who are willing to repeat what needs to be learned in many different ways, and who act "as if" things were better, more workable, and more cooperative are able to triumph over considerable odds. More importantly, these leaders are able to use their own inner resources to help the group move forward.

## Conclusion

Therefore, the greatest challenge of leadership is communication. Without it, all leaders eventually fail. The European business writer, Kets deVries remarked, "The derailment of a CEO is seldom caused by a lack of information about the latest techniques in marketing, finance, or production; rather, it comes about because of a lack of interpersonal skill— a failure to get the best out of the people who possess the necessary information."

The best leaders have courage and kindness; they wait and serve, focus and move, prepare and envision, and when things aren't quite perfect, they even act "as if." As Lao Tzu wrote, when you, as leaders, do all of these things, the others that you lead will say, "We did it ourselves."

A goal for leaders in team situations is to stay on track, not to be perfect or even to be absolutely correct in every situation. Instead, the task of the leader is to courageously take steps forward. Seneca's famous quote, "It is not because things are difficult that we do not dare. It is because we do not dare that things are difficult." Leaders, effective leaders, are at their best with teams when the team perceives the leader to be visionary, knowledgeable, involved, and having the necessary courage to make the next right step.

Leaders of teams are not ruled by others or their perceptions. A large billboard outside Logan Airport in Boston reads, "You can't let praise or criticism get to you. It is a weakness to get caught up in either." Leaders are able to gently manage the fine line between sensitivity and over-sensitivity. When the leader listens and uses a genuine, heartfelt approach, a rare kind of equality develops wherein the team believes the leader is like them and yet different.

Psychiatrist Rudolf Dreikurs remarked to a student of his, "I never listen to people's words… I only watch their feet. Feet point in only one direction, words can go any which way." This "action means more than words" philosophy can be extremely useful to the leading communicator. Noticing the "feet"—the movement and direction of an employee or a team—is a very valuable skill of the leader.

In 460 B.C., the legendary physician, Hippocrates, proclaimed, "It is just as important to know what sort of person has a disease, as to what sort of disease a person has." We are all familiar with professionals who forget that their clients are real people in search of translated technical expertise, not simply information seekers. Those that are the most skilled, knowledgeable and useful are also the ones who make it look easy. These are the leaders who know their craft so well that they can then go beyond technique and translate that expertise for everyone involved. They are admired for who they are and how others become in their midst—the stuff of great leadership. As Dr. Dreikurs was fond of saying, "You never know what you can do until you do it!"

# About Kevin O'Connor, CSP

Kevin O'Connor is a speaker, trainer, and corporate consultant specializing in Team Building, Customer Service and Communication. Kevin works especially well with highly trained technical professionals who know their material, but need equivalent training in the use of interpersonal skills.

Kevin's first-hand knowledge of working with teams comes from his practical experience serving on the boards of directors for three organizations. He is frequently called upon by organizations for his speaking, executive coaching and facilitative skills.

Kevin has attained the designation of Certified Speaking Professional (CSP) from the National Speakers Association. This coveted designation has been granted to less than 300 professional speakers in the world.

For more information, contact:

**Kevin E. O'Connor, CSP**
16 Thornfield Lane
Hawthorn Woods, IL 60047
Toll-free:   800-462-6657
 Website:   http://www.kevinoc.com

# Company Profile

Kevin E. O'Connor & Associates trains professionals in the use of interpersonal skills. They have worked with audiences who at one time or another have to cope with:

- Disappointing sales results,
- Changing markets,
- Diverse personalities,
- Reluctant volunteers,
- Independent colleagues, and/or
- Indifferent customers.

## Most Requested Programs:

*Renewing Your Sales Success*
Coping with a discouraging year—planning for a more successful one!

*Change Management in a Changing World*
Help your staff (and yourself) make change work for them.

*Living and Working with Sometimes Difficult People*
Kevin's most popular seminar teaches "people skills" that encourage and enhance communication.

*Teambuilding... Tactics that Work*
Learn how to develop methods that reinforce strong team support systems.

*Customer Service... with a Twist*
Discover eight specific ways to increase the number of completely satisfied customers.

Some of our diverse clients include: Ameritech, the American College of Physician Executives, the American Veterinary Medical Association, Arthur Andersen, Blue Cross/Blue Shield, Bristol-Myers Squibb, Cook County States' Attorney's Office, Illinois CPA Society, Motorola, RE/MAX, United States Air Force, White Hen Pantry, and many others.

For more information, contact:

**Kevin E. O'Connor & Associates, Ltd.**
16 Thornfield Lane
Hawthorn Woods, IL 60047
Toll-free:   800-462-6657
     Fax:   (847) 438-3421
Website:   http://www.kevinoc.com

❖ **Chapter 10** ❖

# Clues to Communications:

# Bouquets & Landmines

*by*
*Janet Sue Rush*

When we communicate well in our organization
and in our personal lives, we guide the
way for others with inspirational bouquets
instead of blasting the way with bombshells.

—*Janet Sue Rush*

ommunication is as natural as breathing. We communicate with the people around us all the time. We communicate with words; we communicate with attitudes; we communicate with body language. We even communicate with silence. The problem arises when the message we think we are sending to our colleagues, our employees, and our customers is not the message they receive. Certain words antagonize instead of inspire. Certain attitudes promote the very behavior we wish to prevent. In other words, we set out to plant a garden in our organization and end up laying landmines.

The vitality of any group depends on smooth interaction between the individuals who work within it. This interaction, in turn, depends on accurate and effective communication. We may be excellent at our jobs; we may have drive and vision, but, if we fail to communicate well with others in the organization, we jeopardize the entire mission. When we inadvertently antagonize the people we work with, we become a liability to the company. We need to understand the nuances of communication. We must inspire understanding and appreciation of the standards and goals that we set.

With good communication skills, we can clarify the demands of our organization, smooth the road to group cooperation, and speed peak production and service. We can build enthusiasm for the company and each employee's importance within it. Without good communication skills, stray landmines, either verbal or silent, could sabotage our entire operation.

In my career as a professional speaker, I am often called upon to facilitate situations where communication has broken down completely. Sometimes the key offenders are people in top management. I believe, with missionary fervor, that good communication skills can be learned. Learning to communicate is as important as the three R's (Reading, 'Riting, and 'Rithmetic). More important, when we communicate well in our organization and in our personal lives, we guide the way for others with inspirational bouquets instead of blasting the way with bombshells.

# Bouquet number one:
# Telling a good story

A good communicator can transmit information, thoughts, or feelings so that they are understood. We can often get across a point we're making by illustrating it with a good story. Here's one matching rewards with behavior.

A young man approached his father and said, "Dad, when I turn 16, I really want a new car." His father laughed and replied, "Son, you'll be lucky to get any car, let alone a new one."

However, the father reconsidered his response, realizing his son needed motivation to get on track. He thought, "The car seems to have gotten my son's attention. Maybe it could light a fire under him." One evening he called his son into his office and explained, "I've been thinking about that car you want and have decided that you will need to adopt a few changes before you'll deserve it. First, your grades will have to come up dramatically. Then your attitude at home will have to improve; no arguing with your mother, no fighting with your little sister. I want you sitting in church every Sunday with the family, and I want you to cut your long hair."

The son thought over the terms, and finally said, "Okay, Dad, anything for the car I want."

His sixteenth birthday arrived, and he reminded his Dad of their agreement. "I've done everything you asked me to do. Look at my grades, nearly all A's. I'm getting up every morning and singing in the shower— no arguments with Mom and no fights with my sister. I've been in church every Sunday with the family, so how about my new car?"

"Excellent job, son! I'm so proud of you. But you forgot that last requirement. You've still got long hair."

"I know, Dad, but remember how you had me sit in church every Sunday reading the Bible and studying the word? There I learned that Jesus had long hair."

"Yes, son, He certainly did, and He walked everywhere He went."

# Bouquet number two:
# Recognition and rewards

Motivating employees to do their best work is a difficult skill to acquire. Answer yes or no to the following statements concerning company incentives and policies.

    1. Christmas bonuses keep people on their jobs all year long.

2. Having strict rules and enforcing them is appreciated by employees because it lets them know where they stand.
3. Salespeople usually do better when they are competing for prizes in a contest.
4. The four-day work week is a real motivator.
5. Having employees punch a time card ensures that they will show up on time.
6. Threats of punishment for nonperformance are necessary for some people.
7. Company picnics or parties build morale.
8. Giving gold stars for good behavior is one way of keeping children on track.
9. Perks such as a good office and preferential parking builds motivation.
10. Salary increases are the prime motivators for everyone.

According to our best understanding of how people act, the answer to all of these questions is "no," which may surprise some managers.

Everyone needs to feel appreciated. Employees know, and a survey by the Council of Communication Management confirms, that recognition for a job well done is the top motivator of employee performance. However, when employees and a group of managers were given the identical lists of motivators to rank in order of importance to employees, the results were different and interesting.

| MANAGERS' RANKINGS | EMPLOYEES' RANKINGS |
|---|---|
| High wages | Full appreciation of work done |
| Job security | Feeling of being in on things |
| Promotion within the company | Help on personal problems |
| Good working conditions | Job security |
| Interesting work | High wages |
| Personal loyalty of supervisor | Interesting work |
| Tactful discipline | Promotion within company |
| Full appreciation of work done | Personal loyalty of supervisor |
| Help on personal problems | Good working conditions |
| Feeling of being in on things | Tactful discipline |

Although 33 percent of managers surveyed report that they themselves preferred to work where they received better recognition for their achievements. They thought the only rewards appreciated by their employees were those related to the pocketbook—raises or promotions. Certainly money is important, but what tends to motivate most people to perform—and to perform at higher levels—is the thoughtful, personal recognition that signifies true appreciation for a job well done. Numerous studies have proven this fact.

# Bouquet number two:
# Understanding work incentives

1. We will work for rewards—primarily money.
2. We will work for a leader who inspires us.
3. We will work for a cause in which we believe or an activity we enjoy.
4. We will work for psychological satisfactions (recognition, security, friendship, personal fulfillment).
5. We will deliberately keep from working, or at least work less productively, if the activity is unpleasant, poor working conditions are present, physical discomfort exists, irritating people are the norm, or long, tedious hours are required.

# Bouquet number three:
# Writing our appreciation

One of the most successful ways we can make recognition personal is to write a congratulatory letter to the employee and mail it to his home. The recognition can then be shared with family and kept as a memento to show friends and associates for years to come.

When extra congratulations are in order, take the time to write a warm, personal letter. Remember, no one objects to extravagant praise when it concerns himself. Here is an example from my own files:

*Dear Paul,*

*You should be very proud of yourself and of all you've accomplished. I'm very happy for you—and impressed not only with your success, but with the motivation and strength of character you have shown in getting to where you wanted to go. You're someone who deserves the good things that happen. I have a feeling that there are a lot more good things in store for you.*

*Warmest regards.*

Nothing looks better to an individual than written praise. One of the greatest tools I ever saw to motivate people was something I learned when working with Zig Ziglar. Called "I like" notes, they were small, preprinted notepads with blanks to be quickly filled out. Supervisors could watch for employees doing something right, jot a few words about the deed on the note, and give it to the employee on the spot, without the need for a long, detailed evaluation.

| I appreciate | I like |
|---|---|
| _____ | _____ |
| _____ | _____ |
| because | because |
| _____ | _____ |
| _____ | _____ |
| _____ | _____ |
| _____ | _____ |
| You Are a Winner ! ! ! | You Are Special ! ! ! |

Employees tucked them away to read again when they needed a boost and inspiration. The employees had the "I like" notepads, too, and used them to give their peers a quick written pat on the back. Everyone liked to give them and to receive them. We carried the "I like" notepads everywhere, not just in the office. We wrote to our children, relatives, customers, clients, waiters, airline attendants, just about anyone who had impacted us in a positive way.

Americans are not given to flowery pronouncements, and the "I like" notes provide a quick chance to express approval. "I love you." "I like you." "You're special." "You did a good job." "I appreciate your hard work." We need to have only a minute to compose a brief note to motivate one another to be the best at what we do.

A small child's face lights up when we communicate our approval and looks sad when he or she knows we are unhappy. As people grow older, they learn to mask those feelings even though emotions may be festering inside. We need to communicate our approval. Remember the saying, "Give in order to receive."

In today's computerized business climate, customers love a personal touch in our communications. Handwritten notes to clients make a better impression than a typed piece of correspondence. "I like" notes can be written to customers, too. I once wrote Lee Iacocca an "I like" note after meeting him and speaking to Chrysler employees, and he sent back a personal response.

A special word of praise is always appreciated. A written note of praise is always kept. I treasure mine. On days when I need a "hyacinth for the soul," I pull out my notes to remind myself of halcyon days when someone took the time to express approval for my work. Sometime today communicate about a job well done; a thoughtful act. By communicating well and with sincerity, we motivate.

**"And what is as important as knowledge, asked the mind. CARING, answered the heart."**

# Bouquet number four: Saying what we mean

One day I received a call from a prospective client who was searching for a speaker to talk to employees. He began to describe his needs and criteria for the program content and thought I might fit the profile. However, his last comment to me was, "But I don't want one of those motivational speakers."

What did he really mean? That he didn't want a pep talk with no solid advice for action? Certainly he couldn't have meant that he wanted a speaker who was dull and boring. My prospective client clearly needed to improve his own communication skills.

A speaker with fine-tuned communication skills has the ability to influence people to think or act differently. A good speaker knows his audience, knows what makes them click into action, and can use the right words to spur them on. All of us can do that with practice. Managers already have the basic tools for success—common sense, flexibility, and a desire to learn.

# Bouquet basics

Now that we are hooked on the importance of good communicating skills, we need to examine the details. My friend, Barbara Whitman, an insightful and successful communicator, compiled the ABC's of communication simply and succinctly. Read them, remember them, live them.

## THE ABC'S THAT WORK

Ask for ............... instead of ...... Assuming
Build ..................... instead of ..... Belittle
Communicate .... instead of ...... Criticize
Delegate .............. instead of ...... Doing it All
Encourage ........... instead of ..... Exasperate
Feedback ........... instead of ...... Frustrate
Guide .................... instead of ..... Gripe
Help .................... instead of ...... Hinder
Involve ................ instead of ..... Intimidate
Justify ................... instead of ..... Jeopardize
Know how ....... instead of ...... Knowing it All
Listen .................... instead of ..... Lament
Motivate ............. instead of ...... Minimize
Notice .................. instead of ..... Neglect
Observe .............. instead of ...... Object
Practice ............... instead of ..... Procrastinate
Quality ................ instead of ...... Quantity
Recognition ....... instead of ..... Ridicule
Support ............... instead of ..... Solve
Teamwork ......... instead of ...... Turmoil
Understand ....... instead of ..... Undermine
Verify ................... instead of ...... Vocalize
Watch .................. instead of ..... Wonder
Xcellence ............. instead of ...... Xcuse
Yield ..................... instead of ..... Yell
Zip ........................ instead of ..... Zigzag

# Our choices: The big three

Even the best people won't perform up to their capabilities without a motivating environment. Managers choose among three kinds of motivation—growth, incentive, and fear.

**Growth:** Opportunity for advancement or responsibility. Growth, the most powerful and most successful motivator, creates challenges and boosts greater self-esteem.

**Incentive:** Rewards such as money and time off, intrinsic and extrinsic; bonuses, trips, and profit sharing are tangible items that tend to lose their value over time as they become taken for granted, expected rather than earned.

**Fear:** Generally considered a negative motivator, fear can galvanize a person to overcome insurmountable obstacles and perform acts of heroism.

# Five "musts" to motivating and empowering people

Motivators must create:

1. A sense of personal achievement.
2. A belief that the job is challenging. Responsibility must match capabilities.
3. An environment where there is recognition for achievement.
4. The belief that one has control over aspects of her/his job.
5. An environment that allows people to develop and advance in experience and in ability.

Managers must reinforce behaviors and reward results, as simple as one, two, three.

1. Match the reward to the person. Start with the individual's personal preferences; reward in ways the individual truly finds satisfying.
2. Match the reward to the achievement. Effective reinforcement should be customized to take into account the significance of the achievement. Someone who completes a two-year project should be rewarded in a more substantial way than one who does a favor for us.
3. Be timely and specific. To be effective, rewards need to be given as soon as possible after the achievement. Rewards that come weeks or months later do little to motivate employees to repeat their actions. We should always explain why the reward is being given. Communication is important!

# Landmine number one: Demotivating with silence

Once, when I was speaking to a group of managers, I arranged a participation exercise. First, I told them I would give a sample presentation, speaking as I wrote my information on a board. My instruction to them was to pretend the information was exciting and new, and to stop me whenever they heard or saw me doing anything on which they should comment. I proceeded to announce and write on the board these facts: Two plus two equals four. Three plus three equals six. Four plus four equals eight. Five plus five equals nine…. "STOP!"

They stopped me because I said something wrong. Why didn't they stop me after the first fact? They could have said, "Stop, Janet, good job." Or the second fact? They could have said, "Great, Janet, you got two in a row, good job." Or the third? They could have said, "Three in a row. Great job, Janet." No, they did not stop me until I was wrong. Only a lazy communicator waits until something goes wrong to talk about his employee's results.

When we learn to stop people when they are doing things right, to let them know their efforts are noticed and applauded, we become the best motivator of people. When we wait for someone's mistakes before we come to attention, we become the world's best demotivator.

The minute the boss walks up to an employee on the job and says, "I need to talk to you," the first thing that enters that person's mind is, "Oh boy, what did I do wrong?" This kind of thinking derives from having a boss that doesn't communicate when things are going right. When an employee steps out of line, it might profit us to find out where he is going instead of being in a hurry to put him back in line. Most creative thinkers find it hard to conform, and we might get a boost for our organization by listening to them.

# Landmine number two: Only one right way

When basic mores are involved, we can insist that our employees follow the "right" behavior. Inherent in all societies are the taboos against lying, cheating, killing, but not all behaviors that are different are "wrong." We need to expand our understanding of our fellow human beings to keep from criticizing every different mode of action. Consider the following scenarios.

"Honey, every time you fold the towels, you fold them the *wrong way*." Did you know that there are 32 ways to fold towels? Which way is the *wrong way*?

"Honey, every time you load the dishwasher, you load it the *wrong way*." Did you know that there are 132 different configurations on how to load a dishwasher? How many of you go back and reload the whole thing after someone has loaded it?

"Son, every time you mow the yard, you mow it the *wrong way*." I asked the mother how the boy could possibly mow the yard the *wrong way*, and she replied, "Didn't you see the lines? He always mows across the yard instead of up and down."

My all-time favorite scenario is one I'm sure you'll recognize.

She or he is driving the car and proceeds to cross an intersection. The spouse will invariably say, "Where are you going?" "I'm going to the restaurant. Where did you think I was going?" "Well, you are going the *wrong way*." Now, how many different ways are there to get to that restaurant? They could go through the city, across the state, or even across the United States. Would it be the *wrong way*? (If my honey were to answer this question, he would say, "No, it would not be the *wrong way*, just the dumb way!")

The fine art of poor communication—we all stumble into it from time to time even though we know better. Motivating someone to do something our way, rather than his own way, requires a more tactful approach. Even then, it may not be worth the effort. Sometimes we need to be flexible enough to tolerate a *different way*, although it is not our first choice.

# Landmine number three: Stalling explanations

One morning at 8 o'clock, my boss, George, came into my office and asked to see me at 4:30 P.M. What do you think I did for the rest of the day? I worried. What on earth had I done wrong? I kept looking at my watch and dreading the end of the day. I remembered a cynical friend saying he never put anything personal in his office "because if you get canned it makes for a more civilized departure." I gazed around at all the personal possessions I had brought to my office over time and wished I had followed his advice. I felt sick and looked sick by the time my appointment finally arrived.

I sat down in George's office. He prepared me by saying the board had met and had made a few decisions that would affect me. The organization, I thought miserably, is being downsized, and I'm going to be laid off. I had tears in my eyes.

"Janet," George said, "the board decided to give you a smaller raise than you expected. That's why I waited till the end of the day to tell you."

I was so glad to still have my job, I couldn't have cared less about my raise! And I could have killed George for putting me through agony and suspense all day! Judge for yourselves whether George's communication skills were brutal or shrewd.

# Landmine number four: Stereotyping employees

Managing is a lot like parenting—an authority with specific goals tries to motivate an individual or group to move toward those goals. An employee arrives without a manual of instructions on how to motivate him, just as a child does. What motivates one may not spark even a glimmer of interest in another.

A parent's job is to motivate children to do well, be kind, respect others, make good grades, share his toys, and contribute to the good of the family. From the day a child is born, parents constantly strive to positively influence the child's actions, from sleeping all night to graduating from high school.

A manager's job is to motivate employees to do their jobs well, be kind, respect others, use their time efficiently, be team players, identify with the company's goals, fit in with the company's ways of doing things or learn new skills. From the day an employee is on board, a manager constantly strives to positively influence the employee's actions, from arriving at work on time to putting in a solid day's effort.

The first child paves the way for the other children as the parent practices different approaches to strengthen the child's ability to fit into society's demands and expectations. The key word is practice. The parent tries different methods and says different things until that particular individual cooperates. Then child number two comes along and the parent confidently trots out the same techniques used to civilize the first child. They don't work. The parent scrambles to find new ways to motivate child number two. The same problems arise with child number three. No matter how many children we have, each one of them may be motivated differently from the rest. (We say to ourselves, "How could these kids all come from the same family?")

Individuals in an organization, like people in a family, have different needs and respond to different incentives. Managers have to know their employees and communicate to them in ways that make sense and can be heard effectively by each individual. It's not easy, but it is possible.

# Landmine number five: Ignoring different needs

We believe with all our heart and soul that we have hit on just the incentive that will turn our people around, encourage employees to work harder and our customers to buy more. We think everyone will be happy with the "carrot" we have chosen for them. It's disappointing to us when we hear people complaining about it. Suddenly everyone seems to lose their enthusiasm for work.

The first thing we do is ask our employees what the problem is. One answer might be, "I hate carrots. My mother used to make me eat them, and now I gag on them."

We ask, "Well, what would motivate you to get with the program?"

"I really love bell peppers."

"Great. I can throw in a bell pepper."

"Wait a minute," says another employee. "I'm not that crazy about carrots either. I'd rather have cucumbers."

Pretty soon we have a vegetable garden of contented, motivated employees, or at least a mixed salad! And, more important to our company, we also have peak production.

# Ask and you shall receive

We need to understand an ambitious employee in order to plan his rewards.

One day my boss, Zig Ziglar, came along and told me how proud he was of me and all the hours of hard work and travel I had put in over the past year. I had traveled to more than 200 cities that year and I definitely looked and felt like the million mile flier.

I knew he was going to try to motivate me to work even harder, probably to break my record the next year. He was going to hold out a carrot.

I thought, "Oh, this is going to be good."

"Miss Janet," he said. "What I'm going to do is give you two free airline tickets to anywhere in the world you want to go." He smiled, and I started crying.

I travel for a living. The last thing I want to do with my free time is get on another airplane. Put me on a boat, a train, a bicycle. Put me in a pickup truck in Dallas, or tell me I have to stay home for two weeks and I'll get excited.

To be fair, if Zig had offered that incentive to any one of the other 67 employees, it would have worked. We would have heard lots of hollering and celebrating. To learn how to motivate me, all Zig needed to have done was ask me, and I would have told him. Two-way communication works. No need to waste time trying to figure out what reward will motivate a particular employee… ask.

If we know how to listen, people will open up to us. We will learn what is important to the people in our family, in our organization, and in our community. We will have the power to produce dynamic end results.

When my salesperson, Lenore Sordyl, sold a million dollars worth of product, she made history in the company. She had reached that mark faster than any other person, the first woman to achieve that goal. I was proud of her, and I wanted to motivate her to sell two million next time. Believing myself an expert motivator, I began planning her reward. A big sales dinner in her honor, a huge plaque for her office, and her choice of jewelry—a diamond necklace, a ring, or a Rolex watch. Now that would impress anybody!

Later my son, Preston, said to me, "Mom, Lenore doesn't look too excited." I replied, "She's from Chicago; she doesn't show a lot of emotion." Preston responded, "Why don't you practice what you preach, and ask her."

He was right. When I checked, I discovered that most of Lenore's friends and family live in Chicago, and the dinner was planned for Dallas. Lenore also realized that, while her family and friends would bask in her achievement, her colleagues might not be in the "bask" mode. The dinner would only be a reminder that they had fallen short of Lenore's achievements.

"Well," I countered, "what about the plaque?"

Lenore demurred for awhile, then admitted the problem. "It's really nice, Janet, but remember, I don't have an office, just a cubicle, and I won't be able to hang it there."

Almost defeated, I asked, "Well, have you picked out your jewelry?"

"No, but I will sometime soon. It will be a nice memento."

Memento! I stopped dead in my tracks and stared at Lenore. I did not see one piece of jewelry on her. Not a ring, not a bracelet, not an earring.

I was using the wrong carrots. Belatedly, I asked her, "Lenore, what would motivate you to sell two million dollars?"

She answered immediately. "I love to travel, and if I could get two airplane tickets to anywhere in the world… "

"I know right where to get those! Hey, Zig!"

# Landmine number six: Negative responders

Managers who adopt a negative response to work problems by using certain words and attitudes generate, in turn, an uncooperative attitude in their employees, who in turn become "negative responders." Managers with a positive approach, a motivating response, encourage the solution of problems, activating "motivating responders." A review of the attitudes of "a negative responder" and "a motivating responder" is presented below along with a sampling of words that trigger particular responses.

| A "Negative Responder" | A "Motivating Responder" |
|---|---|
| **Irritates** | **Invites Action** |
| ☛ Get the point... ? | ♦ Help me understand.... |
| ☛ Don't you know... ? | ♦ Here's the information.... |
| ☛ I told you once... ! | ♦ To get the best results.... |
| ☛ Buy.... | ♦ Invest.... |
| ☛ I, Me, Mine.... | ♦ You, yours.... |
| **Acts Indifferent** | **Probes** |
| ☛ It's company policy! | ♦ What is your opinion? |
| ☛ I think.... | ♦ What do you think? |
| ☛ I feel.... | ♦ Would you help me understand |
| ☛ Here's what happened.... | what happened? |
| ☛ So what? | ♦ And what happened next? |
| **Denigrates** | **Appreciates** |
| ☛ Jerk! | ♦ Thank you! |
| ☛ Idiot! | ♦ You were very helpful. |
| ☛ Fool! | ♦ It's been a pleasure. |
| | |
| **Creates Apathy** | **Motivates** |
| ☛ There's nothing I can do! | ♦ I will do anything I can to help you. |
| ☛ You will just have to.... | ♦ I can handle that for you. |
| ☛ Whatever.... | ♦ Here's what will happen. |
| ☛ I have no idea.... | ♦ Let me find out for you. |

# Special bouquets: Words that charm

The right words are important!

**Six of the most important words we can use with people:** "I admit I made a mistake." Managers may find these words the most difficult to say. President Nixon failed to use those words after Watergate. How much more accepting the American people would have been had he been able to use them. In contrast, Lee Iacocca publicly apologized for his company, saying, "I admit we made a mistake. We turned the miles back on cars and it was legally, morally and ethically wrong. We're Chrysler and I promise we'll fix that." America applauded him.

**Five more important words:** "You did a good job." What little effort it takes to stop and let someone know that he or she is doing well.

I once suggested that collection agents start their conversations with, "Mr. Jones, you did a really good job by sending in that payment last month." The compliment worked. The customer felt good about meeting his financial obligation and positive about doing it again.

**Four very important words:** "What do you think?" or "What is your opinion?" Plenty of people want to talk, but few know how to listen. We must ask questions of our employees and of our customers and pay attention to the answers. The best salesman in the world knows how to listen to his customers; the best manager listens to his employees. We give true value to the speaker's worth by centering our focus on his opinion.

**Three important words:** "Will you please… ?" We learn this courteous way to make requests when we first learn to talk. We teach it in turn to our toddlers, but in the rush of daily business, "Will you please" is often overlooked. Healthcare workers say that when their most considerate patients ask for things by using the words, "Will you please," the words ease the most onerous duties and soothe the most overworked employee. We need to use these gentle words often with our employees and encourage them to use them with their customers and with each other.

**The two most important words:** "Thank you." Often taken for granted, the words, "Thank you," are most noticeable when they are missing. One day while I was in the check-out line at the grocery store, I noticed the clerk was in a bad mood. In sympathy with anyone having a tough day, I began to bag my groceries for her. It was her responsibility, so when I finished I looked at her expectantly. She ignored me. Her bad mood was contagious. Before I realized what had happened, I prompted, "I expected a thank you." But the clerk had the last word. "It's written on the receipt," she said. I left still needing to hear the words.

**The least important word in effective motivational communication is "I." The most important word is "We."** Starting our day with the word "we" reinforces our realization of the importance of the people we supervise. Using "we" instead of "I" in our letters to customers demonstrates that many persons in our company have an interest in them. The greatest motivational coaches always say, "We did it!"

# Never say "No"

Tactful managers try never to use the word "no." No matter how nicely we say it, the word meets resistance in the listener. The word "no" gives us negative feedback: "No, we don't have that in stock," or "No, that is not available," or "No, I can't see you today." We can eliminate the word "no" by explaining what we can do. Compare the scenarios below.

| SCENARIO | THE "NO" METHOD | THE "WHAT I CAN DO" METHOD |
|---|---|---|
| A customer calls and demands that I be in his office tomorrow at 9 A.M. | "Mr. Customer, I'm sorry but there is no way I can be there tomorrow at 9 A.M." (No matter how nice you are, the reply will be, "Why not? If you can't be here, I'll find someone who can.") | "Mr. Customer, let me check my schedule and see what I can do. The best I can do is to be in your office at 3:00 P.M. tomorrow." |
| An employee wants three weeks vacation in October, the busiest month of the year. | "No way you're taking three weeks in October, unless you quit!" | "You need three weeks of vacation in October. Let me check the calendar and see what I can arrange. The best I can do is two weeks in November and one week in December." |
| The boss needs that report by 2:00 P.M., no later. | "Boss, there is no way I can have that report to you by 2:00 P.M." (His or her reply will always be, "Why not?") | "Boss, I'll be glad to get you that report. The soonest I can have it to you is by 8 A.M. tomorrow." |

| SCENARIO | THE "NO" METHOD | THE "WHAT I CAN DO" METHOD |
|---|---|---|
| A child wants to go ride his bike after school. | "No. You have to do your homework first." | "So, you're going to go to the park with your friends to ride bikes. That sounds great. As soon as you finish your homework, you are welcome to go ride your bike." |

The "What I Can Do Method" works well in most situations, and even when it fails, it reflects our willingness to do our best in the face of an impossible task.

I've been practicing this technique on my son for years. One day, he used it on me.

"Preston, you need to come in and do your chores."

"Mom, super, fantastic, no problem. Just as soon as I finish riding my quad runner I'll be glad to come in and do my chores." What did he just say to his mother? "No, I'm not coming in right now," but notice that he never used the word "no."

# Preparation and inspiration in communication: The best bouquet of all

Neil Armstrong, the first man to land on the moon, was being interviewed by the press before his launch. One reporter presented him with a nightmarish possibility, or rather, impossibility. "Neil, did you know that if your engine goes out after you land on the moon, you would only have six hours of life left? What would you do in that situation?"

The astronaut paused as the press awaited his answer. "Well, I think I'd work on my engine, wouldn't you?" An effective and inspiring remark. His words were unforgettable. He knew how to communicate.

We need to work on our own engines. Although the questions and the demands we meet in our daily work situations may not parallel the pressure Neil Armstrong faced before stepping into his space capsule, our problems demand equal communication skills. We must be wary of sabotaging our goals with careless words. With thoughtful and forceful communication, we can guide our company to success amid the stars of business and industry.

# About Janet Sue Rush

An energetic motivator, educator, and entertainer, Janet has inspired more than a million people with her humorous, fast-paced presentations. Her training sessions result in positive attitudes as well as improved sales, customer service, communication skills, productivity, and teamwork.

Janet travels the country speaking to groups ranging in size from 20 to 2,000, tailoring each talk to the particular objectives of management, the needs of employees, and the expectations of customers. Her dynamic programs have been seen on national satellite television networks and in custom video programs.

With a rich and varied background in sales, customer service and public relations, Janet became one of the youngest female entrepreneurs in America at the age of 32 when she cofounded Strawberry Communications. The company was so successful that, after two years of operation, it was acquired by the well-known Zig Ziglar Corporation, where Janet became a vice president and the company's most sought-after speaker next to Ziglar himself.

As President of The Rush Company, Janet combines a whirlwind speaking schedule with her duties as a mother and brings genuine understanding to the unique problems of women at work. She is the author of *The Magic of Telephone Etiquette, Total Customer Satisfaction, How Are You Feeling Today?, Let's Make Friends and Not Lose Customers, Making a Difference Tomorrow, Today,* and *Zig Ziglar Presents Janet Rush on Customer Service.* Her business topics include service, sales, motivation, team building, leadership, quality management, women's issues, change, entrepreneurship, health care, and education.

# Company Profile

## R.U.S.H.—Real Usable Solutions from the Heart

The Rush Company offers a broad array of services besides customized on-site training. They include television, satellite and video programs, keynote addresses, executive retreats, consulting services, a speakers' bureau, and books, audio and video products.

The Rush Company's impressive client list includes American Airlines, American College of Physicians, American Express, AT&T, BankOne, Bombay Company, Browning Ferris, DuPont, Ford Motor Company, GMAC, Hospital Corporation of America, Hyatt Hotels, Illinois Bell, Louis Vuitton, Mary Kay Cosmetics, Minolta, Neiman Marcus, Nintendo, Snap-On Tools, Southwestern Bell, State Farm Insurance, Texas Instruments, TRW, Waste Management, Westinghouse, Visiting Nurse Association, XEROX, and Zig Ziglar Corporation.

## Powerful Presentation Titles

- *Change... Do I Have To?*
- *The 21st Century Woman*
- *The Corporate Edge*
- *Making a Difference for Tomorrow, Today*
- *How to Enjoy Failure, Be Amused by Rejection and Thrive on Stress*
- *Are You on the Bleeding Edge... or Leading Edge?*
- *Sales is Service... Service is Sales*
- *How are We Feeling Today? Patient Care Relations*
- *From ABC to XYZ... A Primer for Success in Education*
- *Team Building... Are You ON IT or OFF IT?*

For booking information, call Janet Rush at:

THE J.
**RUSH**
COMPANY

**The Rush Company**
9090 Skillman #182-A 203
Dallas, TX 75243-8262
Phone: (214) 383-2434
Toll free: 1-800-781-RUSH
Fax: (972) 473-4733

❖ **Chapter 11** ❖

# Communication
# C.H.A.L.L.E.N.G.E.S.
# of
# Family Businesses

*by*
*James R. Kwaiser*

**Set the Example by your
Attitude, Word and Action.**

*—James R. Kwaiser*

Professional publications and journals have reported that two-thirds of family businesses fail to make it to the second generation. Out of those that do, nine out of ten fail to survive to the third generation. Failure to successfully transfer the family business from one generation to the next is greatly influenced by poor communication between members of the family. Neglecting to address the personal issues surrounding the transfer of ownership is the largest contributor to this failure. Personal issues that deal with questions that include: Who should have ownership in the company? How should ownership be divided? What is equal? What is fair? Who will manage the business? How will the estate of the parents be transferred? Issues usually left unanswered until a family death crisis occurs, when the "what is in it for me" and the "that is not fair" syndromes take over, force the sale of the family business.

Personal experiences over the past twenty-five years have generated opportunities to observe and work with a variety of family business situations. During that time, common denominators have been discovered that have had a marked impact on the success of the transfer of family businesses from one generation to the next. Denominators centered around the communication *C.H.A.L.L.E.N.G.E.S.* that family members face. *C.H.A.L.L.E.N.G.E.S.* identified and defined by the way each family member communicates with, and relates to, one another.

*C.H.A.L.L.E.N.G.E.S.* must be addressed one at a time by family members until a consensus is reached. A consensus that is good for the individual, the couple, the family, and the business. Each of the *C.H.A.L.L.E.N.G.E.S.* are essential components to honest family communication. Communication that is necessary for the successful transfer of the family business from one generation to the next.

The following will identify each of the *C.H.A.L.L.E.N.G.E.S.* and offer suggestions for effective family business communication. Communication that will lead to consensus agreements by family members and minimize the risk of failure when transferring the business from one generation to the next.

# Communicate as Equals

Plans for the transfer of the family business and disbursement of an estate are usually made solely by the parents/owners, and in many cases, just by the father "for the good of all." The father determines how the business will be divided, who will be his successor, how the grandchildren will be taken care of, and many other personal issues that will impact the lives of his adult children, their families, his wife, and the family business. Frequently, it is only when a death occurs that the adult children discover how the business and estate have been divided and often view it as being unfair. This lack of communication leads to arguments and disputes until finally the family business has to be sold in hopes of healing the now strained family relationships. This can be avoided, but it is not easy.

One of the most difficult aspects of effective family communication centers around the mindset of addressing each member as an equal. Parents and children communicating as equals. What a concept! You are probably thinking it could never happen. Communicating as equals is the most important and most difficult of the communication challenges in a family business.

You may have observed or experienced parents who do unusual things to communicate with their children, such as twisting a child's ear to stress a point. Not a practical way for equals to communicate, as it would be difficult to imagine the child communicating with the parent using that method. Examples like this point out that communication between parent and child is not equal. This unequal communication continues as the child grows into adulthood. The parents make the decisions and the father usually runs the business. Including the adult children in the decisions concerning estate or succession planning is not even considered. Why would you ask the opinion of the person whose ear you twisted? You were not equals then, how can you be now? Besides mom and dad have always made decisions for the good of the children.

Childhood memories and perceptions of their meaning on relationships have a profound effect on communication in the family business environment. The communication of parents to children, children to parents, sibling to sibling, and even husband to wife are impacted by incidents experienced and perceptions formed from these memories. Perceptions become unspoken truths and will have a significant impact on whether family members will achieve communication as equals.

The personal interpretation of these memories give children the perception that their parents "just don't understand" or are "too old to know how I feel." At times, the children feel as though mom and dad stick to the old ways of doing things and will never try anything new or different. As adults in a family business, the children have a tendency to bring these feelings—this *emotional stuff*—with them into adulthood, hampering the ability to communicate with their parents as equals.

Communication as equals between siblings can even be harder to achieve. As children, brothers Jerry, Jim, and Dick decided to start a bank at home. The three brothers contributed a portion of their income from their paper route and odd jobs to the bank on a weekly basis. Jerry was the self-designated banker. The stash of saved money would be used for a future, mutually beneficial activity. In most cases, that activity would be centered around a treat of steak sandwiches, fries, and malts at the local Tony's restaurant. This activity became a monthly ritual that was always looked forward to with anticipation. On one ritual day, Jim and Dick went to Jerry to collect their money for the anticipated feast. Jerry informed Jim and Dick that the bank had gone bust because of a bad loan to himself. Jerry, the banker, had drained the bank and spent the money on himself and his friends, for a trip to Tony's! As adults, do not ask Jim and Dick to vote for Jerry as the financial officer of the family business. They remember his cavalier attitude toward money and they certainly do not want him in charge of a bigger bank account now! The fact that Jerry was 12 at the time has little relevance. Jerry took money that was not his and spent it. Situations like this one can instill a negative lifetime perception.

The adult sibling perception of a brother or sister as a kid is a picture that is imprinted in their subconscious and stays with them into their adult lives. Issues such as the home bank incident, when left unaddressed, impairs communication on an adult level. When this impairment happens, trust and openness that is needed for the family business to thrive is next to impossible. Without honest communication, running a successful family business is all but hopeless.

Overcoming the "mindset" of the parent-to-child, and child-to-child dialogue is difficult to achieve. Observations have been made of adults being treated like children by their parents, even when the children are over 50 years of age! In retrospect, there are times when adult children have difficulty relating to their parents as adults, reverting back to the role of child when it comes to decision making in the family business.

A new mindset in family communication must be achieved when it comes to the operation of a family business. In a family business, the children and parents will eventually become partners and one day the children will run the business. Treating your business partners with the mindset most parents and children use will not work. Imagine a business where the decisions of the partners are considered either too childish by the parents, too old fashioned and not up-to-date by the adult children, or too immature by the siblings. Family members that cling to the old ways of family communication destine the company to failure. These same grow-ing-up, family behaviors are handed down from generation to generation, adding to the difficulty of open communication and threatening the con-tinuation of the family business.

A good place to start the family business communication process is by preparing rules of communication. Start early, when the children are young. Assign duties in the family business to each child. No matter how unimportant or how trivial the duty may seem, make each child responsi-ble. Require that each family member gives a report on the progress of their assigned duties at a family business meeting. Assigned duties and family business meetings will foster responsibility and set a pattern that will offer opportunities of "Communicating as Equals." The meetings must be scheduled, have an agenda, and continue even after the children reach adulthood. Keep the meeting professional, follow an agenda, and do not allow petty bickering to enter into the business meeting.

Review the communication in your own family business relationships with an open mind and you will discover where your family fits in the communication picture. This "new" communication requires commitment from everyone involved. A difficult commitment. A commitment that means treating all family members as equals who possess expertise, knowledge, and skills that can contribute to the success of the business and the well-being of the family.

Communicating as equals applies to a spouse as well. Often in a fam-ily business, the spouse is left out of the decision-making process, espe-cially when they are not working in the business on a day-to-day basis. Business issues are not discussed because the spouse is seen as having nothing vital to contribute. A tendency exists to forget that the problems, concerns, and situations of the business are brought home and can adversely affect the marriage relationship. Involve your spouse and try to be open, honest, and clear in your description of business situations, espe-cially if these situations involve relationships with other family members. Ask for their opinions. Additional opinions will enable you to consider sit-uations from a different point of view and this other view can be invalu-able in making sound business decisions.

If this first "communicate as equals" component is not consciously added to the family business, effective working relationships, strategic planning, and consensus decisions will be almost impossible to achieve.

Open communication in a family business is like stirring up a huge pot of liquid that appears to be clear, but at the bottom is sludge and debris. The sludge could be hurt feelings left unsaid and the debris may be misconceptions and misunderstandings that pull the family apart. Every time you address these tough issues, you stir up that sludge and debris.

Some of the *stuff* that is on the bottom floats up and clouds the liquid. For a while, it will make communication seem unclear or even worse than before the stirring. Stirring the pot is necessary. Without the stirring, the hurt feelings, misconceptions, and misunderstandings cannot be addressed and skimmed off. This stirring and skimming for many families has never been achieved and is usually avoided.

Communicating as equals takes commitment. A commitment to allow the emotional sludge and debris that families want to avoid to be stirred up and then to have the courage to address each issue as adults, as equals. Without communicating as equals, family and the family business can easily be pulled in several directions causing hurt feelings and an unsure future.

# Have a Written Vision and Share It

"Have a Written Vision and Share It" is defining, in writing, what the company means to the parents and explaining this meaning to the children. A meaning that is more then just financial opportunities. A meaning that includes the dreams, hopes, and business ethics of the parents.

Continued sharing provides an understanding of why a certain direction for the business was chosen and the role that each parent played in that direction. Sharing the vision also identifies what the parents would or would not do for the achievement of profits or increased business. The vision describes the business values of the parents and passes onto the children an understanding of how the parents feel the customers, vendors, and employees should be treated.

Restating and sharing the vision with the children as they grow, allows for better understanding of the mission, goals, and value positions of the parents, in the language appropriate for each child's age level. By starting to communicate the vision at an early age, the children can formulate a clearer picture of the real meaning of the business. Without this understanding, the children will formulate inaccurate perceptions of the family business by making up their own answers to those questions left unanswered by the parents.

Combining the mission, vision, and value convictions into one philosophy statement, one short meaningful description of what the company means to the parents, is helpful in insuring a consistent explanation to all the children as they grow into adulthood. How each of the children, as they take a more active role in the business, view the philosophy of the company should also be understood by all family members. In this way, parents and adult children are able to identify those areas where there is agreement and also those areas that need additional explanation, before the transfer of the business takes place.

Amazing as it may seem, parents cannot understand why their children may choose a different career, even though the parents have never communicated the positive sides of being involved in the family business. An heir apparent to a successful company was asked why he did not want to enter the family business. He explained that while he was growing up, all he could remember was his dad complaining about the employees, vendors, and customers, while his mother was always upset because his dad was never home at a regular time to eat dinner! The heir apparent stated, "Why would I want to go into a business that made my parents so miserable?" He had made up his own answer to mom and dad's perceived attitude toward the business, as he interpreted it by their words and actions.

Parents either forget or are unaware that their children are constantly watching and listening to them and oftentimes live out what they have heard or observed. Parents disregard the fact that their children will make lasting judgments based on what they, as parents, say and do. These judgments and impressions tend to remain with the children as they grow into adulthood.

Identifying the philosophy and discussing it with the potential successors are vital parts of the communication process. There have been parents/founders who have spent years training and preparing their children as potential successors only to find out too late that the successor never agreed with the existing company philosophy. The end result of this situation is the parents watching their dream become their nightmare. The successor began to use business practices that the parents did not condone causing the philosophy foundation, upon which the company was built, to crack and decay.

Communicating the philosophy and spending the time to be sure that others are willing to accept it, live it, and carry it forward can save a lot of heartache and headaches for the parents and the adult children alike. This is one topic that has been found to be highly neglected when successors are considered and decided upon. This neglect can be tragic, as the philosophy of the parents is usually the heart and soul of the business.

# Address the "Unspeakables"

"Unspeakables" are those feelings and perceptions which have been left unsaid by individual family members in order to avoid conflict, promote harmony, and keep from hurting the feelings of another family member. The result of these unspeakables is just the opposite of what is intended.

Earlier, the problems caused by stirring the pot were mentioned. The sludge and debris are those feelings, impressions, and perceptions believed by members of the family, but never openly discussed. Addressing these unspeakables is when the debris and sludge rise to the surface, as the communication pot is stirred.

The debris may be a misconception or a misunderstanding of an individual who believes they have been hurt or wronged by another member of the family. The unspeakable could be a situation or misconception that happened when they were a child, when they felt mistreated or misunderstood by a parent or sibling. A misunderstanding that imprinted a negative impression of a parent or another family member in their subconscious. An unspeakable that is carried with them into adulthood and, if left unaddressed, can interfere with the decisions, plans, direction, and success of the family business. The story of brother Jerry who took the bank of money as a child and is now passed over for chief financial officer of the family business is a good example.

The unspeakable could be a family member who feels they have been snubbed by an in-law. Instead of addressing this situation, they allow it to affect their relationship with their sibling who is married to the troublesome in-law.

Unspeakables can build and build until one day a small incident subconsciously reminds a person of the other hurts that they have collected. Accumulation of these hurts cause people to lose their tempers and overreact to a minor incident (isolated hurt), primarily due to the unfair way they perceive they have been treated in the past.

In a family business, family members must take the plunge into the communication pot and address those unspeakables. Family members cannot avoid the tough issues. Conflict cannot be avoided. Nothing can be left unsaid when it comes to the personal issues that will eventually affect the ongoing success or lead to the demise of the business. Virtually all festering personal issues left unaddressed will affect the business. In the majority of cases when there are personal unspeakables that are not addressed, trust is compromised, good judgment is second guessed, and immediate decisions are delayed all in the name of family and business harmony.

Family rules do not prepare children to handle conflict as adults. Children are taught not to argue with their brothers and sisters, never talk back to mom or dad, and are often disciplined for being honest. When a young person says, "Aunt Linda's coat is ugly" (and it really is!) mom and dad probably said, "If you don't have something nice to say, then don't say anything at all." Most parents have taught their children to avoid conflict, especially if the message could hurt someone's feelings, even if it is true. Avoiding conflict causes the unspeakables to grow inside of children. As children grow up, there are behaviors of their siblings or parents that have bothered them for a long time, maybe years, but have never been openly discussed. Decisions that mom, dad, brother, or sister may have made for another when they were young and viewed by the affected person as wrong or unfair, can remain an unspeakable for many years. These feelings of unfairness will affect trust, as with the example of brother Jerry, and can hamper effective business-decision making, such as when purchases are stalled due to the feeling that a parent or sibling may not want to spend any money. Bitter battles among family members have occurred not because someone might be wrong or that their decision will be bad for the family or the business, but merely because of the feeling that "I am an adult now and you can no longer tell me what to do." In these battles, most of these feelings can be directly traced back to some unspeakable. Some action, word, or misconception has happened in the past to cause hurt feelings and/or foster the perception of being unable to extend trust to another.

An effective way to uncover the unspeakables is during an "Address the Unspeakables" session. These sessions are conducted by an independent facilitator during which each family member is asked to write a family activity that really made them happy and gave them the feeling of closeness to their other family members. Family members are also asked to write down three things they admire most about each member of their family and three things that really "bug" them about each family member. Finally, add the three ways that each family member hurt them in the past. Just stirring the pot!

After each member has completed their assignment, they individually read out loud what they have written. A facilitated discussion begins to take place after each reading. The unspeakables are stirred up and start rising to the top of the pot in this sharing. For many families, the facilitated discussion is the first time they have ever had an honest, open, in-depth conversation concerning individual feelings and judgments that are often based upon misunderstandings. Also amazing is how families avoid the word "love." Because of this avoidance, the strong positive feelings for each other have never been spoken. Lack or fear of open, honest communication has been the destruction of many family businesses and relationships. Addressing the issues, speaking the unspeakables, being open and honest, loving one another, and voicing personal, often withheld, feelings can have a very positive impact on family members and the family business.

# Learn to Forgive

Stirring the pot leads to honesty, forgiveness, and the healing of family relationships. Stirring the pot also allows a way to open a truthful dialogue that is based on the caring and loving of one another. When addressing the unspeakables in the proper fashion, misunderstandings are corrected, forgiveness is given and accepted, and trust is renewed.

Conflict can be healthy. How people handle conflict will determine whether it is positive or negative. Members of a family business must forgive each other for past hurts. They need to be loving and truthful in their feelings and attitudes about each other and they must honestly communicate with one another. Each family member has to set aside self-interest and place the good of the entire family first with every decision they make. Family members have to unconditionally trust that the motives of each decision made by any family member is in the best interest of the family and business. There cannot be any self-serving decisions being made.

Having, developing, or regaining trust is difficult. In the movie *Robin Hood Prince of Thieves*, Lady Marion says to Robin after his return from the crusades, "All I remember of you is a spoiled bully who used to burn my hair as a child." Robin replies to Marion, "Years in a prison will change a man." The memories of the past can make it very difficult to trust or to have open-minded communication, as the other person may not be fully aware of the experiences that "will change a man." Family members have the tendency to remember the "spoiled bully" and not recognize that people can and will change.

Explaining to others that they are still seen as the "spoiled bully" is the first step in stirring the pot. The debris, the misunderstandings, can now be seen and skimmed off. Even though the water may look clear, the bottom remains full of unspeakables unless the stirring and skimming process continues. When the unspeakables are not addressed, communication will always be guarded and the lack of individual trust will always be an unspeakable issue. A family business cannot survive for long with all the unspeakables still at the bottom of the pot. Forgiveness is how the debris and sludge are skimmed off the top of the stirred pot. Without forgiveness, the water in the pot, the relationships, will never be clear.

# Let Go of the Pecking Order

There was a father who owned a very successful business. He had four children, the eldest being a boy. From the time his oldest son was small, the father spent most of his time preparing him to become chairman of the board for the family business. As a small boy, the son was exposed to the business and began working in various capacities. His father moved him from position to position, telling him war stories and allowing him to experience all types of leadership and decision-making situations. The father introduced his son to the industry by having him join the right professional organizations, allowing him to represent the company at public functions, and placing him on the board of directors of the family business. The father always proudly said, "My oldest son will take over the business. He will be in charge when I am finally carried out of here." The father also was proud of following the right "pecking order" as his father had before him.

The father felt he was doing the right thing, setting the right stage, and properly planning for the future of his company. There was only one thing he did not plan on. His oldest son was killed in a boating accident at the age of 27. The other children were not trained in running the business and they were bitter about not being involved. While they had loved their older brother, they always felt inferior. They had never really been allowed to make decisions, gain the business experiences, or hear the war stories their oldest brother did. They were not communicated with or listened to. Their opinions had not mattered in the past and their attitude toward work and the family business reflected it. They were not prepared to become the decision makers in the company.

The father was getting older and wanted to reduce his work load. He tried to cram all the lessons that had been reserved for the eldest son to the next in line. He was angry that his oldest son died and he vented his anger, sorrow, and frustration on the other children. He was not a patient communicator. He would not *COMMUNICATE WITH THEM AS EQUALS.* He did not *SHARE THE VISION* with them. He refused to *ADDRESS THE UNSPEAKABLES.* Worst of all, he would not *LET GO OF THE PECKING ORDER.* He decided to take his second oldest son and force him into becoming the next heir apparent.

The second son was now pushed into a business he did not like, in a position he did not want, making decisions he was not qualified to make. He was not capable of running the company. However, his younger sister was. She had the business savvy, had studied the industry, and had kept herself up-to-date on the financial and operational condition of the company. The father would not teach, coach, or communicate with her, as she was not "the next son in line."

Because of this refusal to *LET GO OF THE PECKING ORDER,* the father brought in two non-family members to run the company and be mentors to his second son. Bitterness grew, the daughter left the company due to the father's inability to communicate with her as an equal, his lack of sharing his vision, their inability to address the unspeakables, and finally, his refusal to let go of the pecking order. The non-family members fought for control and the business deteriorated. Market share declined, customers began to jump ship, and many of the experienced managers left for greener pastures because of the father's poor communication skills and his adherence to the so-called proper pecking order.

In a family you can be ugly, lack common sense, do stupid things, and still be loved. In a business you can only be ugly. Lacking common sense and doing stupid things can be devastating to a business. What sex you are, where you are in the pecking order, and how old you are has nothing to do with ability, skills, or the "knack" of running a business.

Owners of family businesses need to treat their children coming into the business much like other employees. Sure, some favoritism in the perks and pay may occur, but the children must be given the same learning considerations as other employees. When they are ready, do assessments of their behavioral styles in order to establish a plan for helping them increase their effectiveness. Identify particular jobs for them with defined job descriptions. Allow the children to work together and with other people who can teach them. Enable the children to gain respect for one another by working together and reporting on their progress to one another. Communicate with all the children about the business. Do not show favoritism. Openness of communication, love, and forgiveness will all play a role in who will eventually lead the business. The child with the best overall skills should be the next to run the company, that person may not be the oldest boy.

# Expand Your Board of Directors

When the time arrives to turn over the business, make sure your children have experienced, qualified advisors and, if open communication and trust are not already in place, consider individuals outside the company for the board of directors. These outsiders can become trusted advisors to your children if you are not around.

Non-family board members are not needed in every family business. Families that practice honest, open communication, trust, and forgiveness as key ingredients in family relationships can usually face and resolve any potential differences. Even with these traits, it is important for the parents to remain sensitive to the relationships of their children and consider non-family board members if relationships deteriorate.

The board of directors should always be expanded to include the adult children who will inherit the business, whether or not outside board members are involved.

The selection of outside advisors should be discussed with family members at a scheduled business meeting. Each family member should propose possible board members. The prospective board members should be reviewed, their qualifications discussed, and the list shortened to five prospects. Those candidates should be approached and asked if they would be willing to serve in this role. If there is an interest from the prospects, they should be interviewed by the entire family, as it is important for all members to agree on the selections.

Identifying the roles and duties of the board of directors and utilizing non-family board members can reduce potential conflict issues such as compensation, perks, position, and title that arise due to lack of trust of family members. Appropriate family members, as part of the responsibility of a board member, should participate in constructing the job description of the board of directors. A definite job description will give family members a better understanding of the authority of the board and its relationship to the president and chief operating officer of the company. This job description will also define to the non-family board members what will be expected of them.

Understanding the authority of the board of directors can soften the blow to those family members who may be disappointed that they were not elected to the position of president. The authority of the board includes setting the company direction, which is then given to the president who carries it out. This understanding of the authority of the board allows all family members to understand that, as members of the board, they are very much a part of the decision-making process of the company.

Once the board is established, the members can then develop or review the job descriptions for the other key positions in the company. This expanded board of directors approach for family businesses will help eliminate having any one sibling set the guidelines for the others and can also dispel hurt feelings, perceptions of favoritism, and the buildup of more unspeakables. Using structured communication eliminates feelings of favoritism or "I'm being picked on" by any family member. The use of non-family board members can reduce the amount of decisions based purely on family emotion. This board structure allows for more communication as equals, while helping to minimize sidetracking of important issues influenced by personal emotion.

All board members should be evaluated individually for their effectiveness, opinions, and decision-making skills for the benefit of the entire family and family business, by the other members of the board.

When it is deemed necessary, the recommended composition of the board of directors is to include at least two non-family board members, with the total number of the board of directors always at an odd number for tie-breaking votes. The total number of board members would be determined by the number of family members involved in the business.

Some suggested proposed duties for the Board of Directors are:

1. Declare dividends;

2. Elect officers;

3. Approve the budget;

4. Approve all types of acquisitions, expansions, etc.;

5. Approve major equipment purchases;

6. Approve company objectives, business plans, finances, and the philosophy statement for the company;

7. Approve salaries of all key personnel;

8. Approve bonuses to key employees;

9. Determine how family members enter or leave the family business; and

10. Complete performance evaluations of board members.

The parents had advisors when they came into the business, even if it was just each other. Many times, the next generation does not have a spouse that is active in the business. Observation shows that most parents have never communicated the importance of having advisors for the business with their children, therefore the children end up failing as successors due to the lack of suitable advisors.

Teach your children to recognize who their advisors really are. Jim was a young man from Pittsburgh, Pennsylvania, and Ann, a young woman from Morgantown, West Virginia. Both attended West Virginia University where they met, fell in love, and eventually married. After graduation, they moved to Pittsburgh where Jim became a successful financier, compiling wealth and possessions. After a successful career, Jim retired. Ann asked Jim if they could take a trip to West Virginia to visit the areas where she grew up. He agreed. They loaded Jim's Cadillac with luggage and started driving the back roads of West Virginia, enjoying the sunshine and the countryside. After a few hours, Jim decided to start looking for a gas station. Soon he saw a rickety, rundown gas station and decided to pull in. After asking Ann if she wanted anything to drink, Jim got out of the car. On his way into the station, Jim passed an old, bent over man in dirty, dark blue overalls, a greasy baseball cap, with an unshaven, dirt-smudged face, and told him to "fill it up." Once inside, Jim purchased two soft drinks from an unkempt woman behind the counter and started back to the car. He noticed Ann talking excitedly to the old man, who helped her out of the car where they embraced. As Jim approached the car, Ann happily introduced him to Bob, Ann's first real love. After spending time discussing old dates and school acquaintances with Bob, Jim and Ann drove away. As they started out of the station Jim said, "You know honey, if you had married Bob, you would be living in that old gas station selling candy and soda pop from behind the counter." "No dear," Ann said, " If I would have married Bob, he would have been a successful financier and you would be pumping gas!"

As this story demonstrates, understanding the relationships of advisors to success can mean the difference between success and failure.

Never downplay the importance of advisors. Parents, make sure you recognize who your advisors really were and are and communicate to your children the importance and impact they had and have on your success. The successors will not have the same advisors. Guide them in the selection of their advisors. Teach the business heirs to recognize important qualities, characteristics, expertise, and experience advisors can bring to the business.

Adult children need to understand that they cannot operate a successful, profitable business alone. Having experienced, qualified, trusted advisors, while not insuring success, certainly helps reduce the chance of failure.

As stated in the book of Proverbs 15:22 "Plans fail for lack of counsel." An effective board of directors can help solve that problem.

# Never Dictate Solutions

One of the surest ways of creating mistrust in a family business is for either the parents or one of the adult children to dictate what is going to be done to the rest of the family. Dictating solutions dissipates communication as equals and the unspeakables begin to build again.

The best way to overcome the tendency to dictate solutions is by having regularly scheduled business meetings. Previously, meetings were discussed as an effective way to communicate as equals. Meetings are also the most effective way to reach consensus. Meetings must be planned. A necessary meeting component is an agenda of business topics in which every participant has the opportunity to give input. The president should chair the meeting and be strong enough to keep the meeting focused on the agenda topics. Prior to the meeting, each participant should submit to the president any business items they wish to be addressed. The meeting should be no longer than two hours, starting and ending on time. Every family member involved in the business, plus other key employees in the company, should be involved in this meeting. This key person meeting, held at least every two weeks, will help keep all high-level business participants informed. The meeting also will help to eliminate the feeling of individuals being dictated to by other family members.

Another successful communication idea that has been used is to establish separate family meetings to address hurt feelings or misunderstandings that can cloud judgment and damage the business. Preparation is an important component of these meetings. An agenda that addresses personal issues, a timetable, and a rotating chairperson can all be beneficial in making the family meeting meaningful. Treat these separate communication meetings as vital, important, and as necessary to the business as meetings with vendors, accountants, or bankers. If these meetings to address personal issues are treated as unimportant, family members will place them very low on their list of priorities. When that happens, communication will begin to revert to the old techniques that shut off communication and build conflict.

When personal conflict exists among family members, these once-a-month family meetings can help heal relationships. At these meetings, the chairperson is rotated throughout the family. Each person has 5 minutes to bring up anything that is on their mind. The topic does not have to relate to business, it could be about the previous week's personal activities. The chairperson is charged with monitoring the sharing time of each person. If someone has a serious situation to discuss, a consensus vote can suspend other comments and address the one issue. This meeting needs to have very flexible rules, yet be structured enough that it does not become a gripe session. The family meeting works well as a forum to address, discuss, and resolve the unspeakables. The first few meetings may need to be facilitated by a non-family member in order to help make the time productive and start the process of resolving conflict. Family members have found these meetings to be an invaluable tool in reintroducing family members to each other. Family meetings also enable family members to focus on each other as *family* instead of competitors or just another employee of the business. When relationships improve, so does communication and decision making. Issues that are addressed by the entire family, with the good of every family member as the main focus, will give rise to the proper solutions.

# Get the Priorities Right

When family is placed first, the business has a better chance of flourishing. When the business is placed first, family usually suffers. Which comes first: the family or the business? The answer may seem obvious to you. You may be surprised to find how difficult the answer is for many members of family businesses.

A situation occurred where the parents and the oldest adult child were very instrumental in the building and success of the family business. When the time came for the other adult children to enter the business, the active sibling would not allow it as he stated, "There just is not a place for them at the present time." His decision was made not because of the financial condition of the business, as it was successful, but because he felt that his siblings coming into the business may seem unfair to the employees and may affect the year-end bonuses of the key personnel. Family first took a back seat to bonuses and to what others may think.

Family should always be first. Are family members willing to forfeit their relationships with each other in order to keep the business intact? There are many consultants who profess a "save the company at any cost" philosophy that direct families away from each other.

Family or business priorities must be discussed early in the succession planning process. Family first versus business first can be another one of those unspeakables that must be addressed. Everyone may be thinking about it, but are afraid to bring it out into the open because they are unsure of what the answers might be. If there are marked differences in priorities between members of the family, a different direction for estate planning and a new structure to ensure the continuation of the business will have to be devised. Selling the business to keep the family intact now becomes a viable option.

All family members need to consider the "family first" issue very seriously. If decisions concerning the business are going to tear apart family relationships, pit parents against adult children, adult children against each other, and many times, parents against each other siding with different adult children, the question must be asked, "Is the money worth it?" If a person is persistent enough, a job can be found—a family cannot. People get divorced, lose their health and wealth, and, in most cases, family is still supportive. Unfortunately, ego, greed, jealously, envy, and favoritism enter into the hearts of some family members and the only focus is on "my cut" of the family business. There are times when the spouse of a family business member begins pushing their mate to make sure they "get their fair share" from the business and family estate. Usually this happens because the spouse has never been kept up-to-date on how decisions concerning the family business have been made or what agreements the siblings have made.

Family meetings, including all family members not involved in the business, should be held at least once a year. This way, all family members can understand what is going on within the business, how decisions are being made, and why certain people are in certain positions. The purpose of the family business meeting is to share information, about how the company is run, with those family members not involved in the day-to-day operations. The meeting is not for making decisions concerning the direction of the company. While these meetings may not solve the priority problems, they will promote an understanding of the business and open communication between all members of the family, while stressing that the entire family is important to the success of the business. Additionally, the family-first belief that all family members are important to the family business is re-enforced. When the non-active family members have a better understanding of the business and know that family is first, attitudes toward the business by all family members improve.

# Enlighten with Personal Experiences

When children are young, start telling them about the business. Share experiences with them. Give them responsibility and accountability in the business, no matter how small it may seem.

All members of the family business should share business experiences with each other, tell business war stories, and give examples to one another concerning successes and failures. Past failures become unspeakables because no one wants to embarrass another or to admit there are times where failure has occurred. What a waste of meaningful learning experiences! Shared experiences can save family members from making wrong business decisions a second or third time, possibly saving the company money and customers. Share the stories. Time should be scheduled to do this at regular family business meetings. You can learn from each other if you take the time to listen, yes, even to your parents, youngest brother or sister, or spouse.

# Set the Example by your Attitude, Word, and Action

All communication starts with nonverbals—the example that is set. Honest communication gives potential successors the chance to decide whether or not to enter the business. There are many cases where family members do not enter the family business because of the state of the relationship with parents or siblings. Poor relationships are created by poor communication. This decision to not enter the family business may have been different if everyone in the family set the example by being open and honest with each other, by forgiving one another, and by helping each other to succeed.

Parents must be the first to communicate by their actions. They need to *lead by example*. Usually the example will be copied by the children and demonstrated in their personal and business lives. Whether the child will live out the example in a positive or negative way is impacted dramatically by the person whose example was observed and how it was interpreted as being the right choice to follow. First observed is usually the parents, then the siblings. Attitude toward the business, positive outlook, and positive interaction usually are developed by the communication of example. Helping the children and allowing the children to help each other understand the difference between entitlement and responsibility by example can eliminate much of the jealousy that can grow when one person thinks another has received more then their share from dad and mom. The "what is in it for me" feelings can be especially true in family businesses. The feeling of entitlement also appears to have a strong relationship to each person's feeling of being loved in the family. If a specific child or adult child is perceived to get more from the estate of the parents or from the family business in the form of position, ownership, salary, or perks, the other family members may believe they are not as "favored," are less loved, and were not treated fairly and equally. This perception can destroy family relationships and the family business may have to be sold in order to resolve a misunderstood fairness issue.

If the communication *C.H.A.L.L.E.N.G.E.S.* of family businesses are to be properly addressed it must start with the example set by the parents, passed on to the children, then practiced by the children. Parents must place emphasis on the responsibility for open, honest communication with each member of the family.

Just imagine how successful every family and every family business would be if every family member was totally unselfish, put others in the family first, always set a positive example for others to see and follow, helped others to be the very best they could be, and then took joy in the success others achieved.

The communication *C.H.A.L.L.E.N.G.E.S.* of family businesses can be most successfully addressed by properly stirring the pot, addressing the issues, forgiving, loving, and setting the example.

All solutions to problems that face the family business can be found within the family through communication, if family members get the proper help and follow the process.

## C.H.A.L.L.E.N.G.E.S. (the process)

**C**ommunicate as equals

**H**ave a written vision and share it

**A**ddress the "unspeakables"

**L**earn to forgive

**L**et go of the "pecking order"

**E**xpand your board of directors

**N**ever dictate solutions

**G**et the priorities right

**E**nlighten with personal experiences

**S**et the Example by your
Attitude, Word, and Action

# About James R. Kwaiser

James R. Kwaiser founded K&A Business Planners after twenty-five years of assisting family businesses in the areas of operations, executive development, strategic and succession planning. As a result of these experiences, Jim serves on the board of directors of various family businesses.

Jim's professional experience includes positions with regional family businesses and national corporations. His areas of responsibility consisted of: director of business planning and development, director of business operations, general manager, vice president sales, president and owner of various retail and wholesale businesses.

Jim was born and educated in Michigan and now resides with his wife in Bethel Park, Pennsylvania.

Jim's involvement with professional organizations include: vice president of communications of the Pittsburgh chapter of the American Society of Training and Development, a member of the board of directors for the Pennsylvania Speakers Association, a professional member of the National Speakers Association, a member of Pittsburgh Human Resource Association.

# Company Profile

The major focus of K&A Business Planners is to assist entrepreneurs, corporations and family businesses in resolving the personal issues surrounding estate, succession, and strategic planning, while striving to heal relationships. This is accomplished through a facilitation process that is tailored to the specific needs of the clients and includes a process of conflict resolution and executive coaching.

The mission of K&A is to promote the need for all people to *"Set the Example by your Attitude, Word, and Action."*

Clients and workshop attendees of K&A Business Planners include: ANSYS Inc., Bethel Bakery, Inc., Gold & Company, MED Foods, Inc., VCSI, Inc., Koppel Steel Corporation, CKS North America, Henney Family Services, Henne, Inc., Beitler McKee Optical Company, TEDCO Construction Corporation, Hosner Carpet and Interiors, Southwest Bank, Kapusta Financial Services, Filtech, Inc., Westinghouse Air Brake Company, and U.S. Steel.

Jim is available on a local and national level as a facilitator, executive coach, business advisor, and speaker. His topics include:

- **Is there a virus in your family business?** - *C.H.A.L.L.E.N.G.E.S. facing families in business*
- **What's in a team?** - *C.H.A.L.L.E.N.G.E.S. of team building*
- **People shouldn't follow jerks?** - *Leadership by Example*
- **Who's up next?** - *The process of Succession Planning*
- **It's easy to get lost.** - *Strategic planning, a direction for success*
- **The C.H.A.L.L.E.N.G.E.S. of Executive Coaching** - *Coaching for the future*

For more information, contact James R. Kwaiser at:

*K&A Business Planners*
P.O. Box 751
Bethel Park, PA 15102
Phone:(412) 833-8070
Fax:(412) 833-7725
E-mail:   KABIZPLAN@aol.com

# ❖ Chapter 12 ❖

# Taming the Media

*by*

*Cathy Burnham*

Whether appearing in print,
over the radio, or on television,
the key to success is in controlling
how you are perceived by the audience.

—*Cathy Burnham*

Thump-bump. *Thump-bump.* **Thump-BUMP.** *THUMP-BUMP!* No, that's not the sound of an 800-pound gorilla emerging from the media jungle. The resounding din is merely your own panic-pounding heart as that live television interview draws closer. As if the trepidation of a radio station's microphone in front of your face doesn't stir up enough anxiety, now you must contend with television cameras too.

*Skills, not celebrity, build perception in the media.* On any given day we can read or hear elaborate stories of famous people behaving as complete twits! Loving the limelight doesn't mean celebrities develop the skills to reflect depth or good character. After observing people who enjoy national or even local celebrity status stumble in their media appearances, your dread is amplified. Certainly, as a mere mortal, you will surely land flat on your face. That raging media monster will eat you alive. Not so fast!

Experience is the best teacher, but someone *else's* experience is even better than the best. Even the bravest person alive wouldn't stick his head into a wild lion's mouth without some careful training and assurances. Learning from other people's mistakes and successes can save a lot of time and effort.

# Working the Media to Get *YOUR* Story Out

One basic fact can alleviate much of the mystery the media has enjoyed. Whether appearing in print, over the radio, or on television, the key to success is in controlling how you are *perceived* by the audience. Media moguls despise the criticism that they deal in *perception*, rather than *reality*. Consider all the discourse surrounding televised political debates. Rarely is there serious discussion of the practicality of issues. Rather, we are bombarded with commentary on which candidates appeared more at ease, connected with the audience, demonstrated the best or worst body language, or utilized humor the most effectively.

Armed with the right knowledge, you can also take full advantage of the media arena. Good communication rarely results from art or natural talent. Thankfully, success comes from *learnable* skills.

STEP 1. **Determine the exact perception** you want delivered.

STEP 2. **Reinforce that image** in your total presentation.

Consider for a moment how skillfully polished political candidates follow their *own* agendas during interviews, regardless of what questions are asked. The most remarkable ones have been carefully schooled in the importance of landing two or three key punches. If they want to talk about family values, but the interviewer asks about budget plans, the candidates simply swing the answers to their own desired topics… usually in the middle of their first sentence. "Oh, balancing the budget is paramount, which is why I want to help families gain the control they deserve." Listen carefully, because their next words will have nothing to do with finances, but they will have everything to do with the key point they want to deliver.

Working the media in a smooth, non-confrontational manner is simple savvy. In truth, interviewers typically don't even notice when a guest does this. Sadly, most interviewers are not really listening! They usually have their own agendas, and they are busy concentrating or remembering their next planned question. Thus, few interviews become meaningful conversations. Obvious follow-up questions go unasked, and many media interviews are watched and experienced with frustration.

As a business or civic leader, you probably have not had professional coaching nor extensive public communications experience. Your first shot at a media interview can leave you feeling squashed like a bug, totally drained emotionally, and grossly inadequate at skillfully maneuvering through today's media maze. Such intimidation is 100 percent unnecessary. It's high time some of the mystique and magic of the media get dispelled.

- ♦ *You* know more about your topic than does the reporter or news anchor.

- ♦ Reporters may know a little bit about a lot of topics, but they are counting on *you* to give them the real information on the particular subject at hand.

- ♦ *You* are in complete control over how much or how little you share.

- ♦ In most towns and cities the local media is simply seeking information which may be important or relevant to a given topic. *You* are controlling the potter's wheel and can truly shape the content and thrust of an entire news story or program.

♦ Media reporters seek:
   – sound advice;
   – items to interest the audience; or
   – facts that add a new element to a story's focus.

♦ Take care not to transfer your trepidation from watching pointed *national* news broadcasts or prime time investigative reports to the *local* media. While many reporters may envision themselves to be the next Mike Wallace, Peter Jennings, or Diane Sawyer, this is simply not the case. You actually can control the thermostat on the local media hot seat. If you are prepared, you will not need to be so wary.

♦ Even if your local reporters are *trying* to play network or find a controversial twist to a story, don't help them out. In fact, you can completely defuse most potentially explosive situations and turn many into straightforward, if not positive, scenarios.

♦ Recognize from the start that you *will* be misquoted. Realize that comments *will* be taken out of context. Deliberate maliciousness is rarely, if ever, the cause. Usually, time or space restrictions necessitate summarizing your comments. A reporter or editor must make quick judgement calls and make cuts. Landing on the notorious cutting room floor does not mean you weren't brilliant. You simply may have been long-winded.

♦ Right or wrong, you need to accept that even the very best public relations activities and press releases do **NOT** constitute news to the media. If you can relate your announcement to a vital issue of the day, your chances for success in garnering coverage will be greater.

Watch, listen to, and carefully read reports from your local television, radio stations, and newspapers to get a sense of each media outlet's approach to news. You will probably be familiar with the fairness or the slant predominant in your particular city or region and at each individual media source.

Now you can prepare accordingly. First, observe what local programming and stories utilize area business and civic leaders. Consider the following questions and suggestions.

### 1. Are there regular features showcasing local businesses?

• Observe the themes and highlights of such stories.

• Determine your company or organizational strengths in relation to these features. News media outlets are looking for what they call "news *value*." Because news typically centers around very negative situations, there is an extra challenge when you are trying to do something good.

For example, let's say a group is trying to get media help in finding homes for animals. Three hundred dogs in shelters and pounds across a region might not be outstanding enough on its own to get coverage. An individual or group successfully placing two or three dozen of those dogs in wonderful homes might give the story enough news value to get coverage.

To get a media boost in the pet placement effort, some success must have already been realized OR, you can piggyback on another angle of the same story. Check in with authorities to get specific details on the seriousness of the animal abuse problems in your area. A newspaper or broadcasting station jumps at the chance to cover stories that touch people's hearts. When helpless animals are in trouble, people are outraged and anxious for solutions. By being part of the solution, *you* just became part of some serious news value. Emotional and psychological implications can be of enormous help in getting your story told. Simply forget the old adage, "Just the facts, please."

- Brainstorm to see what specialties or unique traits are present in fellow employees or corporate practices.
- Prepare written bullet points, rather than sentences, to emphasize the most vital aspects.
- Target details that could be of particular use or importance to each media outlet's audience.
- Contact each individual media outlet to get correct names and spellings of reporters, producers, writers, and assignment editors for these features.
- Call and/or write directly to each of these people with a carefully prepared news suggestion, emphasizing expertise and uniqueness.

2. **How often do news reports include comments from people in business that reflect public opinion?**
   - Are these individuals interviewed at *their* places of business, at the media outlet, or on the street?
   - Do some of the same people appear on a fairly regular basis?
   - Is there a void you could fill by representing your particular industry or organization?

- Who on your staff might make a good spokesperson to regularly offer comments?
- Prepare a spokesperson background sheet that emphasizes areas of specialty, credibility and experience.
- Arrange a spokesperson introduction with each media outlet.
- Watch for opportunities to get yourself or your spokesperson included or even featured.
- Consider developing a weekly niche. See if there is a potential column your spokesperson could write, or a TV news magazine on which they could be featured as a regular guest.

3. **Are there any avenues for stories on people's involvement in positive, creative, or innovative programs?**
   - Have your staff provide very accurate and specific lists on all civic and business association memberships and activities, boards of directors, church or school involvement, and other volunteer efforts throughout the local community.
   - Record all of your organization's corporate endeavors to build civic pride, develop the community, or expand philanthropic giving.
   - Compare your compiled corporate and staff lists with columns or programs available through the local media.
   - Emphasize outstanding strengths or uniqueness in the above areas.
   - Research which reporters, editors or producers have specific affinities for various programs, themes, or nonprofit organizations.
   - Step forward confidently as a resource for story subjects or interviews.

Not only will the above steps help start you on the path to getting positive media coverage, but you can also use those tips to overcome some of the common stumbling blocks that are highly prohibitive to good exposure. Instead of getting "worked over" by the media, you can "work the media" and truly make the media work for *you*.

Just remember that what *you* know is a good or even *important*, worthy-of-note story will likely be seen by the media as a desire for self-serving, free news coverage. *Both* parties are absolutely correct, but *you* now have some important keys to presenting your story to the media in ways that fit *their* perceived needs.

# Professional Basics or the Top 10 Reasons Business Professionals Lack Credibility on the Air AND Some Solutions!

If you have the right tools, you can get the job done. The frustration over 20/20 hindsight can be avoided if you look carefully at what aspects of media communication you can control right from the start. Working toward the most commonly overlooked basic, here are the ten most frequent oversights.

10. **Unrealistic expectations.** Most people simply lack knowledge of what constitutes news to the media. The tips detailed previously should help you approach reporters with some solid ammunition to make your desired story both newsworthy and compelling.

    The media's responsibility to report the news does not mean believing or understanding what *you* believe is news. They are literally bombarded daily with press releases filled with good intentions but lacking relevance for a news story.

    Remember to use the three key preparation steps detailed earlier in this chapter in helping build news value and relevance into your stories. They center around observation and analysis to determine the:
    
    - existence of positive news features,
    - frequency of public comments on issues and events, and
    - variety in opportunities for coverage.

    Knowing how to get the media's attention does not mean, however, that the challenge has been overcome. You may well get coverage, but you must be ready for less length and depth than you believe is warranted.

    Some media outlets won't give you any coverage at all. One commonly held news philosophy maintains that positive stories are too fluffy and unsubstantial. Delete all adjectives and descriptive phrases from your press releases, and you have a greater chance of attracting the attention of a media source that limits itself to primarily "hard news."

    Also key to dashing unrealistic expectations in media communications is to be realistic in what you expect from your own performance. When you watch a game show on television, all the right answers seem to pop instantly into your head. You probably wonder how some of the contestants even got selected. Like you, they knew all the answers sitting in their living room. The pressures and strangeness of the television studio can change that in an instant.

Don't set yourself up for failure by expecting to be as calm and competent as Barbara Walters and Dan Rather or as witty (or wacky) as Jay Leno and David Letterman. Your success depends as much on the public's PERCEPTION of your message as on your actual words. Controlling that perception is done in large part by observing, learning about yourself, and taking charge.

9. **Appearing unprepared.** Not *looking* totally on top of your game is unnecessary for most business professionals. The needed skills are all learnable.

Some people seem to have a real talent for making media communication look simple and natural, even fun. Practice and lots of it is required to appear spontaneous and comfortable when dealing with reporters, microphones, and cameras. That's true for full-time media professionals, so why should it be any different for you? Just as the most successful people work very hard for what *others* may see as luck, skillful communicators work very hard to appear totally relaxed, natural, and impromptu.

Remember the analogy for appearances: Glide like a duck on the water—smooth and effortless on the surface, but paddle like crazy under the surface. Said more simply, *Fake it 'til you make it.*

Analyze what telltale signs your own body gives when you are nervous. I used to tremble rather visibly. When the notes were written on a stiffer piece of paper or a 3x5" card, the problem wasn't apparent to an observer. Another woman learned her skin turned red and blotchy at the base of her neck when she was particularly nervous. Thinking about how awful it must appear only made matters worse. Wearing a high-collared blouse, rather than anything open-necked, completely masked the physical symptoms of her nervousness.

You also want to listen to an interviewer carefully. Regardless of what is asked, wearing a facial expression of calmness helps.

A common mistake is trying to get an interviewer to reveal the questions in advance. Most people think to do so would be quite clever and helpful in sounding prepared and competent. Actually, the opposite results will occur nine out of ten times. The reason is simply that you can't help but think up answers to those questions in advance. Now you risk not truly listening and potentially not really answering the question when it gets asked. Far worse is the extremely common result that you cram *all* the answers you had thought up into your response to the very first question.

Wear makeup if you will be on camera. This goes for men and women. Every recent President of the United States has worn makeup for television appearances and interviews. Experienced media professionals will not appear on camera without it. You should enjoy the same advantage.

Vital for men and women is a foundation or base makeup with a matte-finish. That means no sparkles. This is also a must for powder, blush or eye shadows.

Typically, every one needs base and powder. Any makeup beyond that is a matter of personal preference. If you are using blush, don't overdo it. However, television lighting removes pink tones from the skin, so adding a little color is important. Be VERY careful of too much color, especially eye shadows. Colors like blue and green on eyelids look very out-dated on camera. Stick with all neutrals. Lipstick should be neutral, but with a hint of color. Use bright red or hot pink ONLY if this is natural for you and your coloring, because it will stand out to the viewers at home. As a general rule of thumb, the darker your skin color, the brighter accent colors you can handle well. Be aware that fair skin is only complimented by soft, muted colors. Conversely, deeper skin pigments benefit from brighter shades and not pastels.

Makeup also evens skin texture and covers any blotches or blemishes. This is only important if you want to have viewers focused on your message and not distracted by physical facial frailties.

8. **Lack of rehearsal.** The breakneck pace of the typical career path causes most business people to focus little or no attention on media practice. A little diligent and focused rehearsal can make all the positive difference in the world.

Rehearsal doesn't mean turning on the home video camera, pretending to do a live television interview, and then viewing the results. It is virtually impossible to set up a parallel scenario since you can't simulate studio lights, cameras and technicians, the pressure of a real interview, and the unnerving presence of a viewing audience of thousands or even millions.

You can practice easily by *observing other people's interviews*. Notice distracting habits as well as good techniques you'd like to emulate. In interviews that cause you to be bored or distrusting of the person, consider what gestures and body language they used. Did their eyes dart; was their jaw clenched; did they seem tense;

was their voice oddly pitched or their pacing stilted? In successful interviews you would like to parallel, consider their posture, vocal inflection, eye contact, facial expressions, verbal pacing, and enthusiasm. Notice you are paying far less attention to the details of what they may have actually said. If you don't like or can't relate to a person, what they say won't matter.

Make notes about techniques and behaviors in media communication that impress you positively. Review those lists regularly. This sort of repeat planting and nurturing of a positive interview image is a rehearsal technique which can be employed anywhere at any time.

Whether rehearsing in your mind or doing a real media interview, a clever and sometimes very important trick is to pretend you are on camera, even when you are not. Your overall demeanor will become natural and easy with perseverance. In roundtable discussions or multi-camera interviews, you could easily appear on camera at any moment, even when you are not speaking. Keeping what is called an "on-camera attitude" means your manner will never mistakenly reflect boredom, nervousness, or anything else negative. This means making sure you are "on" any time a camera is or could be in your vicinity.

With the growing predominance of television, video cameras are a common part of daily life. You may be totally unaware that a camera is anywhere near you. Polishing the skills to communicate gracefully will make them naturally part of your everyday style, so you never need fear that you'll reflect less than favorably on yourself, your company, or your cause. Even if a camera never catches you unaware, your preparedness can help you shine in everyday situations.

7. **Colors, combinations and prints.** Your delivery can be fabulous, but something as simple as the clothing you are wearing can be distracting or unflattering enough to cause people to miss your message. Some colors, combinations and prints that look great in person simply don't photograph well in print or project well on television or videotape.

   Hey, red is a great color! In black and white photographs it appears black. On live television it is striking. However, on videotape the color can seem to ooze or "bleed" into the picture outside its natural lines. That favorite red sweater may not flatter you. Whether in person, on live television or on videotape, the same risk holds true when wearing bold prints or plaids. Both print fabrics and television cameras can add weight. This entire issue is avoided in radio, but it's best to be armed with the knowledge of what works well on television since we are in such a blatantly video-oriented age.

Blues, whether navy or royal, are commonly accepted as the most flattering on-air colors. They are the easiest for technicians to light and the toughest for technology to mess up. Also safe are neutral taupes, tans and grays.

Most cameras today can handle black and white together, but it's still very risky. The challenge comes in the lighting. White looks VERY "hot" under the lights. In other words, white can appear so bright that it washes out details and makes anything dark near it appear even darker. Have you ever taken a photograph of someone with a window or bright sky behind them? Unless you adjusted the camera lens properly, the person in the photograph probably turned out to look more like a dark silhouette against an extremely bright or "hot" background. To compensate for a bright white, a video camera operator closes the camera's iris to let in less light. However, in doing so, a black jacket will be so dark it will have no definition or detail.

The light and dark contrast challenge is important when considering skin tones, too. The darker your complexion is, the more light is required to show your features. The contrast against a crisp white shirt can simply be too sharp. Try a neutral or pastel shade for more predictable success. A particularly fair complexion demands far less light. Lighting inadequacies either way can make you look washed out or deeply shadowed. Normally lighting is set for the interviewer, not the interviewee. Only very sophisticated studios can handle the professional lighting needed to overcome these issues.

Always risky are small prints, especially if there is any level of striping in a fabric. The resulting effect can be dizzying, like fine zebra stripes jumping around or a swarm of bees buzzing. Such distortion in clothing is uncomfortable to watch and distracting to your message. It is best to avoid small prints, herringbone or hounds tooth weaves, or clothing with fine striping.

You should also be careful not to wear jewelry or accessories that could be distracting, too reflective of light, or noisy against a clipped-on lapel microphone. Eye glasses are totally acceptable, but be aware that large lenses show your eyes far better than small lenses. A non-reflective lens treatment is standard for people in broadcasting. The procedure is not too expensive, so you should consider having your eye glasses treated if you may be making frequent on-camera appearances.

6. **Body language faux pas.** There is really no excuse for falling down here. With all the books that have been written on this subject alone, all professionals should be fully aware of the best body language to deliver positive, confident messages.

You weren't born a media pro, and you probably haven't received professional training for on-air media skills. Watch local and national newscasts, magazines and interview programs, and make note of the impression made on you by such things as tone of voice, verbal pacing, vocal pitch, body language, and facial expressions. These aspects quickly make or break the words being used. It's simply a matter of human nature to believe people or doubt them based on the total delivery picture.

A camera can emphasize actions that are perceived negatively. Beads of sweat starting to form on your forehead could well be the result of heat from the studio lights or not using face powder. Revealed in a really close camera shot, sweat translates as nervousness, discomfort or even guilt. Eyes shifting from side to side can make you look untrustworthy, insecure or like a liar. In truth, you probably just didn't know exactly *where* to look, especially when faced with three or four cameras at the same time.

Physical mannerisms are important to keep in check. I tend to talk with my hands.... frequently and fluently. Hold my hands and I'm speechless. Consequently, when I'm on camera, *knowing* that habit gives me the power to control it. You don't want to appear stiff, so this doesn't mean eliminating gestures totally. They simply must be appropriate to the setting, the tone, or theme of the topic. You want to avoid the opposite extreme, too—do NOT choreograph gestures. Your hands need to look natural and relaxed, whether in gestures, or simply at your side or on a table.

Fidgeting with your fingers or jewelry, avoiding eye contact, tapping your feet, or slouching are all mannerisms to avoid. Fiddling with a pen or papers or jingling change in your pocket can be very distracting. When in doubt about where to look, simply look at the interviewer, just as you would look at anyone else with whom you were conversing. You can look into the camera when that is appropriate or comfortable, but most important is keeping your gaze steady and natural. A person who avoids eye contact is usually misconstrued as untrustworthy, lying, or embarrassed. Your goal should be an overall look that projects confidence, authority and comfort. Movements should *always* be deliberate and visually support your message.

Depending on the situation, simply fold your hands on your lap or rest them on the arms of the chair. Consciously make your hands look relaxed. You don't want white knuckle tension making you look as though you are holding on for dear life. If seated at a table, keeping your hands on top of the table always looks much better. Observe some of the news analysis and roundtable programs, and you'll quickly get a full gamut of the good, the bad, and the ugly in posture and body language.

5. **Intimidation.** The technology and pacing of television or radio are foreign to anyone not in the broadcasting business. Naturally there is a certain awe of such an unknown.

Take some comfort in the fact that most people are intimidated by the very mention of a **c-a-m-e-r-a.** Even a microphone can immediately render normally well-spoken people virtually speechless. Exactly where are you supposed to look when on-camera or how should you speak with a microphone? Such technical media factors are outside the scope of the normal business arena and experience.

Ignore the well-intentioned advice to simply "relax and act natural." Save that for your own backyard or kitchen table where there aren't any bright lights, cameras or makeup. In a media interview or appearance, unlike your backyard, you *will* be nervous. You *will* be uncomfortable. Better advice would be to *appear* relaxed and comfortable.

A great tip to help you triumph over technology is to simply think of the camera or microphone as a friendly *eavesdropper*. You are really having a one-on-one conversation with the interviewer. You are not trying to speak to a million people. This need not be as challenging even as speaking on a stage before a thousand people or in a meeting of a dozen people. Focus on the individual doing the interview and block out the rest. Mind over matter is important here.

One of the best ways to "work a camera" is to *ignore* it. Unless the person interviewing you is in a different studio or location, you don't ever have to look at the camera. Look at and relate to that one person with whom you are directly speaking. Let the camera simply eavesdrop.

If your interviewer isn't present physically, then you need to look directly into the camera's lens. Don't think of it as a live television camera or window through which the world is watching. Just think of it as a person's face. Look at that lens as though it were a human. Try to ignore any people, activity, or television monitors around you.

There's a great technique to help you maintain the appearance of calm, clear understanding, regardless of your terror of the technology. Try repeating or restating a question out loud before answering it. This helps buy a few precious seconds of "thought" time and allows you time to format the answer into a complete sentence, directly related to the specific question asked.

4. **Memorization.** Few tendencies can lead to your failure as surely as memorizing statements in hopes of being able to state them precisely.

In the debate over whether to memorize or not to memorize, there is no question. This is not to say don't plan or rehearse extensively. Just do not memorize. You can easily get rattled on-camera and lose your train of thought. If your mind goes blank, you're lost. You know your subject. Your success rate will be substantially higher if you simply share information as it relates to the questions asked.

Write down one- or two-word bullet points to trigger thoughts on key areas you anticipate discussing. It is unlikely that you could think up all the questions a reporter could pose, so don't even try. Try to come up with general themes. Most questions will have answers within those themes. Remember to parallel the savvy politician's technique and get your key points delivered, regardless of the questions asked. If you jot down anything for notes, it should certainly be the one, two, or three facts *you* believe to be most important.

Another good reason not to memorize is that your words could lack any sense of spontaneity. To be believed, your *conviction* and *sincerity* must be *center stage*. Listeners and viewers will hear it in your voice. They will pick that up faster than whether or not you used just the right term or fit in all the information you had planned to with regard to a particular question.

3. **Blabber mouthing.** Good media communication requires not talking too much. However, you most likely were never schooled in how to talk in "sound bites." That's how the media refer to the spoken comments they actually broadcast from any given interview. Typically, a fifteen- or twenty-second comment is perfect for a broadcast sound bite.

To talk in sound bites, narrow down your thoughts into two or three tightly focused themes or ideas. Then, express those ideas in just one or two sentences.

Related thoughts should be saved for use in answers to follow-up questions. If you delve into important supportive sentences as things pop into your mind, you will not get those two or three primary points into twenty seconds. Remember, you are more likely to end up included in a report if you made good points very succinctly. Less is more, unless you're a guest, by choice, on a "tell-all" talk show. At all costs you need to avoid the tendency to tell your entire story. Plus, if there is even the slightest controversial angle, you could end up talking yourself into a corner and getting undesired negative publicity.

In media communication of any sort, informal, everyday language is most dynamic. You should never use specific industry jargon or buzz words in an interview that will be seen, heard, or read by people outside that particular field. Even if you are trying to educate, choosing terms that are easily understood by the broadest possible audience will positively impact your success. Early in my broadcasting career, a news director advised me not to describe the *choreography* in a musical theatre premiere, but to tell how they *danced*. What initially sounded like silly semantics to me, quickly made sense when I realized he was teaching me to **simplify**.

Success is also greatly boosted when you identify and limit your objectives. You can't possibly tell a broadcast audience *everything* about your industry, event, product, service or good cause in one interview. Time-tested communications lessons are reminders that content is important, but leaving the audience *wanting more* is vital. That doesn't mean leaving unanswered questions. You want to give a complete picture, but you will enjoy greater success if that picture has a distinct focus rather than a broad, all-encompassing spectrum.

2. **Looking and sounding nervous and insecure.** Unfortunately, this translates as lacking knowledge, leadership, and credibility. On the other hand, if you *look* and *sound* honest, sincere, and comfortable, you sparkle.

## "A word fitly spoken is like apples of gold in pictures of silver."
—*Bible, Proverbs 25:11*

A bad scenario is the stuff of which nightmares are made. Your nerves take over; those old "ums" and "uhs" leap gleefully into your speech patterns. Your volume drops off; no matter how hard you try to adjust the controls, there is no response. Your voice escalates in pitch; your pace quickens dramatically; you desperately try to fill every single moment of air space. And, oh, how your mouth feels so closely akin to a sand box! How can you possibly sound confident and credible when you are struggling for survival?

To really level the playing field, you must first remember that media communication is NOT brain surgery. You aren't talking life or death here… it only *feels* that way. Butterflies in your stomach are to be expected. You just want to get them all flying in formation.

For the time being, try to forget all the glitz and glitter that have convinced John Q. Public that television is somehow awe-inspiring. You are simply in a room with a few people, and you're answering a few questions about a topic you know thoroughly.

Don't get all wrapped up in a panic attack over a misguided belief that millions of people are watching and hanging on your every word. A tiny handful of people actually pay attention. A few others focus a bit more if there's a special interest in your topic, or your haircut or the jacket you're wearing. Your life will NOT be destroyed if you open your mouth and absolutely nothing comes out.

Even in volatile scenarios, practice keeping your voice in control. This is an important key and can easily be accomplished whether or not stage and screen acting is your forte. *Everyone* can and DOES act. Growing up, I remember my mother scolding me loudly over one troublesome thing or another I'd done. If the telephone rang, her voice and tone shifted immediately to a melodic peaches and cream, as though everything was just as smooth as could be. She figured the caller didn't need to know she was contending with a hyperactive brat.

Remember to take steps to help you *appear* less nervous:
- Breathe naturally. When nervous, breaths tend to be short and shallow. Take a moment to concentrate on a couple of long, deep breaths.
- Always have a glass of water nearby, just in case of dry mouth or a sudden coughing fit.
- Never chew gum or have a hard candy or cough drop in your mouth during an interview. Nervousness could exaggerate your chewing, and a microphone could pick up the sound of candy clattering against your teeth.

In polishing your technique, remember to slow down your speaking pace and keep your vocal pitch low. Nerves can make you rush and cause your voice to get much higher. Studies show that lower-pitched voices are more comfortable for listeners and are taken more seriously.

You also want to avoid other behaviors which have been found to be highly annoying. Topping most people's lists is interrupting while others are talking. This is one reason it's sometimes frustrating to watch roundtable news analysis television programs. It seems everyone gets talking at once until shouting is all that can be heard. There may be good points being made, but who will know? A good combative technique is to *speak very slowly* to get the floor back and then actually speak more quietly and calmly than others have been. Be sure your point is made immediately and succinctly.

Talking too softly or too loudly can also be annoying. Typically you should try to match your volume level with that of the interviewer. Audible and comfortable, but not annoying or overpowering are good guidelines.

Mumbling is also frequently criticized. If you want people to listen, you must be careful not to make them **work** at it. Basically, you don't want your mouth to get lazy, which is a natural tendency. You want to accurately and naturally enunciate your words. Tape recording your voice and having other people listen specifically for critical areas can be helpful.

Try to detect potential challenges like frequently using "filler" or "thought" words, like "uh," "well," or "um." Starting many sentences with such words is a bad habit that's easy to develop. Concentration and practice can help you substitute a slight pause for the "uh" before a statement. Something this simplistic can immediately make you sound far more articulate and professional.

Another pattern you would certainly want to break is the misuse of inflection, especially at the ends of sentences. Particularly in unfamiliar situations, there is a tendency to let your voice go *up* at the ends of sentences. This inflection is natural and correct only when asking a question. If you do it at the ends of *statements*, however, you sound uncertain or insecure.

The right tone in your voice, appropriate inflection, comfortable pacing, and pausing effectively give you the icing on the cake when media impact is needed. This is very useful in directing public perceptions in everyday business life, and it is vital when situations call for crisis communication intervention.

1. **No counsel or bad counsel.** The number one reason people lack credibility on the air is simply listening to the wrong people. Never mistakenly believe that asking for advice shows weakness or a lack of leadership. Input helps, and it doesn't always have to come from an outside source. Someone on your own staff may have tremendous savvy in this area.

When it comes to media communications, executives are like celebrities and need producers. Left to their own devices, even local "stars" and corporate hotshots can fizzle fast on the air. Why should you risk your credibility and hard-earned community respect by going into a broadcast media situation without counsel. As carefully as you would select counsel for legal or medical situations, you should choose COACHING for media matters. People are traditionally least objective about themselves, so seek out people whose opinions and skills could be very valuable to you.

A good communications coach can quickly analyze your personal delivery style and prescribe foolproof fidget busters, exercises, and technique tips to dramatically elevate the level of your *confidence* and *performance*... without making you appear "coached." In my own speech coaching work, a primary goal is to retain each individual's personal style. If, after a client's public or media appearance, someone questions whether or not they have been professionally "coached," "trained," or "taking lessons," I will give them their money back.

I also guarantee complete client confidentiality. While I would enjoy the benefits of passing around a who's who list of my individual clients, to protect the illusion of naturalness I've worked so hard to create with them, I print no such list.

There is certainly no shame in studying a field to improve skills, but there is a distinct benefit to not announcing your speaking or media training. Certain ingenuous affectations seem to go hand-in-hand with speech training. Anyone who's ever suffered through the resulting presentations is fearful of the cookie-cutter approach to everything from posture and gestures to delivery style.

If you ask other people to review tapes of your previous media interviews, take care to ask people who *know* broadcasting. Our families and coworkers would have your same anxieties about facing the media. They are more apt to praise the job you did on the basis that *they* don't think they could have done as well. Sometimes they're just so proud to see you on TV that their objectivity is clouded. Get unbiased viewpoints and solid input. Also, it helps to compare tapes of your interviews with other people's media interviews that you recognize as very good.

Any coaching you receive, whether from an inside or outside source, should be sensitive to you, your mannerisms, your corporate and community stature, and your personality. The timing of your development should be now. Preparation in advance of any situation is helpful. If you suddenly get thirty minute's notice of the arrival of a television news crew, you are at a distinct disadvantage, unless you have already taken steps to be ready.

Ignoring the nay-sayers is an important key in taking counsel on your media communication skills. One of life's greatest satisfactions comes from doing precisely what people say you *can't* do. Surround yourself with people who say you *can*. Observe good and bad media appearances made by others. Take notes. Analyze what you see and perceive. Get coaching. Ask questions. Rehearse. And lighten up. Don't be too hard on yourself. If you are taking the necessary steps to present yourself and your ideas in the best possible light, you are way ahead of the vast majority of people.

# Bearing the Bad News

**❝No man delights in the bearer of bad news.❞**

*—Sophocles'* Antigone  *440 B.C.*

From time to time, you will inevitably get placed in the undesirable position of bearing bad news. When the message you must deliver is not a favorable one, remember the old expression, "Never let them see you sweat." Bring bad news, and people will listen, but they will also blame the messenger. Bring good news, and people will praise you, even if you had nothing to do with creating the glad tiding. Consider your local meteorologist…. cheered when the forecast is favorable and jeered when it spoils your outdoor plans or travel.

Making points without making enemies has long been recognized as the true art of tactful persuasion. BRIEF anecdotes or light humor can soften a tough stand, while still getting your points across. Better still is to make some obviously popular statements that readers, listeners or viewers would most likely agree with automatically.

For example, assume a tax battle wages in your city over funding for schools. The voters are sharply divided. You've been asked your opinion by the local TV reporter who's now holding a microphone in your face. You want what's best, but you'd hate to say anything to alienate half your customers. You could say something like, "All parents in this town want their children to get the best possible education. All teachers also want to have the most positive impact possible on the students. If we, as a community, can first recognize we all have the exact same goals, we'll realize we're on the same side. Then we can find some compromises to help us all achieve these goals. We all must be willing to give a little to gain a lot. The whole community can then win… both today and in the long run." Like a crafty politician, you've said nothing but precisely what everyone believes. In such cases, you can be perceived as level-headed: the rational mind emerging from the chaos. Waiting for the facts is logical. You gain nothing if you offer frivolous or controversial speculation. At the same time, you can speak up without exacerbating emotional overreaction.

Of course, if a persistent reporter is actually *listening*, you could get pressed for details or suggestions. Side step the dangers here by deferring to others. "Oh, I don't pretend to have all the right answers. No *one* person probably does. Like the other thoughtful, caring people in this town, I look forward to an open-minded discussion of the various ideas and proposals our school board, teachers, and parents' association are developing."

In *"Le Misanthrope,"* written in 1666, Moliere said, "He's a wonderful talker, who has the art of telling you nothing in a great harangue." Such a statement doesn't mean you should *never* take a stand. But when you *do* take a stand, you should *take full control* over *what* you say and *how* you say it. The choice is yours, not the reporter's. Media members cannot force you to say anything. You can choose to take a firm stand at any time. When you do, you are best served by simply stating your position, never apologizing for it. Be honest; be sincere; be forthright. Tact may be preferred, however, your opinion or statement could reflect on your entire company or organization. You must be ready and able to take full responsibility for your statements. Make no excuses.

No one wants to sound like a hot head. Be sure to have thought out your stand clearly ahead of time. When you come from a position of integrity and fairness, honesty and compassion, and you treat people as you want to be treated, those around you can more easily embrace your statements to the media, *even* if there is controversy and bad news.

# Making the One-on-One Connection

When you want to *connect* with an audience, two basic philosophies prevail in broadcasting. One says you are talking to the masses, the entire city, the state, the whole country, the world. The other says you should speak directly, as though to just one person. Typically, people don't watch television or listen to the radio with a crowd. While television ratings services may show viewer satisfaction with huge numbers watching a particular program, no individual wants to be perceived as a mere speck in some huge, faceless throng. When looking at television viewing habits, in fact, national media surveys show that half the audience is watching television *alone*. People often listen to the radio in cars alone or through headsets while jogging, biking, riding the bus, or walking. People certainly read newspapers and magazines alone, unless plagued by others who insist on over-the-shoulder reading.

As a media communicator, you show far greater respect and appreciation for your audience if you address them one-on-one. While either philosophy is acceptable, the one-on-one choice is wise, especially for the *non*professional. Pros, such as sports commentators, are well-versed in talking to masses and can usually make it seem more palatable than someone less experienced.

Regardless of your approach, projecting friendliness is one of the most important things you can do. A smile is easy to see on your face *and* hear in your voice.

Unless you want to risk seeming insincere, your entire *look* and *sound* must be *consistent*. If you are at all nervous, you may tend to get a furrowed brow, distinct frown, or a stiffly set jaw. A sincere, pleasant and not overdone smile helps give the appearance of calm and confidence. Especially in an interview dealing with controversy, your best interests are always served when you *stay cool and conversational*. Smiling in such a negative scenario would be inappropriate and could cause you to look callused or insensitive.

Television and radio are far more intimate settings than a convention hall stage. You need to be conscious of your speaking **tone**, or you could get too enthusiastic and start pontificating rather than talking *with* people. Staying conversational is also aided when you use short, punchy sentences, rather than running all your thoughts together.

Right or wrong, like it or not, the broadcasting business really IS show business. Turning in a good performance means polishing good information with good technique. You never want to get caught dishing out baloney disguised as food for thought. Substance is important, but the image you create is more lasting and has a stronger impact.

In every decade, professionals considered to be "broadcast giants" continue to grow as communicators. The personal development job is never done. One-hundred percent polished perfection is never expected nor achieved, so put aside that pressure.

You also need not fear that anything you say to the media will probably come out all wrong and be headed for the next compilation of television bloopers. Henry Ford's famous line, "Whether you think you can or think you can't, you're *right!*" hits the mark, because it all comes down to ATTITUDE.

Demystifying the media is most easily accomplished by getting your attitude clear. There's no mystery and no magic. Right or wrong, perception is everything. You want listeners or viewers to hear and see you and your message clearly and accurately. Because humans are subjective and highly judgmental, you want to present yourself in the best possible manner.

If you want to tame the media, you must train yourself. The real trick is to enjoy the process, the learning journey. The magic in the media is in YOU, because YOU CAN BE a great media communicator.

# About Cathy Burnham

Dubbed *The Morale Booster*, Cathy Burnham is a professional member of the National Speakers Association and is listed in *Who's Who Among Professional Speakers* in America.

In 1995, she became a founding director for First Alliance Bank and Trust Company. She now serves as Senior Vice President and Director of Marketing and is helping to develop a nationwide community bank system.

A long list of credits includes writing, producing and hosting more than 300 televised *New Hampshire Minutes* on the State's history, culture and folklore. An avid good news enthusiast, Cathy was tapped to write the *Life Matters* column in *New Hampshire Living* magazine. Work as an adjunct faculty member has her teaching both persuasive speaking and video communications to college students. She is also featured in the **Miss America Cookbook,** published in 1995.

Recognized as a versatile broadcaster and award-winning journalist since 1983, Cathy's news coverage has ranged from presidential primaries to the opening of the Berlin Wall. Cathy also hosted and produced a highly rated, live studio audience talk show. She was named the Granite State's favorite media personality for eight consecutive years.

Since 1983, she has been the anchor host for New Hampshire's national award-winning Easter Seal Telethon/Celebration. In 1997, she also began hosting the nationally televised Easter Seal program from New York City. Honored over the years by numerous organizations as Woman of the Year, Cathy is a strong supporter of charitable work and actively promotes the *First Love America* business program to benefit not-for-profit organizations.

# Company Profile

IDS is a multi-faceted communications program, founded by Cathy
Burnham, which focuses on decisive development of a powerful competitive edge through speaking and media skills mastery. A natural
extension of her broadcasting career, the development of fellow anchors
and reporters initially exposed Cathy's training prowess.

The success of Image Development Systems came from customer-
tailored programs with long-term impact. Coaching fulfills the newest
management prerequisites of solid media and speaking skills. Standard
training packages include:

- **Complete Communications:** media savvy and public speaking
  polish for a highly tangible business advantage.
- **Attitude Development:** techniques to predetermine success, shape
  public and personal perceptions, and build leadership skills.
- **Public Appearance Management:** strategy development, making
  events effective, and community service with sincerity.
- **Piggyback Public Relations:** making press releases positively
  newsworthy, becoming "the" expert in demand, and getting repeat
  exposure.

High energy, high content keynote, and motivational presentations are
fully customized with powerful, practical messages that champion the
American "Can-Do" spirit. Speaking from experience, Cathy Burnham's
talks are positive and upbeat, focusing on action and solutions. In addition
to speaking and media skills, popular topics and components include:

- *The Future is in Good Hands... YOURS!*
  (Ten confidence commandments)
- *Twisting Like a Pretzel Without Losing Your Salt*
  (Key elements to cope with change)
- *Growing GREAT Leaders*
  (Developing leaders at all levels)
- *Kowabunga Dude! Riding the Age Wave*
  (Business success with aging Baby Boomers AND Generation X)

*Image Development Systems*
*First Alliance Bank and Trust Company*
1750 Elm Street, Suite 102
Manchester, NH 03104
Toll-free:  1-800-568-0568
Phone:  (603) 624-6676
Fax:  (603) 624-6717
E-mail:  www@firstalliance.org

# ❖ Chapter 13 ❖

# Your Voice—
# Your Signature

*by*
*Judy Tobe*

Your voice IS your signature—
it presents your ideas and your personality
to a judgmental world.

—*Judy Tobe*

T he authors of the previous chapters have addressed subjects that are of utmost importance as they relate to the topic of business communication. You have learned about understanding personality types, about the importance of asking the right questions and about the necessity of knowing what to say and when to say it. Armed with this information on business communication skills you have thought about, maybe even rehearsed, what you are going to say at your next meeting, business introduction or media interview. All of your efforts can be undone, however, unless you have also given thought to how your voice sounds when delivering your message.

You can be confident and always know what you are talking about, yet your voice may send a very different message to others. You can be very fond of another person, respect, admire, even love them, yet your voice inadequately or incorrectly reflects such emotions. You can be pleased, angry, excited, worried or sad, but your voice tells a different story. The voice is your primary tool of communication.

An inappropriate or inadequate voice can counteract all the learning and rehearsing of other communication skills. What you sound like is what people think you are. For example, a man who may make others edgy at a board meeting because his voice sounds nasal and tense may be viewed by colleagues as nervous and jumpy. Or the woman who speaks in such a high pitched, child-like voice that nobody takes her seriously. Nancy, for example, is a realtor who spoke in a "little girl" voice that she believed was the voice that she was stuck with. In fact, Nancy had acquired this voice as a child because her parents had reinforced it by always telling her that it was cute. Later, her dating companions continued to reinforce it by saying they found her voice to be sexy. In business interactions, Nancy's clients questioned her credibility and her sales were directly affected. Once Nancy learned that this voice was not permanent and discovered techniques to use her optimum pitch, people paid attention to what she said and respected her opinions.

YOUR VOICE IS YOUR SIGNATURE—it presents your ideas and your personality to a judgmental world. Is your voice communicating what you want it to? Does it project confidence, authority, sincerity, enthusiasm?

# Factors Affecting Your Vocal Signature

How you sound and the message you communicate is related to a number of factors:

1. The amount of relaxation or tension in your voice.
2. Your ease of breathing.
3. Loudness of your voice.
4. Pitch of your voice.
5. Precision of your articulation.
6. Resonance of your voice.
7. Rate of your speech.
8. Your use of pauses and intonation.

Together these voice and speech characteristics comprise what is distinctly YOUR VOICE—YOUR SIGNATURE. The most important thing to understand is that you are not stuck with the voice you use. One often assumes that their voice is something they were born with and that it cannot be changed. Most inappropriate or inadequate voices, aside from those voices that are the result of a physical inability/disability, are related to things you do or fail to do that prevent a better voice from being heard or that prevent you from communicating who you are or what you want to say.

A conservative estimate is that 25-30 percent of adults (without a voice disorder; i.e., one that needs to be treated for medical reasons), are unhappy about the way their voices sound and with the way their voices affect their careers and social lives. Take the following voice self-awareness test to determine if you have a voice problem that may affect your ability to communicate affectively.

1. Are you often short of breath when you speak?
2. Is it difficult to control nervousness in your voice when you speak?
3. Is there tightness or soreness in your throat after prolonged speaking?
4. Do you clear your throat often?
5. Do you think that your pitch is too high or too low?
6. Is your voice monotonous and/or uninteresting?
7. Do others often misunderstand what you say?
8. Do you have a nasal-sounding voice?
9. Does your voice get tired as you use it, often sounding weak and distant?
10. Does your voice sound dry and scratchy after prolonged speaking?

11. Do people on the telephone think that you are younger or older than you are?
12. Do people have difficulty hearing you occasionally?
13. Do people on the telephone think you are of the opposite sex?
14. Do you speak too quickly or too slowly?
15. Do you use adequate pauses and intonation?

If you answered "yes" to any of the above questions, you are using a voice that is preventing you from being effective in your business and personal communication.

Again, you CAN do something to change your YOUR VOICE—YOUR SIGNATURE.

There are many factors, both physical and environmental, that can adversely affect your voice. You must be aware of these factors in order to minimize their negative effects and change those that can be changed.

## Noisy Environments

Certain environments such as cars, airplanes, restaurants, social gatherings and night clubs are inherently noisy. Special care needs to be taken to use your voice less often in these adverse speaking situations. Alternatives include facing the listener, overarticulating rather than increasing loudness, slowing the speaking rate to avoid the need for repetition, and speaking at a normal pitch. A tendency exists to raise pitch and loudness when background noise levels are high. A normal or slightly lower pitch often cuts through the ambient noise, naturally decreasing the need to speak more loudly.

## Humidity

Humidity, either too low or too high, can affect the vocal mechanism. In regions where relative humidity is low, special attention to improving environmental hydration is needed. The relative humidity on airplanes tends to be very low and special precautions should be taken. Superhydrate prior to and during air travel. That means drink a ton of water! Use a humidifier and travel with one, if possible. Minimize talking on the plane and increase humidity in hotel rooms by running a hot shower and letting the steam permeate the whole room.

When humidity levels are too high, too much moisture is added to the airway causing continuous throat clearing. An easy solution is to use air conditioners and furnaces with dehumidifiers.

# Fatigue

General body fatigue manifests itself in a weak voice. Optimal vocal efficiency cannot be achieved when you are tired. Therefore, try to get more rest and a full compliment of sleep prior to increased use of your voice. Be particularly careful of jet lag. In order to counter the effects of jet lag, allow time for a short nap prior to important speaking engagements whenever possible.

# Hydration

A good voice depends upon careful attention to hydration. Adequate hydration is accomplished by drinking water every time you eat, keeping water close at hand at all times and avoiding caffeinated beverages, e.g., coffee, soda and tea, especially before heavy voice use. In addition, be aware of voice-changing side effects due to dryness caused by over-the-counter and prescription drugs. Check with a physician or pharmacist to obtain information as to whether or not an over-the-counter or prescription drug that you are, or will be taking, can affect hydration.

In addition to physical and environmental factors affecting your voice, your own vocal abuse and misuse will cause many voice problems.

# Throat Clearing

Excessive mucus, associated with gastric reflux, postnasal drip and allergies, often causes constant throat clearing. More often, however, throat clearing results from habit rather than need. Trauma to the vocal folds caused by clearing your throat should be eliminated. Listed below are useful alternatives.
1. Dry swallow.
2. Take small sips of water.
3. Use a "silent cough;" i.e., push air through the throat as if producing an "h" sound. The strong airflow blows mucus off the vocal folds.
4. Pant lightly, then swallow.
5. Hum lightly.
6. Laugh gently or giggle, then swallow.
7. Talk through the mucus. The natural vibration of the vocal folds may rid them of any secretions.

## Grunting or Noisy Vocalization

Grunting when lifting or exercising creates a forceful and traumatic closure of the vocal folds. An example of grunting is very obvious when watching professional tennis. Instead, exhale slowly on the exertion phase of any exercise and close the vocal folds gently prior to initiating each exercise such as a sit up or weight lift.

## Yelling, Screaming or Loud Talking

Yelling or screaming is often used as an expression of anger, frustration, elation or joy. Take time to educate family members about the harmful effects of yelling and screaming and change this abusive behavior all together as a family activity. Try to use facial expression to express emotion. Be aware of how much loud talking you can tolerate before experiencing vocal fatigue and change your mode of expression from verbal to nonverbal. Finally, use soft, well-articulated speech.

## Whispering

Forced or "loud" whispering is harmful to the vocal folds. Avoid whispering at all times in order to prevent damage to the vocal mechanism.

## Excessive Talking

Outgoing people sometimes find that excessive talking is a difficult habit to curb. Moderation can be achieved by using several strategies. First, schedule vocal rests. Observe 20 minutes of silence two or three times per day. Next, set the beeping signal of a watch to sound every ten minutes. Use the beeping to create awareness of the amount of time that you are using your voice and modify your vocal activity accordingly. Finally, limit interrupting others in conversation—be a good listener. Listening is not only an important communication skill but an important tool for decreasing your tendency to talk excessively.

## Poor Posture

Poor sitting and standing posture can interfere with good voice production. Posture which adversely affects your voice includes rounding the shoulders forward, protruding the abdomen and holding the chin down.

Poor posture prevents adequate breath support. The result is often a weak and hoarse voice.

The success of your communication is also affected by additional factors.
1. Increased tension in the neck and face.
2. Inappropriate breathing patterns.
3. Inappropriate use of loudness.
4. Inadequate pitch.
5. Misplaced resonance.
6. Misarticulation.

These six factors constitute several separate yet related processes. Speech processes include respiration, phonation, resonance and articulation. Interaction and integration of these processes create efficient and effective use of the voice. You will then be able to present yourself, your product or your service in a manner that accurately reflects who you are. You may have a vocal characteristic that you do not like but may be unaware of how bad your voice really sounds or may assume that nothing can be done about it. Such beliefs will cost you a lot in both social and business situations. Paul was a sales representative for a pharmaceutical company. He had always been in sales and had changed jobs frequently. He attributed these job changes to the nature of the business. When Paul started a new position he always enjoyed initial success, but then his prospects would slowly begin to lose interest. Paul's clients were "too busy" to see him, they failed to return his phone calls and he had difficulty scheduling appointments. When Paul complained to his sales manager that, "Nobody wants to talk to me anymore," he was shocked to hear his boss' response. "Maybe they don't want to listen to you." After completing a series of voice coaching sessions which focused on integration and appropriate use of the vocal processes, Paul found that his clients were happy to talk to and listen to him.

# The Processes of Speech and How to Create Your Signature Voice

## Relaxation

Relaxation, although not a speech process, is an important prerequisite to success in mastering the four speech processes.

Muscular tension, especially in the throat, prevents a pleasant and pain-free speaking voice. Use relaxation techniques to reduce muscular tension and to energize those muscles used in voice production. The goal of the following exercises is to teach you to speak without unnecessary tension in the head and neck area. The first step is to become aware of the presence of tightness and pain in the head and neck region. Then perform effective relaxation techniques to alleviate tension. The following relaxation exercises should not be done by anyone who has a history of head and/or neck injuries, back pain, spinal cord problems or cervical arthritis.

## Relaxation Exercises

### 1. Head Rolls

Sit in a chair with both feet placed flat on the floor, or on the floor with your back straight and your legs crossed Indian fashion.

a. ○ Inhale and bring your head forward, touching the chin against the chest.

○ Roll head slowly to the right.

○ Open mouth, relax jaw and look at the ceiling.

○ Exhale and roll head back around to the front—let the mouth close.

○ Repeat to the left.

b. ○ Look over the right shoulder as if there was something behind you and hold for 10 seconds, feeling the stretch of the muscle.

○ Look over the left shoulder and hold for 10 seconds.

### 2. Tensing and Releasing (Progressive Relaxation)

Tensing and releasing exercises involve contracting a particular part of the body and then slowly relaxing it in order to appreciate the feeling of relaxation.

Sit in a chair with both feet placed flat on the floor, or on the floor with your back straight and legs crossed Indian fashion.

### Jaw Relaxation

a. ○ Inhale through the mouth, hold your breath and close the mouth.

○ Press the lips together tightly.

○ Press the upper and lower molars together tightly.

○ Press the tongue up onto the palate.

○ Hold for five seconds and release.

b. ○ Inhale and hold your breath.

○ Open your mouth very wide.

○ Hold for five seconds and release.

### Chin and Throat Extension and Compression

a. ○ Inhale and hold your breath.

○ Point chin straight up toward the ceiling.

○ Hold for five seconds and release.

b. ○ Inhale and hold your breath.

○ Bring your chin to your chest.

○ Hold for five seconds and release.

*Continue by tensing and relaxing any muscle where tension is found.*

After doing the above exercises several times to establish the contrast between tension and relaxation, you will be able to achieve the same feeling of relaxation if it is required quickly. Being in a relaxed state is important in many speaking situations. For example, when being introduced to speak, when introducing yourself at a networking event, or when giving an impromptu report. Begin by breathing in, holding your breath for a few seconds, concentrating on any tension in the mouth, jaw, throat and upper body and then releasing your breath and feeling the relaxation.

## Respiration

You are born with an innate ability to breathe correctly for the production of normal speech. If you watch an infant breathe quietly, the abdomen expands when inhaling and the abdominal muscles contract during vocalization such as crying. Adults often lose the natural ability to breathe effortlessly. You can take conscious control of your breathing when you speak.

Unfortunately, particular breathing habits have been developed during speech which fail to produce voice very effectively. There are two types of breathing which cause problems. The first is upper thoracic breathing. Upper thoracic breathing means that the upper part of the rib cage is lifted and expanded as you inhale. The second, clavicular breathing, involves actually lifting the shoulders and collar bone to increase the chest cavity size and cause inhalation. Both of these breathing styles interfere with adequate speech production. Inappropriate breathing patterns cause laryngeal tension, can reduce the potential for good resonance quality, and increase the difficulty in controlling speed and duration of the exhalation. The effect of inappropriate breathing patterns is a hoarse, muffled voice and/or decreased loudness when speaking. Instead, abdominal/diaphragmatic breathing is the pattern that results in the production of normal speech. In abdominal/diaphragmatic breathing, the shoulders and upper chest remain still while the lower abdominal wall and lower ribs expand.

1. **Breathing Exercises—Non-speech Tasks**
   a. ○ *Checking for abdominal/diaphragmatic breathing*
      ○ Place one hand on the chest and one hand on the abdomen.
      ○ Inhale to the count of eight, exhale to the count of eight.
      ○ Monitor the chest to ensure no movement is present.
      ○ The hand on the abdomen should rise on inhalation and fall on exhalation.
   b. ○ *Developing abdominal support*
      ○ Inhale to the count of eight.
      ○ Hold your breath using abdominal muscles, not the throat.
      ○ Release the air.
   c. ○ *Developing controlled exhalation*
      ○ Begin with slow, steady, abdominal breathing with one hand each on chest and abdomen to monitor movement.
      ○ Inhale for eight counts.
      ○ Stop the inhalation using the abdominal muscles, not the throat.
      ○ Produce a hissing sound "sssss" very softly, slowly and steadily.
      ○ Sustain "sssss" for as long as you can.
      ○ Practice until exhalation can be sustained for 20 seconds.

2. **Breathing Exercises—Speech Tasks**
   a. ○ *Controlled speaking*
      ○ Breathe in through the mouth quickly for one count.
      ○ Count to five as you exhale slowly and with control.
      ○ Immediately take a quick breath and continue counting to 10.
      ○ Take another quick breath and continue counting to 15.
      ○ Take a quick breath and count from 1-15 as you exhale.
      ○ Count from 1-50, this time inhaling when it feels comfortable.
      ○ Make sure that the abdomen and lower ribs are expanded. Begin the exhalation low in the abdomen. Ensure that there is no upper chest movement.
   b. ○ *Phrasing*
      ○ Phrasing is an important component of using appropriate breath control and support in ongoing speech. Begin practicing with short sentences and then move to paragraphs. Any book or magazine can be used as a source for sentences and paragraphs.

○ Mark the material for appropriate places to pause. Any natural punctuation such as a period, semicolon or comma is a good place to breathe. A poor place to breathe is between an adjective and a noun; i.e., "New York is a big (breath) city," or between a verb and an adverb; i.e., "The noise was really (breath) loud."

○ Read material without marking it then practice phrasing using adequate breath control and support.

○ Use a tape recorder to listen to yourself. If the phrasing did not sound natural, try the sentence or paragraph again pausing in another place.

# Phonation

Phonation is the process of creating vocal sound by passing the exhaled air between the vocal cords and causing them to vibrate. Creating vocal sound, which involves increasing loudness and changing pitch, must be done without creating tension in the larynx.

### 1. Loudness

Creating a louder voice is accomplished by coordinating relaxed phonation with an increase in the speed of the exhaled air.

a. ○ *Relaxation of the larynx*

○ Place your thumb on one side of the larynx and two or three finger tips of the same hand on the opposite side.

○ Relax your throat and jiggle it from side to side.

○ Begin to hum and keep jiggling the larynx—your voice will quiver.

○ If you can shake the larynx easily while humming you know that your throat is relaxed and that you are not pressing your vocal cords together.

○ Increase the loudness of your voice by increasing the speed of movement of the exhaled air with increased contraction of the abdominal muscles.

○ If you are able to continue shaking the larynx easily while getting louder, you will know that you are avoiding any throat tension. If you are tightening your vocal cords, you will not be able to continue the shaking.

○ Practice single words ten times each, gradually increasing the loudness on each word.

○ Practice short (four- to five-word) sentences again gradually increasing the loudness within the sentence.

○ Decide which word or words in the short (four- to five-word) sentences carry the important meaning and increase the loudness only on that word.

○ Continue to monitor the throat tension and use faster abdominal movement to increase the loudness.

## 2. Pitch

As a result of vocal cord size and shape, each person has a certain pitch at which sound is produced most efficiently and with the least likelihood of vocal tension. This optimum pitch is the point from which the pitch departs and to which it returns most frequently. Optimum pitch, therefore, is not the only pitch produced. When changing pitch two problems can occur, which result in creating tension in the throat. First, the tendency is to place great tension between the closed vocal cords when raising or lowering pitch. Second, pushing the entire laryngeal structure higher in the throat when raising pitch and pulling it down in the throat when lowering pitch is a common occurrence.

a. ○ *Finding your optimum pitch—the "Um-Hum" method*

○ The "Um-Hum" method proposed by Morton Cooper in 1973 is an ideal method for finding your optimum pitch. Here is how to find your optimum pitch.

○ Read the question below aloud and then answer with "Um-Hum" as though you are spontaneously and sincerely agreeing with what was just said.

"Do you think Americans would like more paid vacation time from their jobs?"

Notice what pitch you used to respond to the question. This note was in the optimum pitch range for your voice.

○ In order to appreciate the difference between the pitch you are currently using, your habitual pitch and your optimum pitch, use a tape recorder to record as you read, in your habitual pitch, a short paragraph that can be taken from any book or magazine. Now, find your optimum pitch, as described, then reread the paragraph. As you listen to the tape, can you hear the difference in pitch?

b. ○ *Pitch change without tension*

○ Place your thumb and fingertips on your larynx so that you can monitor the larynx for tension.

○ Begin humming and slide the pitch up gradually.

○ Check to make sure that the throat does not tighten and also that the larynx does not push up in the throat as the pitch rises.

○ Let your fingertips massage your larynx very lightly to get rid of any tension.

○ If the larynx elevates, massage using a slight downward motion to resist the upward movement.

○ Repeat the above, this time starting at optimum pitch and moving down without tension and without downward laryngeal movement.

○ If the larynx is pulled down, place your fingers low on the larynx and create a very light massaging motion in an upward direction.

○ Practice sentences four ways.

1. optimum pitch
2. several notes above optimum pitch
3. several notes below optimum pitch
4. varied pitch jump

○ Monitor the larynx to ensure that there is no tension or movement.

c. ○ *Varying pitch—vocal variety*

○ Pitch changes contribute significantly to ensuring an interesting voice. The normal voice should go up and down around one's optimum pitch. Professionals who are interesting to listen to use a general pattern of pitch change. An important word is said very early in the sentence at a higher than optimum pitch level. On the very next syllable, pitch is lowered syllable by syllable until optimum pitch is reached. Patterns such as this are then repeated again wherever there is an important word to emphasize. The sentence is ended by a larger drop in pitch to emphasize the final idea in the sentence.

Practice these sentences trying the suggested pitch variations:

```
              weather
1. The             in
                      August
                             is
                               hot.
```

```
          probably
2. We will          start
                        at
                           six.
```

```
                  simply
3. The bakery smells
                       delicious.
```

```
          buses
4. City          are       crowded
                   often          and
                                      noisy.
```

○ When greeting someone or recording your greeting on your voice mail, practice using the method described above. Again, tape record yourself as you read sentences and paragraphs from newspapers or magazines. Replay the tape recorder and see if you like the pitch variations as they are or if pitch changes would be more effective if used on different words.

# Resonance

After leaving the larynx, sound becomes enriched by bouncing around the cavities above the vocal cords. Resonance of the voice is produced in three resonating cavities—the throat, the mouth and the nose. These cavities are the only ones that can be consciously controlled in order to improve resonance. Improved resonance leads to a richer sounding voice. As you open or close the passage of air into the nose, the quality of the resulting resonance will change. To appreciate a change in resonance, read aloud and record the following two sentences. *Mama makes lemon jam. My name is*

*Norm.* Still recording, read the same sentences this time holding your nostrils closed. Both sentences contain many nasal consonants. When you did not squeeze your nostrils the normal response would be for the sentences to sound nasal. As you squeezed your nose, however, there should be a significant change in resonance. Resonance will also change as you stretch, tense or soften the walls of your throat and mouth. Any movement of the lips, cheeks, tongue and soft palate will affect vocal resonance.

### Oral Resonance Exercises
1. **Relaxing the Front Mouth and Opening the Back**
   ○ Let your jaw move slowly down and up, down and up, keeping your lips relaxed.
   ○ Experience the movement in the back by opening up the space in the middle and back of the oral cavity, keeping lips and face relaxed.
   ○ Drop tongue and jaw to create an "ah" sound.
   ○ Count from 1-10 with a relaxed mouth at front and feel the openness at the back.

2. **Opening the Oral Cavity**
   ○ Several vowels and diphthongs have an inherent openness when pronounced and naturally facilitate more vertical space in the oral cavity.
   ○ Use the following words in sentences and experience the openness of the oral cavity.

| | | | |
|---|---|---|---|
| top | ask | sky | powder |
| opportunity | ladder | isolate | cloudy |
| lock | laughter | dice | howl |
| tolerance | hangs | arrive | hour |
| locked | capacity | how | town |

# Articulation

In addition to quality phonation and rich resonance, vocal sound has to be shaped into small units of recognizable speech to achieve clear and understandable speech. The precise production of sounds is accomplished through subtle but specific use of the lips, tongue and teeth. The process of creating clear, recognizable vowel and consonant sounds is called articulation. Exercises for providing correct articulation of the vowels and consonants are too numerous for the scope of this book. Articulation patterns are one of the most noticeable features that distinguish your speech from the speech of others. Often it is your articulation, the way that you pronounce a certain sound or sounds, that attract others to you. Just as often, however, it is your articulation that distances you from others and distracts from what you are saying. As with the other speech processes, this, too, is an area that can be changed.

# Putting It All Together

After practicing all of the exercises you are now able to produce a relaxed, interesting, well-projected and resonant speaking voice. All the techniques and exercises that have been presented are essentially worthless, however, if they are not used in your business communications. Newly learned speech behaviors rarely carryover by themselves into everyday use. You must now follow a process in order to systematically teach yourself to speak with your new voice—the one that is to become your signature.

## Carryover Exercises

It it not realistic to expect to use the new breathing, phonation and resonance behaviors all the time. Your first attempts at carryover should be brief (less than one minute) and should occur a few times each day.

1. **Greetings:** Use appropriate speech techniques for short greetings (five to ten words) in all face-to-face and telephone conversations. Practice this for several days.
2. **Lengthier Utterances:** Gradually increase the length and frequency of speech attempts, increasing to ten per day with each situation lasting five minutes.
3. **People and Places:** Identify three situations (i.e., work function, social gathering, shopping) and three people (i.e., personal relationship, social acquaintance, a stranger) with whom you will practice your new speaking techniques.

   Select a speaking situation and person that is the most comfortable for you. Practice your new speech behaviors in this situation first. Practice the more difficult speaking situations as you become more competent mastering your new speech techniques.
4. **Daily Living Reminders:** Identify the activities you carry out during the course of a typical day. Choose five events during the day and use these times to check vocal technique; i.e., while you are talking to a co-worker, having dinner with your spouse or talking to a client on the telephone.

5. **Reading:** Read aloud three to four times weekly and tape record these speech samples.

Having practiced all of the voice production exercises outlined in this chapter, you are aware of the feeling associated with proper breathing, relaxed phonation, and adequate oral resonance. The goal throughout the carryover exercises is to create these feelings every time you speak. Carrying out these techniques will feel uncomfortable at first. The more you practice your new speech behaviors, however, the quicker they will become second nature.

If your speech attempts feel uncomfortable as you first begin these carryover exercises, it is likely that the new speech patterns should be produced with greater effort. Try to focus more intently on using abdominal breathing, relaxed phonation at your optimum pitch and opening up the space at the back of your mouth.

If you find that while speaking you are breathing improperly, are tightening your throat, or are returning to former mouth movements, begin your next utterance by using your new speech techniques.

If communication skills were a giant puzzle, effective use of your voice would be the last piece. Proper use of your voice is a vital piece and the puzzle cannot be completed without it. All of the chapters in this book comprise the business communications puzzle, but information obtained from the previous chapters cannot be effective unless your voice portrays the message you are attempting to communicate. Your voice is often the first judgment that a prospective client makes in determining whether or not to do business with you. Let this first impression be a positive one. Practice the speech techniques and exercises and you *will* perfect YOUR VOICE—YOUR SIGNATURE.

# About Judy Tobe

Judy Tobe is a qualified voice coach/ consultant and holds a Master's degree in speech-language pathology. With over 15 year's experience as a communications specialist, she has worked with hundreds of people with voice and speech challenges. Judy has traveled throughout the United States, Canada, and Europe, conducting seminars and workshops at conventions and meetings. She also provides one-on-one or small group coaching to executives and other professionals either in her Pittsburgh, Pennsylvania office, or at their place of business.

Judy's clients include professional speakers/trainers, telemarketers, salespeople, CEOs, architects, financial planners, and many others. Tobe's philosophy embraces the idea that "...anyone, in any walk of life, can benefit from improving their communication skills." She is a member of the American Speech Language Hearing Association and the Pennsylvania Speakers Association.

Judy resides in Pittsburgh, Pennsylvania, with her husband, Jeff, and their two daughters. She completed her undergraduate degree at the University of Western Ontario and her graduate studies at the State University of New York at Buffalo.

# Company Profile

**W**ork and social life present you with many voice challenges—challenges which, if handled with skill, can advance you personally and financially. It might be as important as making a major presentation to your boss, to your client or to a large audience, or as informal as a social interaction. At YOUR VOICE—YOUR SIGNATURE, we know that success depends on you gaining attention, holding interest, being understood and finally, being persuasive and credible. In short, your communication skills will determine your effectiveness. The stakes could be high enough to determine financial gain, a possible promotion, a large sale or personal satisfaction. A good communicator is always in demand.

### M I S S I O N :

- To help clients, in any walk of life, better their communication skills;
- To develop a custom, individualized program of voice coaching to ensure proper use of the client's vocal mechanisms; and
- To use our knowledge of the science of speech to partner with our clients in practical applications.

At YOUR VOICE—YOUR SIGNATURE, each client receives an individual evaluation of the use and effectiveness of their voice. Areas of specific concentration include, but are not limited to: breathing techniques, controlling nervousness, pitch and intensity, resonance, rate of delivery, gestures and facial expressions, and articulation. Using this information, we develop experiential exercises and techniques which address specific areas of concern. A step-by-step program is tailored to meet the needs and schedule of the individual with the goal of turning an ordinary voice into a "signature voice" without using a one-size-fits-all model.

For more information, contact Judy Tobe, M.A., CCC at:

Your Voice — Your Signature
1144 Colgate Drive
Monroeville, PA 15146
Phone: (412) 373-5945
Fax: (412) 373-8773

THANK YOU! We hope you enjoyed reading *THE COMMUNICA-TION COACH...Business Communication Tips from the Pros.* We trust that you are now well-armed to face your communications challenges with a new arsenal of effective, bottom-line approaches. If you would like to order additional copies of this book, please fill in this form and forward it to us.

*Allow 2-3 weeks for delivery.*          *Note discount available on volume orders.*

Name:_____

Company:_____

Shipping Address:_____

_____

Phone: (_____) _____    Fax: (_____) _____

**PRICE PER BOOK:**     $19.95 usd / $27.95 cnd

| QUANTITY | COST PER BOOK | TOTAL |
|---|---|---|
| _____ | _____ | _____ |
| _____ | _____ | _____ |

|  | PA residents add 6% sales tax | _____ |
|---|---|---|
|  | Add $3.00 per book shipping | _____ |
|  | **TOTAL DUE** | _____ |

**PAYMENT:**

☐ VISA     ☐ MasterCard     ☐ Check enclosed (payable to author's name)

*Credit card billing appears under* **COLORING OUTSIDE THE LINES**

Credit Card # _____

Expiration Date_____

Billing Address_____

_____ Zip Code _____

**SEND ORDER TO:**          (Author's name on the front of this book)
200 James Place, #400
Monroeville, PA 15146

          —OR— Fax order to:    (412) 373-8773
          —OR— Call toll-free:   1-800-875-7106
          —OR—        E-mail:    cre8iva@aol.com

THANK YOU! We hope you enjoyed reading *THE COMMUNICA-TION COACH...Business Communication Tips from the Pros.* We trust that you are now well-armed to face your communications challenges with a new arsenal of effective, bottom-line approaches. If you would like to order additional copies of this book, please fill in this form and forward it to us.

*Allow 2-3 weeks for delivery.*          *Note discount available on volume orders.*

Name:_____

Company:_____

Shipping Address:_____

_____

Phone: (_____) _____     Fax: (_____) _____

**PRICE PER BOOK:**     $19.95 usd / $27.95 cnd

QUANTITY               COST PER BOOK               TOTAL

_____     _____     _____

_____     _____     _____

                        PA residents add 6% sales tax        _____

                        Add $3.00 per book shipping          _____

                                    **TOTAL DUE**            _____

**PAYMENT:**
☐ VISA     ☐ MasterCard     ☐ Check enclosed (payable to author's name)
*Credit card billing appears under* **COLORING OUTSIDE THE LINES**
Credit Card # _____

Expiration Date_____

Billing Address_____

_____ Zip Code _____

**SEND ORDER TO:**          (Author's name on the front of this book)
                            200 James Place, #400
                            Monroeville, PA  15146
        —OR— Fax order to:  (412) 373-8773
        —OR— Call toll-free: 1-800-875-7106
        —OR—     E-mail:    cre8iva@aol.com